For Lynn, Josephine, Dexter, Brooke and Spider

ADRIAN FRANKLIN

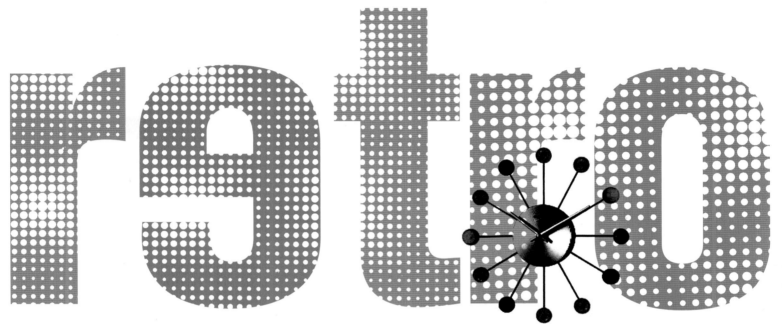

retro

A GUIDE TO THE MID-20TH CENTURY DESIGN REVIVAL

'.... A UNIQUE POSTWAR TENDENCY: A POPULAR THIRST FOR THE RECOVERY OF EARLIER, AND YET STILL MODERN PERIODS AT AN EVER-ACCELERATING RATE. BUT THIS TENDENCY SHOULD NOT BE DISMISSED AS MERELY A SERIES OF REFLEXIVE STYLISTIC GESTURES. INSTEAD, IT MIGHT BE MORE USEFULLY SEEN AS REPRESENTING A KIND OF SUBVERSION IN WHICH THE ARTISTIC AND CULTURAL VANGUARD BEGAN LOOKING BACKWARD IN ORDER TO GO FORWARD. THESE GROUPS, A KIND OF "RETRO-GARDE", SAW THEIR APPROACH TOWARD THE PAST SPREAD QUICKLY.' ELIZABETH GUFFEY, *RETRO: THE CULTURE OF REVIVAL*. LONDON: REAKTION BOOKS

BLOOMSBURY
LONDON · NEW DELHI · NEW YORK · SYDNEY

ACKNOWLEDGMENTS

This book would not have come together so well without the involvement of a lot of people. First and foremost I have to thank my Publisher at NewSouth Publishing, Phillipa McGuinness, Dawn Casey, Director of the Powerhouse Museum Sydney and Judith Matheson, Manager, Editorial & Publishing at the Powerhouse Museum, for their encouragement and support in setting this project up and seeing it through to completion. The excellent contributions from the Powerhouse Museum curator team give a rare and valuable glimpse into the making of an aesthetic movement like retro, and thanks are due to Glynis Jones, Debbie Rudder, Erika Taylor, Melanie Pitkin, Angelique Hutchison, Anne Marie Van de Ven, Campbell Bickerstaff, Eva Czernis-Ryl, Margaret Simpson, Christina Sumner and Paul Donnelly. Paul Donnelly was a great sounding board, source of inspiration, fellow traveller and my main collaborator at the Powerhouse Museum and I am indebted to him in many ways. I would also like to thank the excellent team at NewSouth Publishing particularly Chantal Gibbs, Emma Driver, Rosie Marson and Uthpala Gunethilake. Thanks also to Fiona Sim for the very best copyediting and to Jon Jermey for an excellent index. An extra special thanks is due to Diane Quick for working so closely with me and for such dedicated and exquisite design work. Pulling the book together at the end and having such a great talent to work with was an unanticipated joy.

Behind the scenes there has been a large group of people, a veritable retro-garde who have provided information, photographs, suggestions, inspiration, enthusiasm and encouragement. These include Geoffrey Hattie, Andrew Shapiro; David, Maxine, Eleni, Suzy and all at Vampt Design; Peter Kelly, Jake Smith, Peter Kearns, Charlotte Smith and the Darnell Collection; Claudia Chan Shaw, Gordon Brown, Peter Faiman, Roger Leong, Alan Smalley, Phil Colechin, John Blain, Paul Dean, Maggie Walter, Jean and Gordon Paddock, Brooke Franklin-Paddock, Melinda Clarke, Susan Cohn, Andrew Mitchel, Claire McGreal, Richard King, Terry Holt, everyone at Space Furniture, Sydney; Industria, Melbourne; Keryn Fountain, Suzy Moore, Diana Forsyth at the ABC, Nicola Sault (*Grandma Takes a Trip*, Sydney), Daryll Mills (*De Mille*); Shag, Melbourne; everyone in the vintage scene in Exeter, Frome, Canterbury, Alfies (London), Blandford Forum, Hobart, Chapel St Bazaar, Camberwell Market, Salamanca, Geelong Mills; production, crew and cast of *Collectors* and all the collectors who have come to the party, and Todd Alexander from eBay.

Thanks also to my family, Lynn, Brooke, Dexter, Jo, Spider and Miffy. Their patience and forbearance knows no bounds. Thanks to my mother, Gladys, for running the UK office and dealing with too many unexpected parcel deliveries.

I know I have forgotten too many people. To them I send extra special thanks, hugs and kisses.

CONTENTS

INTRODUCTION

IT IS UNFORTUNATE THAT A WORD LIKE *RETRO* has attached itself to the mid-twentieth century modern period. After all, retro can be considered a contradiction of the word 'retrospective' and this might refer to a retrospective celebration of any period in history. However, it is more than that. While we would expect antiques to retain their aesthetic aura I think it has surprised people that modern objects (of all things) have had such a strong aesthetic afterlife. Does not modernity supersede things and move on? Were modern objects not designed for a limited life? Were many not throwaway or disposable? Were they not designed with 'built-in obsolescence'? So, this period has surprised us precisely because of our persistent love affair with its (superseded) material culture. For this reason, it had to have a name. Retro is a daft one, but it will do.

So far, few books have attempted to explore this newfound love affair. There are guides to mid-twentieth century collectables that do little other than list and value; then there are books on design that document a period of design and production without making any connection to the contemporary consumer. This book bridges these two genres and therefore reaches out to collectors and enthusiasts in a way that is meaningful to them. It is alert to what is important now, and why, but it also provides an account of those key designers and manufacturers who fire the contemporary imagination. In this way it aims to be both an inspiring collector's sourcebook as well as a collector's 'context book', providing a deeper appreciation of the things they love.

In a way, retro not only refers to renewed interest in this unique era of the twentieth century and its objects, it also refers to the way in which this period has *shaped* contemporary lifestyle, design, aesthetics, architecture and interiors. Its influence on contemporary popular culture has been profound and is probably more than just a fashionable come-back. At a time when anxiety, risk and uncertainty are omnipresent spoilers of our happiness, the giddy aspirations, unlimited imagination, and carefree hedonism of the mid-twentieth century are like a tonic. This era has it all. Politically it aspired to the extension of rights, equal access to life-chances and liberation from stifling tradition. Commercially it succeeded in extending luxurious consumption to all; and not only luxury but a truly diverse, culturally rich abundance of things. Above all, it finally realised the dream of all modernists: to provide the means and the supply of an aesthetic existence for all. Even the humble chair was to change now: as designer Eero Saarinenn pronounced, 'A chair should not only look well as a piece of sculpture in a room when no one is in it, it should also be a flattering background when someone is in it'. We cleave to its music as we do to its fashions, furniture, tablewares, graphics, glass, metal and lighting. It reminds us of values that have

IS NOSTALGIA STOPPING OUR CULTURE'S ABILITY TO MOVE FORWARD, OR ARE WE NOSTALGIC PRECISELY BECAUSE OUR CULTURE HAS STOPPED MOVING FORWARD AND WE INEVITABLY LOOK BACK TO MORE MOMENTOUS AND DYNAMIC TIMES? BUT WHAT HAPPENS WHEN WE RUN OUT OF PAST?

SIMON REYNOLDS, **RETROMANIA** 2011:XIV

been temporarily mislaid but which we hope to regain; it reminds us that energy and vision are still required to power the modern world; it teaches us that play and escape still have a place in our workaholic, bureaucracy-entangled life-worlds. This is why a house or a lifestyle without some retro content would be missing something. There is nostalgia for retro but it is the sort of nostalgia where we can relive or 'perform' our treasured lost time. Sadly, we are destined to go forwards in time; happily though, these magic objects can travel with us as well as transport us back. Most of these objects have an aura of the familiar even if they were produced some forty to fifty years ago. These days we are used to nearly every consumer object coming from overseas, in particular from China, but the retro period is almost defined by more evenly distributed origins and particularly by its more local production. Of course,

during the retro period, some nations became design and manufacturing leaders with global exporting industries: Sweden, Italy, the USA, the UK, Japan and France. However, it is also true that almost every country is included in the united nations of retro.

I should also say that, looking back, one must remember that cherishing and restoring are not necessarily new sentiments. One does not have to think very hard to find major objections to the arrival of the very objects of our retro passion. In his 1966 volume of poetry *High and Low* (John Murray, London), for example, John Betjeman writes the disturbing lines of 'Inexpensive Progress'. He sees the Britain of the mid 1960s as one in which hedges, lanes, old villages, willows, elms and ancient inn signs will all be swept aside for obscene modern amenities: airports, roads, chain stores and power stations. He does not mince his words:

Encase your legs in nylons,

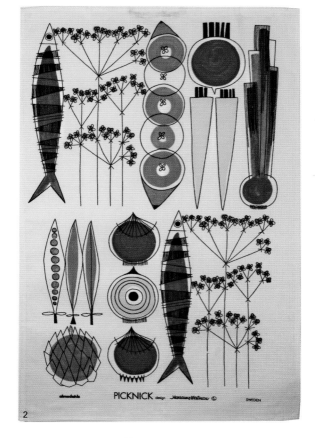

2

3

1
Alfies Antique Market of Church Street, Marylebone in London was an influential leader in the emergence of retro. Its original interest in antiques (30 years ago) is now all but abandoned in favour of mid-twentieth century design

2
'Picknick' design on linen tea towel by Marianne Westman for Almedals, Sweden, 2011

3
Glafey ruby red salt, Germany c. 1960

4

630 244 items listed under 'retro' or its analogue, 'vintage' (Carter's Guides define vintage as post-50s objects, although I make allowances for fuzzy boundaries). We are seeing antiques shops disappear before our eyes and their premises taken over by twentieth century emporia. Go to Fitzroy in Melbourne, Surry Hills in Sydney, or Notting Hill or Alfies Antiques Market in central London and see for yourself. Some antiques dealers now make the switch before they go under. As it develops, we see its commercial side grow: there are now exhaustive op-shop guides to New York, London, Paris, Sydney and Melbourne; television has realised its popular appeal with a new suite of programming spanning its entire range, all obtaining top ratings; and there is a massive new manufacturing base built on continuing series of retro designs and reissues. Of course, a lot of this is made in China, but the estate of Abram Games the poster designer from the 1940s to 80s now sells reissues, Arabia in Finland do the same with

Bestride your hills with pylons
O age without a soul …

Here the church loving Betjeman is expressing the love of his own past, his memories and his cultural identity, which he does not want to see destroyed. He worked extremely hard to make sure vital elements of it *were* saved, and was a pioneer conservationist who prompted the retro sensibility, but at the same time one sees an accommodation to the new. Besides churches, his other great love, immortalised in his poetry, was for modern trams and their suburbs, and trains.

The current enthusiasm for retro things is astonishing. It accounts for a massive part of the global internet market just as it drives a global love affair with second-hand markets, charity shops and car boot sales. While there were 115 342 objects described as 'antiques' at auction on eBay when I looked in March 2011, there were

5

4
Magic Roundabout mug. *Magic Roundabout*, written by Serge Danot, broadcast in UK by BBC 1965–77; this merchandise mug produced in 1967 by an unspecified English (probably Staffordshire) pottery

5
Futuristic cigarette case from the 1933 Chicago World Fair. It was something of a manifesto for modernism with its motto: Science Finds, Industry Applies, Man Adapts

6
Unlicensed Chinese copy of Eames Dining Chair, China, 2009

6

many of their choice vintage designs, as does Jobs the bespoke Swedish fabric designer/maker. In fact, one does not have to work the charity shops to find vintage Lucienne Day fabrics or Florence Broadhurst wallpapers. Most of the top furniture manufacturers have continued to make many of the designs we hunt down in top auction houses.

This enthusiasm has an important demographic dimension. It is a fact universally acknowledged that a large proportion of collectors 'return' to collect something from their own past. Those born between 1950 and 1980 are currently aged thirty to sixty, which includes the most affluent sections of the working population, and it is they who have driven retro rather than those older or younger. On the other hand, half of those born after this period are aged between fifteen and twenty-nine, which happens to be an age where fashion consciousness combines with relative poverty – another reason why this cohort is also completely at home in the second-hand world of retro. While they have not experienced this period

directly *themselves*, the fact that their parents were moulded by it creates an intense curiosity. Sociologists have discovered that this generation have a lot in common with and enjoy similar cultural influences to their parents.

As we look back with this renewed passion, we find ourselves having to learn a great deal that we actually did not know about this time and its material culture. Arguably, consumption was far more stratified in the mid-twentieth century and, although almost everyone participated in the popular mass-produced world of objects, only very few had access to its most illustrious designers and manufacturers – who also happened to be among the most audacious and extreme modernists. Time and fashion whittled away at the value of these objects (in many cases turning them into 'junk') and for long periods made them accessible and affordable to new audiences of collector-enthusiasts. If they are not careful however, and they never are, they will make these rare and wonderful objects inaccessible once more by creating new markets for them among collectors. Researching and publishing books on the back catalogues and manufacturing histories of these objects become key elements in their enjoyment; and so we consume them this time around as aesthetic, historic objects. Whereas their first purchaser was frequently blissfully and happily

7
Aldo Lundi, 'One-armed' figure, Bitossi, Italy, 1950s

8
Door chime with psychedelic ceramic tile by Friedland of Stockport, England, 1968–73

9
Glass 'hobnail' vase by Rudolf Jurnikl for Rudolfova Hut, Czechoslovakia, 1964

10
Fleronde pedestal chair by Fred Lowen for Fler, Melbourne Australia, 1966. Restoration by Maypole Upholsterers, Hobart; woollen fabric supplied by Australian Wool Innovation

10

11

12

ignorant of an object's designer and its manufacturing provenance, not so the contemporary collector. Thus are we now dependent on and addicted to guides, but also more aesthetically attuned than the first wave of consumers. Part of this interest stems from the esteem extended to a number of the more successful designers from this period. It is only in retrospect, at the end of their careers, that we can evaluate their contribution and influence. Some of the earliest pieces by Stuart Devlin for Wiltshire, the Australian cutlery company, passed by unnoticed when they were first sold in the early 1960s. Today, however, the fact that he became the Prime Warden of the Worshipful Company of Goldsmiths and was appointed jeweller and goldsmith to Queen Elizabeth II has made a significant difference to how we appraise his earlier work. The same might be said of the young Terence Conran, Lucienne Day, Arne Jacobsen, Mari Simmulson or Jessie Tait.

Objects with compelling histories of design and manufacture compare favourably to what is currently on sale *new* in shops. While there is a vibrant design market, where similar details of pedigree and provenance are craved, it is a fact that as we stopped being a manufacturing culture, the vast majority of things around us are produced overseas

13

11
Nils Landberg 'Off-Centre' vase for Orrefors, Sweden, 1956

12
Wall plaque by Ninnie Forsgren (she signed herself NIE) for Bromma Keramik, Sweden 1963–68

13
St Clements fish platter, France, 1960s.

THE BRIONVEGA RR126 RADIOGRAM, 1965

CAMPBELL BICKERSTAFF = CURATOR, SCIENCE AND INDUSTRY, POWERHOUSE MUSEUM

The Brionvega RR126 was nicknamed the 'Musical Pet'; a moniker drawn from its zoomorphic features – the symmetrical arrangement of the dials and controls, pedestal legs on casters demonstrating certain 'mobility' and speakers that hang like ears on the sides of the body.

Designed by the Castiglioni brothers, Achille and Pier Giacomo, the radiogram reflects their maxim that design must restructure an object's function, form and production process. This belief led them to reinvent many of the products they were commissioned

to design. Over the latter half of the twentieth century, they produced a body of work that influenced product designers internationally, and their work is represented in public and private collections in Europe, North America, Asia and Australia.

Brionvega was one of many Italian manufacturers of domestic consumer goods that encouraged flamboyance in product design, without deviating too far from function. The company engaged outstanding Italian industrial designers of the time, including Marco Zanuso, Rich-

ard Sapper, Mario Bellini and Ettore Sottsass. Many examples of Brionvega products designed in the 1960s rejected existing forms in favour of startlingly new interpretations, using new production methods and materials, and positioning the company as avant-garde. As a result, many Brionvega designs continue in production today, including a contemporary variant of the RR126 – the RR226 – which includes a CD player. This kind of longitudinal product lifespan validates the Italian manufacturer's commitment to modernism.

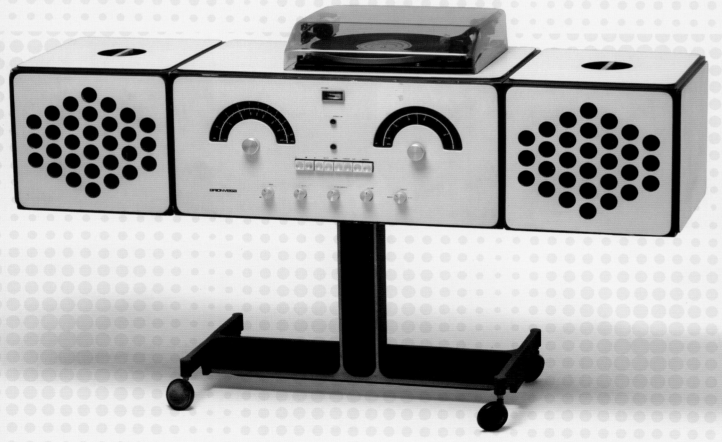

'RR126' stereo radiogram, designed by Achille and Pier Giacomo Castiglioni, manufactured by Brionvega, Milan, Italy, 1966. While other manufacturers of high fidelity equipment were at this time exploring the separation of components, the Castiglioni brothers went against this trend, seeking to mould this domestic technological product into a piece of furniture that would sit comfortably alongside forms coherent with (1960s) modern interiors and furnishing
Powerhouse Museum collection

14

15

by people we do not know, in towns and regions we have never heard of, and under conditions that we might well disapprove of. The marks, back stamps and labels that once described the geography and society of our own modern world have been replaced by the anonymous ciphers of global producers, saying as little as possible so as to avoid whatever discrimination exists in faraway markets. Such is the complexity of many objects and the myriad origins of their various parts that it becomes impossible to talk about them as produced 'any*where*' or by 'any*one*'. This complexity may not worry us unduly but it does confound our ability to track an object and have a sense of it as a coherent thing. Thinking about it tends to fragment the thinker too, dismantling rather than providing a sense of self. So here is another reason why retro objects can range from 'throwaway' to studio pieces but still, ironically, provide a centre, a focus and an identity. The sociologist Walter Benjamin said that the significance of collecting to modern cultures is that it prevents the liquefying, fragmenting and discarding tendencies of modernity from inflicting permanent damage. Left to itself, modernity might eliminate times, periods and

16

14
Three-legged table
in rosewood,
glass and chrome,
designer unknown,
country of origin
unknown

15
Philippe Starck
digital P1092 watch
for Fossil, country
unspecified

16
Official Star
Wars™ watch,
Lucasfilm Ltd,
Hope Industries,
USA, 1999

17
Tandy Poodle
Transistor Radio,
Korea, 1960s

17

18

objects in its onward march towards better futures and better products. However, Benjamin said that collecting is a form of memory, holding still in a rather beautiful manner, the look, the feel, the technology, the actual materiality and culture of times past. This is why there is such a strong moral and conservational dimension to the collecting impulse. Objects ought not to be forgotten, for this is to forget people. The machines that once produced rail, road and other connectivities were formative of many nations and ought not to be allowed to rust away. Old Australian electric fans were the very sound of an Australian summer, prior to air-con.

This book aims to provide a useful explanation of the retro phenomenon, as well as a sourcebook for a representative range of objects from this period. Rather than aim to be an exhaustive catalogue (for that

would be practically impossible, given the great diversity of production in this era), it seeks instead to give its reader a solid grasp of the forms of objects that comprise the retro genre as well as influential designs, innovations, factories and designers. To do this, it considers each of eight key collecting areas (furniture, ceramics, glass, metal, plastic, fashion, graphics and technology) in turn and delivers a concise description of the range of design alongside an account of the direction and form of innovation and change, including key or defining exhibitions. Curators at the exceptionally well stocked Powerhouse Museum in Sydney have been invited to contribute small vignettes that illustrate how particular objects have been recruited into the retro period, and how this has indeed influenced museum acquisitioning. This will be illustrated by a generous selection of

18
The ultimate Mod footwear: Hutton of Northampton deerskin shoes, all leather soles, handmade, England circa 1968

19
Jaguar XK-E or E-type; Series 1 (3.8 litre), UK, 1961. According to Enzo Ferrari this was 'the most beautiful car ever made'. This one is owned by Peter Kearns Photo Peter Kearns

20
Keyhole surgery instrument bought from Industria, a new type of retro shop specialising in industrial items from offices, hospitals etc.

19

20

21

representative examples, referred to in the text. In each section we will see both continuity and change: how 50s glass morphed into 60s glass and how to identify the distinctiveness of 70s glass. This enables us to see how the output of particular designers and factories changed over time and to understand why. It also avoids the rather unfortunate separation of decades when in fact they often overlapped and related to and referenced each other in important ways.

22

23

24

25

21
KHI plastic beakers, Hong Kong, 1950s

22
Mickey mouse themed tin bucket by Willow, Australia, c. 1940 Courtesy Peter Kelly

23
Attributed to Stig Lindberg, 'Vinga' for Gefle/Upsala-Ekeby, Sweden, 1950s

24
Marine-themed TV light that featured on ABC TV's *SeaChange*, USA, 1950s

25
Brevettato 'Necchi Mini' children's sewing machine, Italy, 1960s

CHAPTER 1

FURNITURE

EVEN BEFORE MODERN ARCHITECTS had finished perfecting a contemporary look to buildings, they had turned their attention to designing furniture that would be compatible with the look they were after. Simply put, sets of older furniture looked terrible in modern buildings and although these days we can insert the odd antique here and there to very good effect, we mostly don't. Harry Seidler went even further: he said there had to be a design integrity that linked the exterior with the interior and the lines of the building with the lines of anything inside it. At Rose Seidler House in Sydney, Seidler therefore designed everything or bought it himself (and what he bought was typically designed by other modern architect/designers).

It is a very exciting time for retro furniture buying and collecting because although many people love it and prices are rising, they have not yet reached the impossible prices of antiques. Some of the really beautiful pieces are prohibitively expensive but it is a still a good time to buy and bargains are out there as some people still regard retro furniture as worthless and ugly. I can remember when art deco was also being dumped, so this golden era of collecting won't last. Nonetheless, it is still a relatively new area and there are designs, designers and manufacturers whose work has yet to be fully documented, appraised and understood.

Retro furniture design was not simply about finding modern expressions for older furniture forms but also creating designs that had never existed before, such as modular and stackable furniture, storage shelving and the coffee table. Most significant here was an ever-growing range of new materials like tubular steel, wire, plywood, plastic, fibreglass, foam rubber, glass, webbing, cardboard and paper.

When seen together in an interior this mixture of forms and materials produced a brilliant technical and aesthetic ensemble that was such a refreshing change from the all-over 'brown wood' look of antique and Victorian furniture. It offered the modern person more than rest and function. Take one look at the more extreme experiments of the 1970s and you will see designers aiming to stimulate intellectual discussion, 'community', family life, leisure and sex. This furniture played a profound role in new ways of living.

FOR A BRIEF SPAN IN A DECADE AND A HALF, MASS-PRODUCED FURNITURE REACHED A DESIGN PINNACLE ACHIEVED NEITHER BEFORE NOR SINCE.

CARA GREENBERG, **MID-CENTURY MODERN** 1995:9

1, 2, 3
Design integrity at
Rose Seidler House,
Sydney, Australia,
c. 1948–51

4
Butterfly chair on the
deck at Rose Seidler
House, Sydney,
Australia

The modern chair

The modern chair is something of an architectural movement in its own right and after the Second World War competition was stiff to consolidate home markets or, even better, establish export industries. Leading the pack in the 1950s were the USA, Denmark and Italy, with Britain and France producing their own versions of the broader modern look.

In the 1950s a significant break was made with the domestic look of the first half of the century. The thickly upholstered look, with richly patterned and darkish tones was replaced by leaner, cleaner more architectural lines in which the structure or frame of chairs and sofas became a more prominent part of the aesthetic appeal. Instead of an all-engulfing comfort zone, the designers of the 1950s created more architectural, technical and dynamic lines that still delivered the comfort and support that a human form required, but using minimal materials. In order to make that possible more thought was put into the structure, mix of materials and the relationship that the design had with the interior design.

The postwar period, even as early

5
Ernest Race
'Antelope Chair',
England, 1951
Powerhouse
Museum collection

6
Metal chair, Charles
Eames for Herman
Miller, USA,
c. 1951 Powerhouse
Museum collection

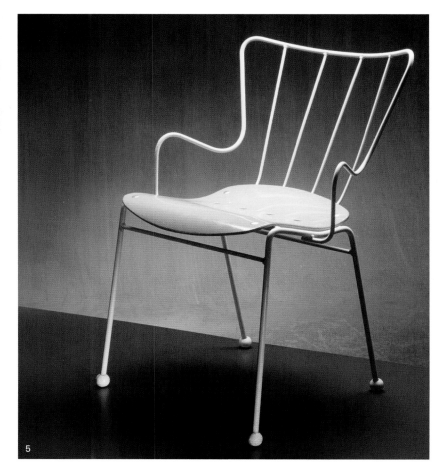

5

6

7

8

9

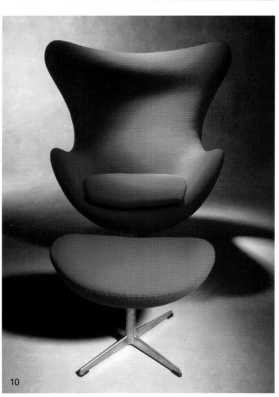

10

11

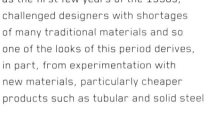

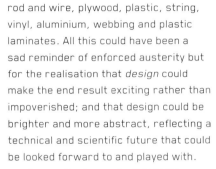

as the first few years of the 1950s, challenged designers with shortages of many traditional materials and so one of the looks of this period derives, in part, from experimentation with new materials, particularly cheaper products such as tubular and solid steel rod and wire, plywood, plastic, string, vinyl, aluminium, webbing and plastic laminates. All this could have been a sad reminder of enforced austerity but for the realisation that *design* could make the end result exciting rather than impoverished; and that design could be brighter and more abstract, reflecting a technical and scientific future that could be looked forward to and played with.

Among the key materials to be used initially were metal rods and plywood, and in the early 1950s all-metal furniture, as well as all-plywood constructions, abounded. The key designers to achieve this and thus inspire many others to follow their lead were Charles and Ray Eames. Later in the 1950s this austerity was modified considerably with the appearance of revolutionary designs in such new materials as aluminium, steel, fibreglass and formica. Here, luxury and architectural panache could be achieved relatively cheaply. A popular new form, the chair and footstool or ottoman, became a core genre of this period and again it was American and Danish

7
Charles and Ray Eames lounge chair and ottoman, Herman Miller, USA, 1957 Powerhouse Museum collection

8
Wooden chair, Charles Eames for Herman Miller, USA, c. 1946 Powerhouse Museum collection

9
Arne Jacobsen 'Ant Chair', Denmark, 1952 Powerhouse Museum collection

10
Arne Jacobsen 'Egg Chair' and footstool, Fritz Hansen, Denmark, 1958 Powerhouse Museum collection

11
Danish sideboard in rosewood, Kofod Larsen , c. 1955 Vampt Vintage Design

12
A softer modernity? Hans Wegner wooden 'Peacock Chair', Denmark, c. 1952

12

14

15

13
A cosy but modern
corner: Fred Lowen
'SC55' chair, a
palette-shaped coffee
table and atomic-
style magazine rack,
for Fler, Australia.
All items from mid-
1950s

14
Oak 'CH28' chair
by Hans Wegner
for Carl Hansen &
Son, Denmark, 1951
Vampt Vintage
Design

15
Wing chair by Illum
Wikkelsø, Denmark,
c. 1950 Vampt
Vintage Design

16
Arne Jacobsen
'Swan Chair' for Fritz
Hansen, Denmark,
1958 Vampt Vintage
Design

17
Teak and fabric
armchair and
footstool by Illum
Wikkelsø, Denmark,
c. 1952 Vampt
Vintage Design

16

17

18

designers who one thinks of as leaders here. These include the iconic designs of Charles and Ray Eames and Arne Jacobsen.These have been so popular in recent years that they are often used as symbols of retro design itself and, to their detriment if not to that of sales, have become something of a cliché.

The highly influential publication

Decorative Art: The Studio Yearbook 1951–52 (Studio Books, London, 1951) provides a glimpse into this modern world as it emerged. It is quite breathtaking to see how liberated these new designers were; how soon that distinctive *retro* look became established. In it, we see how the Scottish designer Dennis

18
Beech and fabric chair by Magnus Olsen, Denmark, c. 1955 Vampt Vintage Design

19
Oak table by Børge Mogensen, Denmark, c. 1954 Vampt Vintage Design

19

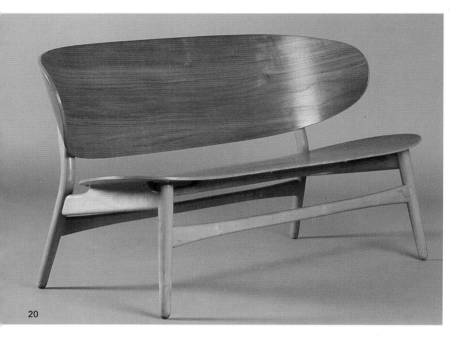

20

Lennon created a light, open structure of pressed aluminium to support a seat and back, then mounted this on a fine beech wood frame, and upholstered foam-rubber cushions with textured Scottish tweed. Although it had a recognisable sofa shape it was also refreshingly new.

The book also shows how the Danes created new lighter structures with wood, but augmented pure structure with daring new angles, often incorporating historical and nautical lines. Their structures became more and more organic, culminating in the futuristic shapes produced by Finn Juhl for Søren Willadsens Møbelfabrik. Niels Vodder designed the most audacious look of all: a curling, asymmetrical sofa

21

20
Hans Wegner 'Shell' sofa by Fritz Hansen, Denmark, 1950 Vampt Vintage Design

21
Teak dining suite by Kai Kristiansen, Denmark, c. 1956 Vampt Vintage Design

22
Dining chairs by Ib Kofod Larsen for Christensen & Larsen, Denmark, 1950 Vampt Vintage Design

23
Teak nest of tables by Johs Andersen, Denmark, c. 1962 Vampt Vintage Design

24
Spanish chair by Børge Mogensen, Denmark, c. 1958 Vampt Vintage Design

25
'CH27' easy chair in oak and cane by Hans Wegner for Carl Hansen, Denmark, 1955 Vampt Vintage Design

22

23

24

25

26

27

28

26
Borge Mogensen
teak/oak 'Hunting
Table' and 'Shell'
chairs, Denmark,
c. 1958 Vampt
Vintage Design

27
'CH25' easy chair in
oak and paper cord
by Hans Wegner,
Denmark, 1951
Vampt Vintage
Design

28
Mahogany, cane
and steel tubing
chair by Peter Hvidt
and Orla Mølgaard
Nielsen, Denmark,
1959 Vampt Vintage
Design

29
'Ax' chair by Peter
Hvidt and Orla
Mølgaard for Fritz
Hansen, Denmark,
1947 Vampt Vintage
Design

30
Armchair by Ib
Kofod-Larsen,
Denmark, c. 1950
Vampt Vintage
Design

31
Dining suite in
rosewood by Niels
Møller, Denmark,
c. 1953 Vampt
Vintage Design

29

30

back, upholstered in solid red wool that floated above a seat upholstered in boldly striped wool, the entire ensemble made possible through an organically shaped iron frame. Many people might think this was from the 1970s or even the 1990s. While the Americans and British produced a hard-edged, modernist, industrial design aesthetic,

the Scandinavians designed a softer, organic and more human-centred comfort zone out of practically nothing more than wood and clever design. Australian designers did both, though many are hybrids of the these two influences – a case in point being Fred Lowen's designs for Fler in the 1950s.

Meanwhile in the UK, Robin Day and

Ernest Race produced a slicker, flatter rectilinear look for sofas, using steel rod structures to support minimalist wedge-shaped superstructures covered in leather and vinyl. In fact, these sofas began to resemble the new buildings they were to grace.

Despite improvements in transport after 1945, furniture produced

31

32

32
Illum Wikkelsø pair of
easy chairs 'V11' for
Holger Christiansen,
Denmark, c. 1960
Vampt Vintage
Design

33
Illum Wikkelsø
'V-Series' sofa for
Holger Christiansen,
Denmark c. 1960
Vampt Vintage
Design

34
Gordon Andrews,
'Rondo Chair', Gordon
Andrews, Australia,
1957 Powerhouse
Museum collection

overseas, rather like rock bands, was
expensive to ship to Australia, which
meant that Australia did her own thing.
Modern styles had an international
look but there were interesting local
variations. Even within Australia,
furniture was too expensive to ship
around the country and so every city
tended to develop its own. Australian
designers were talented and had an
affluent market to produce for.

The Historic Houses Trust of NSW
owns a photo of Marion Hall Best's

shop in the exclusive Sydney suburb
of Woollahra, taken in the late 1950s.
Best was Australia's queen of interior
design at this time and this photo
features piles of fantastic fabrics with
Australian motifs (native animals, flora
and Aboriginal designs) and the work
of furniture maker Gordon Andrews.
Apart from co-designing the Woollahra
shop, Andrews also designed two of the
chairs that feature in the photo. The
first, his 'Gazelle Chair', is typical of this
period. It has a tripod of cast aluminium

33

legs; a moulded plywood seat base in a rounded triangular shape with an aluminium stem connecting to a seat back which is also a rounded triangular shape. Triangles, tripods, aluminium and plywood: all new things that made the chair lighter and somehow crisper. But then Andrews adds a touch of pure Australian luxury: a richly textured tangerine woollen fabric. Even more astonishing was his sumptuous 'Rondo Chair'. This features a squared-off cone of moulded plywood, upholstered in jazzy wool with four splayed legs. It looks like a feat of space-age engineering combined with a very organic, soft, womb-like body.

Gordon Andrews was influenced by contemporary French design – by people such as Pierre Paulin – and this is what gave his work something of an edge because most makers at the time were influenced by Scandinavia and America. Clement Meadmore, for example, was clearly under the influence of people like the American Harry Bertoia, who worked a lot with wire-rod framed chairs. Unlike the upholstered 1930s settee, the structure of this kind of chair was the thing to *see* not the thing to hide!

Meadmore had a productive period in the 1950s, making delightfully playful and well-engineered chairs. His 'Michael Hirst Chair' from the late 1950s is made of white, plastic-coated steel wire, formed in a grid shape that rises to a triangular-shaped back. It was perfect for outdoor living in Sydney. The Norwegians and Danes liked the traditional 'rigging' look of

34

35

36

string (which happened to be cheap and available) and this inspired an entire series of Meadmore's best work that includes strung chairs and stools. They are deceptively simple, beautifully appointed and an absolute must-have.

Douglas Snelling is another big name. He was clearly taken by the Finnish designer Alvar Aalto, whose bentwood recliner was famously upholstered in twin-tone parachute canvas webbing. One of these will now set you back around $8000–10 000 but you can buy a Snelling chair, which

showcases Australian hardwoods, for a lot less. His dining chairs look remarkably like those designed by Jens Risom in 1946 (for Knoll International, USA), but no matter, because he went on to design other furniture for Functional Products Pty Ltd in Sydney to match them, and this really became a recognisable look of the 1950s Australian interior.

In Melbourne, Fred Lowen started Fler (with Ernest Rodeck), and from the very beginning their furniture had a Scandinavian arts and crafts

35
Gordon Andrews,
'Gazelle Chair',
Gordon Andrews,
Australia, 1957
Powerhouse
Museum collection

36
The simplest is
the best: Clement
Meadmore
stool with steel
construction,
moulded plywood
seat with vinyl cover
printed with cool-
modern pattern,
Australia, c. 1957

37
Clement Meadmore,
'Michael Hirst Chair',
Michael Hirst Pty
Ltd, Melbourne,
Australia, 1959
Powerhouse
Museum collection

38
Douglas Snelling,
chair and footstool,
Functional Products,
Australia, 1957
Powerhouse
Museum collection

look about it. However, they only used native Australian timber and found a clever way of making chairs with a handcrafted look and finish using newly modified factory lathes. Hence, for the first time, most Australians had access to this quality of chair. His important chairs from the 1950s are the 'SC55' and 'SC58' and, just into the 1960s, the Norwegian influenced 'Narvik' range. In the 1970s he founded Tessa with yet more high quality but affordable chairs. This time the emphasis was on using native timber plywoods and ultra soft leather.

Melbournians liked this European 'modernised arts and crafts look' and studio designers like Schulim Krimper and Dario Zoureff were kept very busy, largely with intricate commissioned works where their skill as cabinet makers could shine. Both favoured native hardwoods and showcased the beauty of structure and engineering. Zoureff armchairs had real design pizzazz and were unashamedly showy

38

and expensive looking – often with flowing, organic-shaped arms.

Grant Featherston is one of the few Australian designers to be well recognised internationally. In 1947 Featherston began making chairs that used surplus parachute webbing (similar to the Snelling chairs) but then he fell under the spell of the great Danish architect designers like Arne Jacobsen and Verner Panton. Both looked for new materials and forms rather than trying to adapt the look of wood for the modern era.

Featherston's 'Contour' range of elegant chairs and sofas were so called because their form was designed to follow closely the contours of the human body. So, while they bore an unmistakable similarity to Arne Jacobsen's famous 'Swan' and 'Egg' chairs, there was an important improvement.

Featherston, Panton and Jacobsen were leading international figures in the transition into 1960s furniture making, although by then French and Italian modernism was beginning to really take the lead. Pierre Paulin's work in metal, foam and fabric was revolutionary and established a freer architectural imagination among chair designers. It may also have been influential in the French government investing heavily in French design by setting up CCI (Centre de Creation Industrielle) in October 1969. Two of Paulin's early works, his '577' chair and the '582' Ribbon chair, mark a turning point in European chair design that gave great scope to designers such as Gaetano Pesce, Piero Gatti and Cesare Paolini. Their furniture was updated to the pop art era, which in turn inspired the idea of

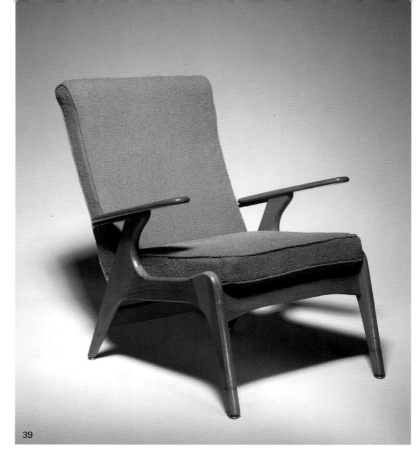

39

40

39
Fred Lowen, 'SC55' chair, Fler, Australia, 1956 Powerhouse Museum collection

40
Grant Featherston, 'R152 Contour' chair, Australia, c. 1951 Powerhouse Museum collection

41
Pierre Paulin, '577' chair, Artifort, The Netherlands, 1965 Powerhouse Museum collection

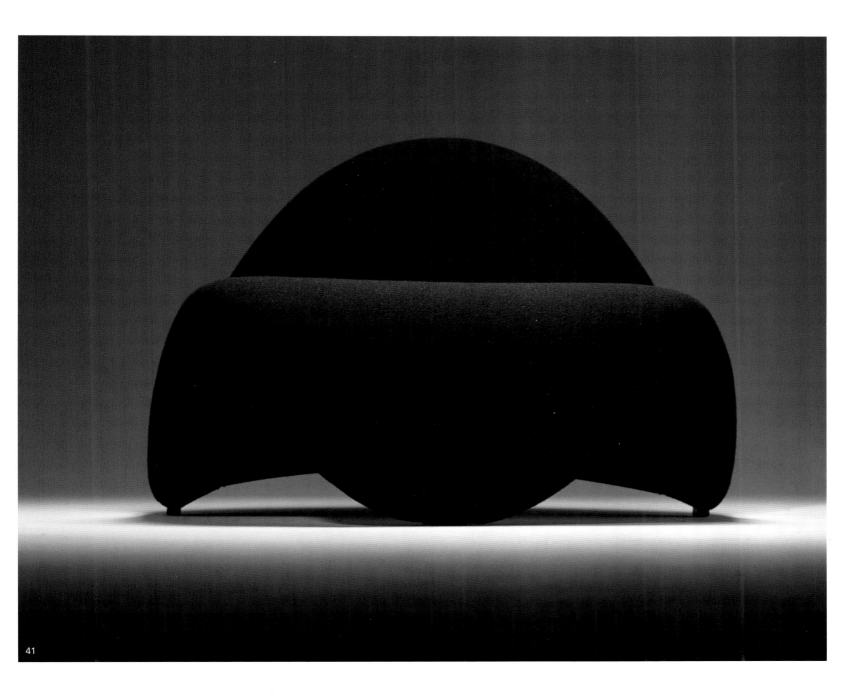

41

new interiors and new ways of living in them.

Pop art belonged to a social movement that questioned how we live and introduced collective and social themes that challenged the socially isolated, introspective and privatised world of the modern nuclear family. This era of retro design used furniture to explore and suggest new ways of living in homes with other people and modes of interacting in household and other spaces. Furniture and other design was linked to other art forms such as painting, sculpture and music.

Featherston's 'Mark I Sound Chair' is a case in point. First unveiled at the 1967 Montreal Expo in the Australia Pavilion, it suggested a futuristic space-age and chimed well with the work of Stanley Kubrick in his film *2001: A Space Odyssey*. At first sight it seems like a version of Verner Panton's 'Cone Chair' from ten years earlier. However,

THE 1960s CHAIRS OF OLIVIER MOURGUE AND PIERRE PAULIN

PAUL DONNELLY = CURATOR, DESIGN AND SOCIETY, POWERHOUSE MUSEUM

The Powerhouse Museum opened in Australia's bicentennial year of 1988. One of the new and much-anticipated exhibitions was *Take a Seat*, a chronological look at the history and development of the chair. Chairs are ideal objects for discussing design through a single genre, as their complexity reflects – perhaps more than any other single item – the adoption of available materials, skill and fashion from a regional through to an international level. The chair is a barometer of architecture and interior design, offering a snapshot of any decade's societal values, lifestyles, and aspirations: 'a society and city in miniature' to quote influential British architect Peter Smithson.[1]

In this way, the sinuous and sculptural chairs distinctive to the French designers Olivier Mourgue and Pierre Paulin were exemplars of the 'groovy' 60s, which made them ideal for the *Take a Seat* exhibition.

Olivier Mourgue's 'Djinn' chaise longue of 1963, along with Pierre Paulin's 'Ribbon' chair no. 582 of 1965 and 'Tongue' chair no. 577 of 1967, were bought specifically for this exhibition and were most recently displayed in the *Mod to Memphis: Design in Colour 1960s–80s* exhibition at the Powerhouse in 2002–03.[2] The 'Djinn' ceased production in 1976, so an example was bought at auction in London. The Paulin chairs were (and still are) made by Artifort in Holland and were purchased new in 1987 from Artes Studios – one of Sydney's prime sources since the 1950s of modern international furniture.

The 'Djinn' series was already famous by the time of its celebrated role in Stanley Kubrick's 1968 cult film, *2001: A Space Odyssey*. Along with the Paulin chairs, its French aesthetic of transparency of form continues to evoke the optimism and youthfulness of the period, which makes them attractive to buyers today.

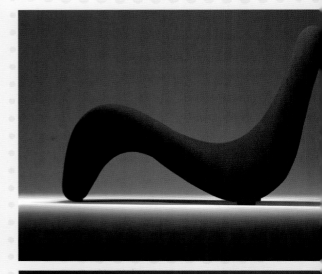

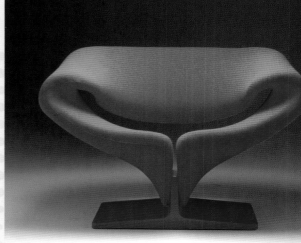

Pierre Paulin, '577' chair, Artifort, The Netherlands, 1965 Powerhouse Museum collection

Pierre Paulin, '582' chair, Artifort, The Netherlands, 1966 Powerhouse Museum collection

Olivier Mourgue, 'Djinn' chaise longue, Airborne, France, 1963 Powerhouse Museum collection

42

42
'Up 1' chair, C
and B Italia, Italy,
1969 Powerhouse
Museum collection

as with the 'Contour Chair', Grant
Featherston took what was clearly a
great design and made it better – and
more popular – in this case by inserting
a sound system into the wing backs.

Inflatable plastic divans and sofas
made an appearance at this time and
enabled a crossover/hybrid between
furniture and sculpture. De Pas,
Lomazzi and Scolari's 'Divano Gonfiabile'

and De Pas, D'Urbino and Lomazzi's
'Joe Chair' are good examples but many
more followed.

Along the same sculptural lines,
the world very much enjoyed the
'Marilyn' sofa design by Studio65 in
1970, Magistretti's 'Veranda 3' sofa
in 1973 and Frank Gehry's playful and
surprising 'Wiggle Chair' that was made
from cardboard.

THE 'SACCO' BEAN BAG AND OTHER ANTI-DESIGN FURNITURE

PAUL DONNELLY = CURATOR, DESIGN AND SOCIETY, POWERHOUSE MUSEUM

It is hard to imagine the ubiquitous bean bag as a political statement, but the original bean bag or 'Sacco' was an anti-design statement calculated to question conventional taste. Among examples of 'manifesto furniture', the 'Sacco', by Piero Gatti, Cesare Paolini and Franco Teodora, is by far the most commercially successful; there are countless imitations of the original, which was first produced by the Italian manufacturer Zanotta in 1969. The bean bag's status over the past forty years as the ultimate in cheap and informal furniture belies the novelty and innovation of the original 'Sacco'. The museum's example was displayed from 1988 to 1993 in the exhibition *Take a Seat* and from 2002 to 2003 in *From Mod to Memphis.*

At the other end of the spectrum is the 'Mies' chair by Archizoom Associati, founded by architects Andrea Branzi, Gilberto Corretti, Paolo Deganello

Piero Gatti and Cesare Paolini, 'Bean Bag Chair', Zanotta SpA, Italy, 1968 Powerhouse Museum collection

and Massimo Morozzi, and industrial designers Dario and Lucia Bartolini. The 'Mies' chair was a targeted criticism of the revival of 'classic designs', such as those by Mies van der Rohe and Le Corbusier. Using the materials typically used by these architects, in combination with a transparent form, the 'Mies' is a parody of the 'less is more' aesthetic of the modernists. Perplexingly, the dramatic angled silhouette of the 'Mies' appears to offer no support until the tight web stretches under the weight of the sitter. This particular example of the chair was shown in the exhibition *100 Modern Chairs* at the National Gallery of Victoria in 1974.

Furniture designed less for commercial success and more for socio-political commentary might be thought an unlikely candidate for collecting. However, items like the 'Mies' chair, which embody the complexity of an era and provide comparisons with the mainstream, are eagerly sought by serious collectors and museums. The success of the 'Sacco', of course, makes it the most unusual of these statements; but to truly experience the original intent, it's best to get the original. Even a bean bag is not just a bean bag!

'Mies' chair and footstool, Archizoom, 1969 Powerhouse Museum collection

In the 1980s the Memphis design group formalised what had really occurred very widely in the 1970s – the absence of rules and formulae for furniture making – although at the same time it is curious how the 1980s pieces share the same basic look! Just compare, for example, Toshiyuki Kita's chaise longue of 1980 with John Smith's coffee table and Michele de Lucchi's 'Lido' couch. Here we have a love affair with blocks of strong, contrasting colour, an almost toy-like simplicity of design and a great passion for an engineered architectural look. This all comes together in a dramatic way with the 'Sunset in New York' sofa by Gaetano Pesce.

Regardless of the different aspirations of the four decades of retro chair design and their obvious differences, the fact that they all sit

43
Jonathon De Pas, Paolo Lomazzi and Carla Scolari, 'Divano Gonfiabile' inflatable plastic divan, for Plasteco Milano Senago, Milan, Italy, 1965
Powerhouse Museum collection

43

THE 'MARK I SOUND' CHAIR

MELANIE PITKIN = ASSISTANT CURATOR, ARTS AND DESIGN, POWERHOUSE MUSEUM

The 'Mark I Sound Chair', or 'talking chair' as it was colloquially referred to, was designed by Melbourne-based furniture designers Grant and Mary Featherston for the Montreal Expo 67 Australian Pavilion. Only 250 chairs were produced, and all were given to the city of Montreal at the exhibition's end. In line with the brief set by the eminent Australian architect Robin Boyd, the chair encapsulated Australia's youthful and forward thinking spirit through its combination of modern design with innovative materials and technologies (each chair featured an inbuilt audio system playing recorded stories about the Australian way of life).

In the words of Mary Featherston, the use of plastic in furniture production at the time was part of the 'shock of the new'. The 'Mark I' had a dramatic horn-shaped form, produced as a single piece in a mould. This was a formative moment in Australian furniture design and manufacture, which subsequently landed the Featherstons with a reputation for being cutting-edge in their field. This standing, coupled with the prestige attached to a Boyd-affiliated Montreal Expo, made the 'Mark I' chair (and its commercial successor, the 'Mark II') highly sought-after by private collectors and museums alike.

The Powerhouse Museum acquired a 'Mark II' in 1986, while remaining watchful for a rarer 'Mark I' to surface. Quite serendipitously, one of these chairs became available when the museum was developing the major retrospective exhibition *Modern Times: The Untold Story of Modernism in Australia*. In recognition of this special acquisition, both chairs came to feature prominently in the museum's exhibition marketing campaign as representative examples of Australian modernism and the shift into the swinging sixties. The chairs are also the subject of an important chapter in the accompanying exhibition catalogue.

Grey chair:
Grant and Mary Featherston, 'Mark I Sound Chair', Aristoc Industries, Melbourne, Australia, 1966
Powerhouse Museum collection

Red chair: Grant and Mary Featherston 'Mark II' chair
Powerhouse Museum collection

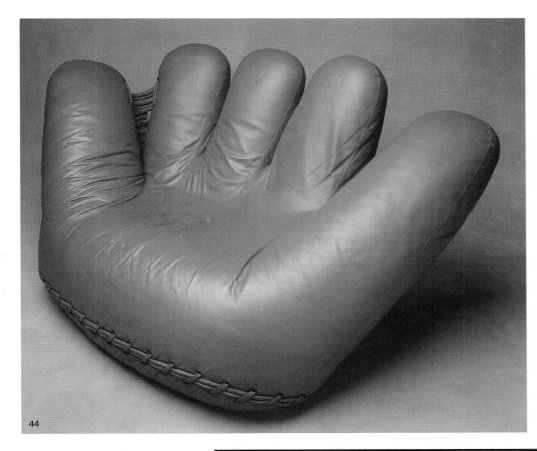

44

well together in contemporary living spaces is an indication of the great design integrity of the period. There *were* common threads, in terms of the designers' aims, the kind of society they were designing for and the kind of society they hoped to bring into being through their designs. They coped very well with tight budgets, new materials and a continuous stream of new ideas and criticism. In fact, it was this intellectual undercurrent, forever there and forever churning the ground on which these designers stood, that kept their output fresh, exciting and life affirming.

45

44
Jonathon De Pas,
Donato D'Urbino,
'Joe Chair',
Poltronova, Italy,
1970 Powerhouse
Museum collection

45
'Marilyn' sofa,
Studio65 for
Gufram, Turin, Italy,
1970 Powerhouse
Museum collection

46

47

48

49

50
Philippe Starck and
Eugeni Quitllet, 'High
Cut Side Chairs'
in polycarbonate
plastic for Kartell,
Italy, 2007
Space Furniture

51

46
Philippe Starck 'Cafe
Costes' chair, made
by Driade, Italy,
1985 Powerhouse
Museum collection

47
Memphis-style chair,
Australian designed
and sold from Roar
Gallery, Melbourne,
c. 1988

48
Frank Gehry,
'Wiggle Chair',
Vitra, Germany,
1972 Powerhouse
Museum collection

49
Toshiyuki Kita,
chaise longue,
for Cassina, Italy,
1980 Powerhouse
Museum collection

51
Michele de Lucchi,
'Lido' couch,
Memphis, Italy,
1982 Powerhouse
Museum collection

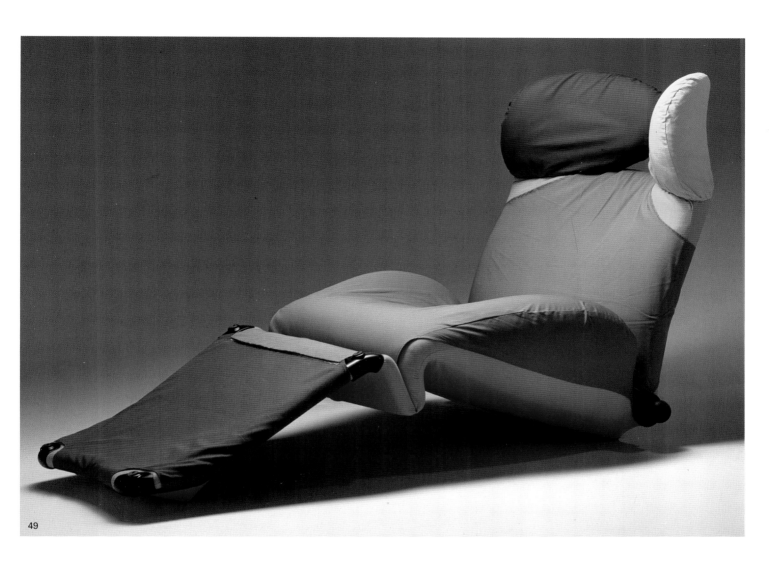

49

50

51

Storage

One of the easiest ways to create a retro look in a sitting room is to add a long, low-slung sideboard in teak-coloured wood. But it is more than just a look. The sideboard, which often combined storage for a cocktail cabinet and formal dining equipment, promised the prospect of parties, entertainment, fun and a leisure-rich life. Along with the coffee table, the sideboard was part of that lowering of the eye-level and our position in living room areas, that was not unrelated to sitting comfortably in

order to hear a radio or see a television screen. The long, slimline profile of the retro sideboard was of course in stark contrast to the higher solid-looking sideboards and dressers of the early twentieth century (and before) and produced a less cluttered, minimalist look. There was a place for the odd piece of choice pottery or artful glass perhaps but the idea was to keep walls and spaces clean and clear. The only structure that was allowed (or that looks good) above it was the very

architectural 'storage unit' which often seemed to be built from a sideboard-style base or, in the 1950s, built in. Even late 1940s cocktail cabinets, that were approximately piano-top height, no longer fitted into this emerging modern aesthetic. Certainly, pianos had had their day too.

The archetype for this new space revolution was designed in 1953 by Charlotte Perriand, Jean Prouvé and Sonia Delaunay at the Jean Prouvé Workshop in Italy. At around $80 000

at auction, these are not suited to every budget. Nor is the 'ESU 420N' storage stack designed by Charles and Ray Eames in the early 1960s (worth around $30 000 today), but in my view the very best of these is Dieter Rams's '606 Universal Shelving System' for Vitsoe in 1957. This actually seems to float because all of the modules of the unit fit onto a wall-mounted grid-structure so that shelving or cupboard units can be placed anywhere on it. Best of all, it combines an unapologetically hi-tech look with great poise and beauty.

However, because these units could be produced in factories and self-assembled, affordable versions of them were soon available. G-Plan in the UK was quick off the mark producing one of the first ever 'whole house' modular systems of furniture. Their 'Form Five' system was hugely advertised on TV and backed up by swanky showrooms in London W1. G-Plan collecting has assumed cultic proportions among contemporary collectors. In Australia, Douglas Snelling also went modular, establishing his 'Snelling Module' range (manufactured by his Sydney-based Functional Products Pty Ltd) in the early years of the 1950s.

The 1980s was a golden age for storage and particularly so since it aimed to reintroduce a playful 1950s modernism. This is very much the case with Memphis's most iconic piece, Ettore Sottsass's 'Carlton' room divider from 1981. It is a show piece whose role is to show off other objects, and although it would do this very well I have yet to see one that has any object on it all.

53

54

52
Hans Wegner wall units for Ry Møbler, Denmark, 1953
Vampt Vintage Design

53
Paul Kafka, cocktail cabinet with cubist marquetry, Australia, 1947 Powerhouse Museum collection

54
Teak veneer sideboard, unknown designer, Chiswell, Australia, c. 1955

55

The coffee table

If there is one item of furniture that is completely modern, it is the coffee table. As far as I can tell, there were no Greek or Roman coffee tables to inspire later European makers of antiques, partly because coffee drinking was unknown in classical antiquity. But then again, they didn't watch TV either, and it was the combination of drinking coffee and watching TV that gave the impetus for the coffee table.

Although coffee was imported into Britain in the sixteenth century, it took a while to catch on and was not instantly popular. One (anonymous) woman detractor argued that it '*Eunucht* our Husbands, and Crippled our more kind *Gallants*, that they are become as *Impotent*, as Age'. I suspect this poor woman's husband had the odd nip of whisky besides his java, but I digress.

By 1675 there were 3000 coffee-houses in the UK, but not a single *coffee table*, or at least, not as we know them. This is because, until the twentieth century, people drank their coffee sitting on fairly normal dining chairs at tables that were dining table height. You can find antique long, low tables which are even described as coffee tables but, believe me, most of them have had their legs shortened *after* the modern coffee table became popular. So what prompted their design in the first place? There are several theories. One has it that low tables popular in the Ottoman Empire were imported and became fashionable. This may be true, but they did not become an established feature of western homes until later, when people began to favour sitting on much lower sofas. From the late 1920s and 1930s, one sees a few low tables that are probably the ancestors of all coffee tables. One of the first to be called a coffee table was produced by Mies Van Der Rohe in 1929 and was constructed, somewhat outrageously, of chromed steel with a glass top.

However, it was not until television held people in specially designed low-slung chairs and sofas for such long periods of time that the idea of eating and drinking at this elevation became feasible or popular. Tea was still drunk mainly at the table but coffee somehow detached itself from dining formality and wandered about the house more. It is therefore sculptor Isamu Noguchi's coffee table of 1944, just at the beginning of the TV era, which is often considered the ancestor of all coffee tables. Like Mies Van Der Rohe's earlier piece, it was glass topped, but that's where the resemblance ends. Noguchi's design was warmer and softer, with a free-form wooden base of ebonised walnut. It fitted in well with the relaxed, comfy space of the modern 'television room' and allowed coffee cups and the odd magazine to be within each viewer's reach.

Australia was onto the coffee table very early and Paul Kafka's coffee table of 1940 is a masterpiece of modern design. Made

58

59

60

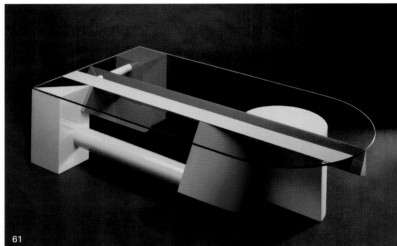

61

62

63

58
Coffee table, Paul Kafka, Sydney, Australia, c. 1940 Powerhouse Museum collection

59
Sofa table by Peter Hvidt & Orla Molgaard for France & Daverkosen, Denmark, c. 1956 Vampt Vintage Design

60
Clement Meadmore, glass coffee table, c. 1958, Australia

61
John Smith 'Colourblock' coffee table, Australia, 1984 Powerhouse Museum collection

62
Inspired by the coffee table? Philippe Starck's 'table vase' 'Quatre etrangetes sous un mur?' ('Four Curiosities Below a Wall') for Daum Crystal, France, 1988 Powerhouse Museum collection

63
Douglas Snelling, coffee table in freeform shape, Functional Products, Australia, 1955 Powerhouse Museum collection

64
Robert Klippel, plywood coffee table, Australia, 1954 Powerhouse Museum collection

65
Solid hardwood coffee table, designer unknown, mid-1950s, Australia; Fred Lowen, Fler 'Narvik' blackwood chair, Australia, 1950s; lamp, designer unknown, 1950s, USA

of walnut veneer and sapele wood with a peach mirror-glass top, this three-tiered coffee table would fit into any modern interior, from Art Deco to Memphis. After Kafka, every major Australian furniture designer offered a coffee table. As a piece of furniture, the coffee table offered the designer the opportunity to identify the clearest expression of their times.

Robert Klippel's 1954 design for a coffee table that could be made from one sheet of wood demonstrates not only the cleanest of interlocking lines but also a design that could be easily translated into industrial art. A year later he produced one of the best coffee tables ever: his 'Boomerang' coffee table. Again, there is a smoked-glass top that provides a good view of its amazing sculptural base structure, comprised of two black and two white boomerang shapes that cleverly provide both the legs and the supports for the top. All four boomerangs articulate around a large red atomic sphere that focuses the entire design. If ever there was a design crying out to be reissued, this is it.

1955 was a good year for the factory of Functional Products in Sydney who were making Douglas Snelling's coffee table: a simple free-form shape in maple

with confident diagonal legs.

Through the 1950s to the 1970s the coffee table began to inhabit almost every home as a required element of furniture. The ubiquitous kidney-shaped coffee tables of the 1950s seemed to remind everyone of the new pleasures that took place around them but, by the 1970s, they appeared to have become stale, as simple rectangular shapes in teak, cane or pine lost all sense of playfulness and fun. The artists' palette-shaped coffee table, mostly set on three unsteady legs, was widely manufactured or made at home during the 1950s. Although one feels that these were ubiquitous, it is nonetheless true that not many have survived into the present day. In fifteen years of searching at my local markets and garage sales, I have only ever found one.

Through the 1970s, few coffee tables excite. They became generic and pedestrian, and for a ghastly period were made from cane and pine. These have very little retro interest. Enter John Smith in the 1980s, then under the spell of Memphis Design from Italy. His hard-to-ignore 'Colourblock' coffee table from 1984 brought back so much colour, art and excitement to the television room that I cannot imagine myself watching TV if I had that to look at instead.

64

65

66

The office

During the retro years, the interior of most homes became more diverse. To my knowledge, few people had home offices in the 1950s but by the 1980s they were a standard feature. In between, offices became more necessary as fewer of us worked in manufacturing and more were engaged in information and service industries. In addition, the cost of a home office became more affordable through the use of cheaper materials, telecommunications and word processing technologies and printing. Once perfected, the home office made it possible for many to work from home. With more time spent in the home office, it became the focus for more competition and better design. Meanwhile, corporate offices in the city also became lavishly designed and appointed and much of this furniture is now available for the enthusiast to buy.

Desks quickly caught the eye of the top designers and there are some classy names and designs to dream about. Maybe it was Marcel Breuer's astonishingly new desk from 1935 that set it all off. This was a glass-topped desk supported underneath by a loop of tubular chrome steel that dipped down at the end to form a paper clip–like leg. The other end cantilevered on a tightly designed block of drawers in sycamore-veneered wood. Made for Isokon (one of *the* names to look for) and manufactured by P.E. Gane, this became the inspiration for many other daring takes on the desk.

Into the 1940s we start to see stylish acts emerging from France and the USA. Jean Prouvé's 1940s design in steel and wood for a secretaire desk matched his *beautiful* 'Standard' chair. Then, into the 1950s, it was George Nelson for

Herman Miller who really set the tone, especially his lovely 'Model 4658' that seems to have been an inspiration for Harry Seidler, since a lot of his one-off designs for Rose Seidler House in Sydney bear a striking resemblance to it. Its dainty Bauhaus-influenced lines are composed of an ensemble of blocks of separated colour and shapes, connected to an engineered structure rather than a cabinetmaker's frame. From certain angles, it is more like a Miro painting than a solid object.

George Nelson's desk designs for Herman Miller carry right through into the 1970s and these are typically more affordable through his mass-produced 'Action Office' range. That said, his rosewood 'Action Office 1' desk on a green aluminium base will set you back at least $4000. In Australia, the most eye-catching modern desk in the arts

67

and crafts style was by the Melbourne-based German designer Schulim Krimper, but others also produced striking designs, including Fred Ward, Parker and Module.

In 1959 Joe Colombo's father died, leaving him in charge of an electrical equipment firm in Italy. He was just twenty-eight. Over the next ten years or so, he exploited the growing market for office and desk-related equipment by designing a new generation of desk and floor lamps. His success, particularly with new materials, launched him as a designer; and by 1970 he was turning out a staggering range of bright plastic furnishing innovations, including the famous 'Boby' trolley, which was designed to hold a vast range of office equipment but avoid the need for drawers. This surely inspired de Pas, Lomazzi

and D'Urbino to come up with large, brightly coloured Lego-style bricks with which one might build anything from a console table to a set of shelves.

The ultimate desk from the 1970s is also Italian: Parigi and Prina's 'Oryx' desk for Molteni and Co. This is in bright red plastic on a tubular steel

chrome base, and it is truly space-age in conception, combining a glass-topped desk lid, moulded storage pods for contemporary desk equipment and a flip-up chrome light. Sold from the very best showrooms in Europe and not out of place in a Tardis, these still turn up occasionally, so keep your eyes peeled.

68

CHAPTER 2

CERAMICS

THIS STREAMLINED, FUNCTIONAL, SOLID-COLOUR WARE COULD BE BOUGHT IN CHARTREUSE, GRANITE GREY, SEAFOAM, CANTALOUPE, CEDAR GREEN, CORAL, WHITE, BEAN BROWN, GLACIER BLUE, BLACK CHUTNEY AND STEUBENVILLE BLUE.

PAUL ATTERBURY ET AL, DESCRIBING RUSSEL WRIGHT'S **AMERICAN MODERN** DINNER WARE FOR STEUBENVILLE, OHIO, 1999

IN THE RETRO PERIOD THERE were several important changes to housing and domestic organisation that created the basis for a very new look and feel to modern life. Combined, they transformed the historic role of ceramics as functional and decorative objects to something that demonstrated style, an aesthetic sensibility and the successful insertion of art into everyday spaces. Designs became lighter and airier and expanded domestic spaces provided opportunities to introduce colour and attention-grabbing decorative objects. For the majority of people, rather than just the wealthy few, it became possible to live in a space that was both beautified and artistic. In a relatively short space of time the home changed from being barely big enough, dry enough and healthy enough for human habitation, common enough up until the 1930s, to a place that people found genuinely exciting and a reward in itself. This is why so much modern life came to centre on the home. It wasn't that community had died, as was commonly believed at the time, but more that people were simply less reliant on public, communal spaces. Childhood gradually moved indoors, teenage culture developed the space of the bedroom, and adults created party spaces, dining spaces, leisure spaces and other social spaces out of what had previously been the rather cramped space of cooking and eating.

This functional differentiation inspired designers to provide a wide range of decorative objects to enhance these new activities. Various new resources made this possible. First, the population of artists and designers was significantly increased by a massive investment in new colleges of art and design. New factories with modern mass production techniques improved output and reduced unit prices to levels that most people could afford. At the same time, new light-weight materials such as plywood, ABS plastic, tubular steel, spun aluminium, fibreglass and laminates reduced prices of raw material and transport costs still further. These materials were often combined into system-built or modular packages that provided an integrated look. Through the flat-pack, self-service revolution pioneered by companies such as IKEA, consumers contributed to cost reductions by becoming home-based constructors. While not a new industry or material, ceramics proved to be a highly flexible and versatile medium for modern design. They provided a diverse range of functional and decorative objects and their surfaces were loved more than any other by a new generation of trained artists. In many ways, ceramic surfaces became the new canvas for modern art and design.

In post-1945 England, the so-called Parker Knowle government standards laid down new construction quality standards and minimum sizes for domestic spaces in public housing. This dramatically increased the average space available to householders. Similar norms were established in Scandinavia, Germany, Holland and elsewhere. In the New World, land prices were considerably cheaper and domestic spaces that had always been generous grew even bigger. Most Australians, Americans and New Zealanders could afford to live in detached housing, typically on large building blocks. The cluttered domestic interiors of the early part of the twentieth century gave way to a more open-plan space, and a more selective use of decorative display. The mass ranks of photographs disappeared, as did the space-hungry piano, the strangely preserved 'parlour', 'front room', 'best room' or 'holy of holies' and the china cabinets for objects 'too good to use'. These spatial arrangements of genteel poverty were to be superseded by the more strident aesthetics of 'the affluent (or consumer) society'.

A new form of furniture arrived in the 1950s that personified this new aesthetic. Often built from floor to ceiling and delivering a dramatic aesthetic spectacle, system-built shelving units required householders to choose and display far more decorative objects, and a diversity of forms. No

1
Affordable luxury: 'Ketchup Boy' ketchup pot, USA, c. 1953

2
Modern art from the factory: Eve Midwinter 'Sun' dinner plate for Midwinter Pottery, Staffordshire, England, 1973

3
'Earth' and 'Sun' mugs by Eve Midwinter for Midwinter Pottery, Staffordshire, England

1

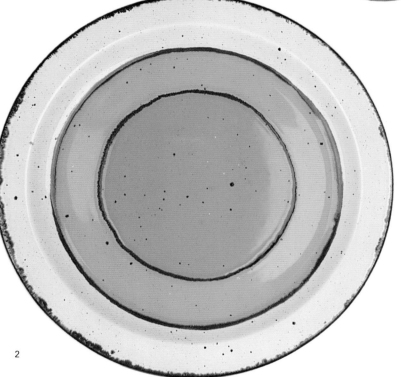

2

3

4

5

6

4
Midwinter Pottery
'Stylecraft' jug,
England, 1955

5
Russel Wright's
'American Modern'
coffee cup and
saucer in Granite
Grey, Steubenville
Pottery, Ohio, USA,
1939

6
Midwinter Pottery
'Fashion' jug,
England, 1958

7
Cover from *New
York World's Fair:
The World of
Tomorrow*, New
York, 1939

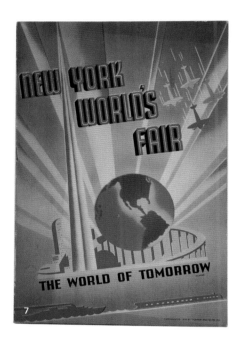

7

longer displaying a motley and disjointed
collection of heirlooms and surviving
wedding gifts, these shelves supported
the household's growing and changing
collection of decorative arts. This
gave rise to a new connoisseurship in
choosing and matching domestic wares;
and their greater prominence meant
that this competence was there to be
noticed and, importantly, judged. Taste
became an important quality for modern
consumers and was used to express
and evaluate social belonging and rank.
Understanding and expressing an
emerging modern taste was no easy
task, however. There was a great deal
of variety in modern designs as well as
a degree of continuity with the past.
However, we can see in the catalogue of
modern ceramic design some commonly
expressed values, and, arguably, these
were first clearly expressed in the 1939
New York World Fair.

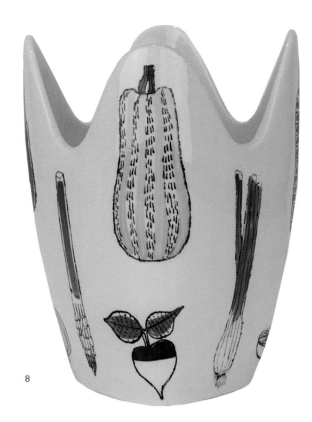

With its slogan 'The Dawn of a New Day' the 1939 World Fair set the tone for what we associate with retro. This was the first world fair to be based on 'the future' and the social character of this future was clearly set out inside its centrepiece, the Perisphere. The sphere contained a diorama called *Democracity*, a futuristic vision for a utopian city. By the end of the Second World War, this demand for utopian thinking created a keen sense of a new starting point, and as this deepened, so consumers eschewed designs that reminded them of the past and embraced things that embodied the new. In ceramics, Russel Wright's 'American Modern' tableware echoed around the world, demanding emulation. Produced by Steubenville Pottery, Ohio, between 1939 and 1959, this tableware sent a dramatic message to ceramic companies around the world to change. 'American Modern' introduced a totally different shape to tableware that was simply exciting to behold; it stood out, it was bold and exuberant. Streamlined, organic and machine-age; it was, at the same time, very solidly built, sober and finished in earthy, plain colours. It was modest and affordable for the average family and yet it also welcomed them to the possibility of a more stylish world. As a design it was a masterstroke; it

8

9

10

11

8
Terence Conran
'Saladware' celery
jug for Midwinter
Pottery, England,
c. 1955

9, 10, 11
Jessie Tait 'Tonga'
coffee cup and
saucer and coffeepot
for Midwinter
Pottery, England,
1955

12
Jessie Tait 'Astral'
plate for Midwinter
Pottery, England,
1957

13
Sir Hugh Casson
'Cannes' plate for
Midwinter Pottery,
England, 1960

12

13

sold 400 million pieces and is still in production today.

The implication of 'American Modern' for tableware manufacturers was picked up loud and clear by Roy Midwinter in the UK. With sales slumping, he realised that he could no longer rely on long-established designs or shapes and maybe even the in-house ceramic designers. One reason why Midwinter survived and is a retro favourite is because he decided to introduce artists and recently trained designers to bring his products into the future. This innovation became a core element of Midwinter philosophy and began in 1953 with the 'Stylecraft' shape (the mix of new and old is established clearly in this name) and then the 'Fashion' shape of 1955. While distinctive, these shapes combined the shockingly new and exuberant with more familiar organic lines. Where 'American Modern' remained distinctly puritanical and plain, Midwinter let rip with colour and decorative audacity.

In the 1950s Midwinter design was dominated by Jessie Tate, who was inspired by the experience of travel that was opening up in the 1950s. She brought renditions of the exotic, indigenous art and colourways of southern Europe, Africa and Polynesia to the dining tables of Britain. Designs such as 'Sienna', 'Tonga', 'Zambesi', 'Madeira' and 'Hawaii' suggested an emerging cosmopolitanism and sense of openness and adventure among consumers. Gone was any sense of upholding tradition or stability; these designs embraced change by being open to others, and in this sense they embodied a form of tolerance that was

new. Tait's other abstract and floral designs were similarly strong, vivid and eye-catching; her work never became tired because she always applied a modern eye to even the most familiar object.

Although Jessie Tait was a success, Roy Midwinter seemed to understand that the modern world was going to be strongly differentiated by age, and while Jessie Tait designs covered a broad demographic, he also wanted to engage youthful designers fresh out of college. The young Terence Conran came to Midwinter with little other than his experience of the 1951 Festival of Britain behind him, but he brought an appreciation of Scandinavian traditions to the Midwinter catalogues, which became very successful. His 'Saladware' was a mixture of the familiar and the exotic; a spring onion alongside a chilli, an avocado alongside a radish. Other designs such as 'Nature

14
Meakin Pottery 'Fisherman's Cove' plate, England, c. 1955

15
Meakin Pottery 'Fairground' plate, England, c. 1955

16
Jug, bowl and pepper pot by John Clappison for Hornsea Pottery, England, 1957

17
Meakin water jug in their 'Holiday' pattern, with clear 'American Modern' styling, England, c. 1950

17

18

19

Study', 'Chequers' and 'Plant Life' and designers such as Marianne Westman and Stig Lindberg extended the Scandinavian influence.

Other potteries tried young designers in the 1950s, often with stunning success. John Clappison was still at Hull College of Art when he designed the 'Elegance' range for Lancaster-based pottery Hornsea. With its Scandinavian influenced two-tone lines and its stunningly polished yellow and black glaze, it has become, in retrospect, a defining look of the period and is much sought after. It was launched in 1957 with the hope that it would find a niche in the lucrative wedding present market, consumers being tempted to buy a complete set rather than single items.

Midwinter also engaged the artist Hugh Casson to produce designs based on the French Riviera. As with 'Salad Ware', his 'Riviera' and 'Cannes' are suggestive of a leisure-rich life where a sojourn in France is within everyone's grasp, whereas only thirty years previously it had been the exclusive playground of the aristocracy and celebrity class. What a democratising difference the modern car and cheap air travel made. Motifs from the exotic edges of people's experience projected them into a future where such places, foods and culture would become more familiar. In the meantime, these featured on many decorated surfaces of the home, from these tablewares to furnishing fabrics and wallpaper.

The more mainstream and popular-taste orientated Meakin and Meakin Studio also opted for leisure themes, although their take on 'American Modern', 'Meakin Studio', was also impressive. Meakin's 'Cornwall' and 'Devon' designs were popular with all classes in the UK and their vividly stylised 'Fisherman's Cove' design was a hit through the 1950s, as was their Paris-themed 'Moulin Rouge'. Other leisure themed series include an indoor 'Cactus' pattern, a 'Fairground' pattern, and a 'Tally-Ho' hunting pattern.

It seems odd that it was through young designers like Conran that many British people were introduced to Scandinavian design, but import taxes kept most of it out of the country and few people ventured that far on their holidays in the 1950s. The contemporary world of retro collectors knows no such boundaries and although people face the impediment of higher postage costs, eBay has at least allowed them to see what they missed the first time around. The Scandinavians completely

18
Marianne Westman 'Picknick' lidded pot for Rörstrand, Sweden, 1956

19
'Barbecue' plate by Ridgway of Staffordshire, England, mid-1950s. This design was made primarily for the Australian market

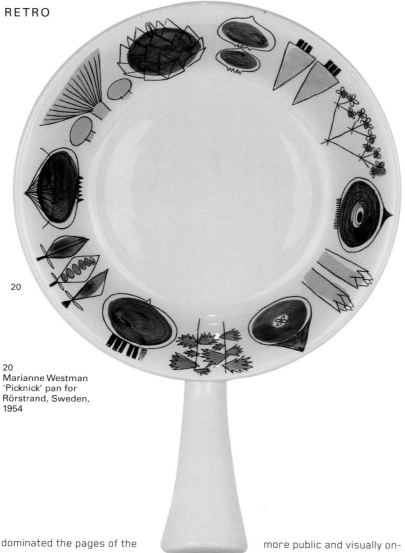

20

20
Marianne Westman
'Picknick' pan for
Rörstrand, Sweden,
1954

had always been an occasion for shows of fine craftsmanship, often in silver, the emphasis being on demonstrating rank, the modern, popular take on this was to celebrate and elevate the beauty of the everyday, the commonplace and popular. It is hard to imagine a bourgeois silversmith using the humble carrot as the design focus for a major table feature in the same way Westman did. But here is clear evidence that new values were in play, and this is a defining feature of retro. At the same time, there is a wry, somewhat muted playfulness and humour in these designs. They *are* fun, possibly because they were so audacious, so 'out there', so fresh and new.

Conran's botanical and zoological subjects were previously explored by Gustavsberg and Arabia which both released several designs for the everyday staple in Scandinavia: fish. They vary from the rich stylisation of Gustavsberg's pike laying in wait among the reeds and their seascape of plaice, crab, whelk and seaweed, to the more figurative style of Upsala-Ekeby's shoal of perch and freshwater vegetation. Less abstract designs such as this still had a market and seem to have inspired British designers such as John Russell who also did natural history designs for Midwinter in the 1950s, and Richard Drake who did exquisitely mannered designs for Crown Lynn in New Zealand.

In France, major potteries such as St Clements, which had specialised in sumptuous majolica wildlife absinthe pitchers since the late nineteenth century, were given a new lease of life in the fifties and found a ready market for their strikingly lovely but quirky ducks,

dominated the pages of the Design Yearbooks of the 1950s, and among their many companies Gustavsberg, Upsala-Ekeby, Rörstrand and Arabia stand out.

Marianne Westman's 'Picknick' designs for Rörstrand were particularly significant here, not least because they won prizes at the Milan Triennales in 1954, 1957 and 1960. Here again is a similar formula of new, audacious shapes coupled with sharp designs using abstract renditions of fine foods. The message was clear enough: food preparation was now going to be socially significant and dining a

more public and visually on-show affair. The Swedes and the Norwegians developed an important series of 'oven-to-table' tablewares that illustrated that cooking and eating not only took place in a common nexus of spaces but that the entire process was now open to scrutiny and appreciation. Gone was the foundation for plain, merely functional cookware that remained simply tools in the background, and gradually more and more cook- and tablewares became mantled with aesthetic qualities or 'aestheticised'. Whereas for the bourgeoisie, dining

MARTIN BOYD POTTERY RAMEKINS

DEBBIE RUDDER = CURATOR, SCIENCE AND INDUSTRY, POWERHOUSE MUSEUM

These ramekins were mass produced by Martin Boyd Potteries, a company established in 1946 by Guy Martin Boyd (a member of Australia's artistic and literary Boyd family) and Norma Flegg. When new, the ramekins were valued for their fresh appearance and solid practicality. Many examples have survived and are traded today both online and via op-shops.

Their varied colour combinations and lack of decoration differentiated these bowls from the dinnerware that was most valued in mid-twentieth century Australia: matched sets of fine porcelain or bone china with intricate applied decoration. In such formal dinner sets, soup bowls lacked handles and were intended for use at a dining table. In contrast, handles made the Boyd ramekins appropriate for use at the kitchen table, in front of the television or outdoors, while their cool design and good quality finish set them above other crockery suitable for such informal meals.

The appeal of these objects to a new generation could be put down to their mix of Bauhaus-inspired simplicity and unusual colour combinations. Or it could be simply that they are cheap and cheerful. But why do examples in good condition keep turning up for sale? Perhaps, after a first flush of use, they were reserved for special occasions, consigned to a high shelf and forgotten for years. More prosaically, they could have moved gradually into the dim depths of cupboards, replaced in everyday use by bowls that stacked more compactly in dishwashers. It is thus perhaps appropriate that the museum's ramekins are still in their original packaging and have never been selected for display.

'Australian Modern': These earthenware ramekins were made in Sydney by the Martin Boyd Pottery, 1946–63. The museum holds several pieces made by this pottery company and two machines used to make them Powerhouse Museum collection storks and herons, and added well-designed fish platters to their range (see page 11). Seafood and an interest in marine life came together strongly in the seaside holiday experiences of modern people everywhere. Located at the English epicentre of seaside holidays, Poole Harbour, Poole Pottery did more than sell to a passing seaside trade: it exported its soft, two-toned loveliness and free-form shapes to major department stores around the world. The two scallop dishes pictured on page 63 were clearly designed to add a quirky note to a party table, but any reference to the seaside had the power to relax the social tone. In Australia, where an entire civilisation was spreading out along its interminable coastlines, seafood became almost as entrenched as in Scandinavia, and thus gave rise to similar 'good life' wares

21
Bristol Pottery (est. 1652) beaker commemorating the coronation of Queen Elizabeth II on June 2nd 1953, England, 1953. Exquisite colour and hand applied gilt

22
Bourne of England (for the Medici Society) Half Pint tankard to commemorate the coronation of George VI, May 12th 1937. This very fine salt glaze vessel by Bourne (later Denby Pottery) is hand thrown and glazed in a very old style – superb and rare

23
New Hall pottery,
Hanley, Staffordshire
beaker made to
commemorate
the coronation of
Edward VIII prior
to his abdication in
1937. These were
withdrawn from sale
and so are much
rarer than other Royal
commemoratives.
England, 1937

24
New Hall pottery,
Hanley, Staffordshire
mug commemorating
the coronation of
Queen Elizabeth II
on June 2nd 1953,
England, 1953. Carries
the backstamp of the
British Pottery

25
Carlton Ware kneeling
cup commemorating
the Silver Jubilee
of Queen Elizabeth
II on June 2nd
1977, England,
1977. This is a rare
example from their
hugely collectable
Walking Ware range
designed by Danka
Napiorkowska and
Roger Michell

26, 27
Gustavsberg 'Pike'
plate, and 'Plaice
and Seascape' plate,
Sweden, c. 1950

28
Upsala-Ekeby 'Perch'
plate, Sweden,
c. 1950

29
Wade Pottery dish
commemorating
the coronation of
Elizabeth II in 1953.
This delightful dish
was clearly earmarked
to be sold across the
'British Empire' and is
nicely decorated with
animals representing
the Dominions

30
Purbeck Pottery dish
commemorating the
Wedding of HRH The
Prince of Wales and
Lady Diana Spencer,
July 29th 1981,
Dorset, England, 1981

26

27

28

29

30

ARGENTA WARE CERAMICS

EVA CZERNIS-RYL = CURATOR, DESIGN AND SOCIETY, POWERHOUSE MUSEUM

In 1917 Sweden's Gustavsberg ceramics factory engaged the painter and graphic designer Wilhelm Käge as its new artistic director, with a mandate to modernise the company image. During his tenure, Käge developed a range of modernist lines for both the everyday and luxury markets. In response to a demand for more ornament, he also introduced more decorative designs, known as 'Swedish grace'. Käge was awarded a grand prix at the 1925 International Exposition in Paris.

Soon after his success in Paris, Käge developed art deco stoneware with a matt, blackish-green glaze, resembling the patina that forms on bronze. The glaze became decisively green from about 1927, when it was paired with gold motifs. When gold was replaced with silver, the 'Argenta' range (from Latin *argentum*) was born: a luxurious, silver-inlaid ware for the table, kitchen and the desk, first exhibited in 1930. Käge's designs evolved over two decades, drawing influence from Swedish folklore, modernist painting and classical mythology. His repertoire of imagery included dancing maidens, mermaids riding seahorses, nymphs resting among sea grasses and fantastical sea creatures and fish blowing bubbles. Delicate silver bands, lines, tiny flowers, stars and leaves also featured.

Argenta's popularity waned in the mid-1930s, but had a resurgence the following decade, its round shapes and stylised naturalistic decoration fitting perfectly with the 'organic' modernism of 1940s Scandinavia. Blood-red, blue, brown and white glazes were used alongside a spectrum of greens. Production ceased in 1953.

Argenta ware first appeared on the radar for collectors with a revived interest in art deco in the late 1960s and again in the 1980s. Collecting enthusiasm has continued ever since with many items now sporting the 'retro' prefix on the international market.

'Argenta' line platter and two bowls, glazed stoneware with silver inlays, designed by Wilhelm Käge (1889–1960), made by Gustavsberg, Sweden, about 1953 Powerhouse Museum collection

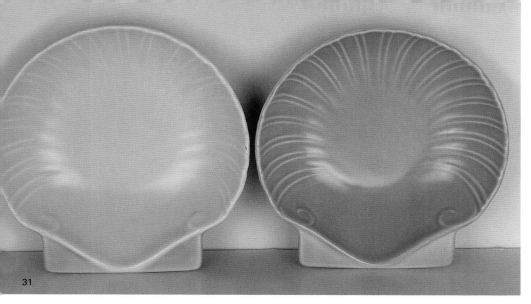

31

32

33

34

such as Elischer Pottery's fabulous 'Oyster' platter.

Smaller potteries, such as Rye in southern England, also followed the lead of Scandinavia, particularly in their choice of colourways and shapes. Simple symmetrical patterns in purples, reds and blues on little bowls and the much sought-after avocado dishes were reminiscent of patterns and shapes attributed to Stig Lindberg for Gefle. Lindberg would be an obvious candidate to attribute the richly stylised fishing motifs for a lidded fish pot, presumably for pickled herrings. It remains an understated masterpiece in tableware design for this period.

This new 'with-it' mood caught on everywhere and can be seen, for example, in the designs of Albert Colledge for Denby. His 'Flair' gravy jug (1947–69, pictured on page 65), shows a humorous scene of an angry chicken chasing away a bird. Again, such a

scene would not have been deemed appropriate to the formal tables of the 1930s, and note also the extravagant handle, borrowed directly, it seems, from Russel Wright's 'American Modern'.

The early 1960s continued many of the 1950s themes and only changed in relation to the counter-cultural movement that became the inspiration for design after 1965. The challenge to the sober, standardising, conservative and industrially-focused modernity of the 1950s came swiftly and on a number of fronts. As usual it was among the youth, and especially among very influential art school and university circles that change was brought in and normalised. Experimentation with drugs and consciousness-changing techniques such as meditation produced a more emotionally receptive human subject, interested in 'mind expanding experiences'. Art and design obliged

31
Poole Pottery 'Scallop' dishes, England, c. 1954

32
Attributed to Stig Lindberg, lidded pickled herring pot for Upsala-Ekeby, Sweden, 1956

33
Elischer Pottery 'Oyster' platter, Australia, 1956

34
Rye Pottery pot, England, 1958

35

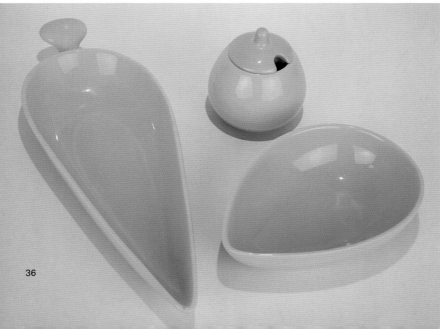

36

by taking people outside the realm of the familiar and into a dreamlike, psychedelic reality. This dreamlike quality can be seen in the designs of John Clappison for Hornsea Pottery that became a global success in the 1960s. A shift in consciousness and values seemed to require a shift in shape as well as decoration. One of the key innovations of the 1960s, and a form in which Clappison excelled, was the mug. Mugs had been around for a while but they became more commonplace in the 1960s. Mugs referenced the arrival of instant gratification: no longer willing to wait for formal dining times, tea and coffee could be taken whenever people wanted. Nescafé instant coffee emerged at the beginning of the Second World War and was so popular among the armed forces that the entire output of its US plant was reserved for military use until the end of the war.

Coffee was the teenage drink of choice and coffee bars their distinctive social space in the 1950s. In 1955 a new instant version of Blend 37, a richer continental coffee, came onto the market but it was only in 1961 that the familiar brown jars of Nescafé coffee became a household staple; and only in 1964 that a truer coffee aroma was captured in the drying process. Thus, cheap, better quality instant coffee came onto the market at a time when the new art colleges and universities were coming on line around the modern world. With jars of coffee and then tea bags, students casualised hot drink consumption. Because it could be taken without the need to brew for an entire household or gathering (this was, after all the role of the teapot or coffeepot)

35
Kaj Frank 'Flounder' platter for Arabia, Finland, 1958

36
Stig Lindberg dishes for Gefle/Upsala-Ekeby, Sweden, 1955; Arabia mustard pot, Finland, 1950s

37
John Clappison, 'Heirloom' and abstract animal mugs for Hornsea Pottery, England, 1965

38
Albert Colledge 'Flair' gravy jug for Denby, England, 1947

39
A collection of abstract animal designs by John Clappison for Hornsea, c. 1967

37

and because it was relatively cheap, more of it could be drunk in a serving. This is why the mug came to replace the tea and coffee cup on all but formal occasions. Hornsea mugs by John Clappison really define this period, not merely by their new mug shape but through the architectural form, particularly when it came to depicting abstract animals. Because mugs were associated with youth, fashion and 'with-it' leisure, they were also an ideal form for giftware, particularly for the affluent younger generations. Mugs could be bought as gifts for friends, the very people one lounged around drinking coffee with into the small wee hours, and soon these gift-mugs were mantled with personalised attributes. So, Clappison, for example, did a series of birth sign mugs followed by another series of 'Best in the World' mugs. The informality of the mug played against the less fashionable formality of the cup and saucer, and so became an appropriate canvas for the expression of humour. Clappison used industrial design techniques that had been deployed for adverts and public

39

38

information for the 'Best in the World' series to create attention-grabbing, humorous logos and catch phrases. From his 1970s 'Best Babysitter in the World' mug, the magnificent 'Best Woodworker in the World' mug and the still popular 'Smarties' Easter mug, it was a short step to the proliferation of merchandise mugs in the 1980s. Everyone, from the risqué *Viz* comics

40

41

42

43

40
John Clappison
'Best Woodworker
in the World' mug
and 'Best Babysitter
in the World' mug
for Hornsea Pottery,
England, c. 1970

41
Susan Williams-Ellis
'Totem' storage
jar for Portmeirion
Pottery, England,
c. 1950

42
John Clappison 'Leo'
astrological mug
for Hornsea Pottery,
England, c. 1967

43
Susan Williams-Ellis
'Jupiter' mug for
Portmeirion Pottery,
England, c. 1969

44
Susan Williams-
Ellis 'Totem' cup
and saucer for
Portmeirion Pottery,
England, c. 1969

45
David Queensberry
'Queensberry'
teapot for Midwinter
Pottery, England,
1962–78

46
John Clappison
'Smarties' mug for
Hornsea Pottery,
England, c. 1968

to Greenpeace produced merchandise mugs. For the ceramic industry, this removed the risk associated with new and untested designs because the wares were already tied to popular products.

Taken together, these various innovations enrolled ceramics into the fast-expanding popular cultures of the postwar period. In the 1960s and 1970s, tableware design was also influenced by the growing architectural use of texture and this was demonstrated by many of Portmeirion's designs by Susan Williams-Ellis, including 'Jupiter' and 'Totem', as well as Gill Pemberton's 'Chevron' design for Denby.

By the 1980s the long tradition of postwar modern tablewares in Europe was beginning to wane especially as a result of increasing competition from cheaper sources overseas. Many tried to adapt to new circumstances and markets, but slowly; many simply folded. One associated leadership in new design more with the resurgence in studio potteries and the sculptural licence that the 1980s seemed to offer them; the work of Jenny Orchard being a case in point.

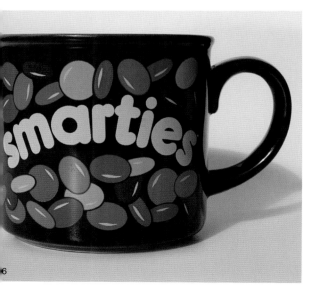

Around 1966, Midwinter launched David Queensberry's (Marquess of Queensberry) mod-styled shapes 'MQ1' and 'MQ2' alongside some breathtakingly cool patterns. These have to be the quintessential 1960s look, before design descended into the flower power, neo-traditional, psychedelia and Pythonesque whimsy that characterised the 1970s. Gill Pemberton's 'Chevron' for Denby can be included among this rarefied community of design.

Queensberry's 'Queensberry' pattern is a *very* sharp, understated pattern consisting of lines in olive greens and dark and pale greys. David Queensberry was professor of ceramics at the Royal College of Art in London between 1953 and 1989 and has left a powerful legacy in his designs for Midwinter alone.

After 1967, Clappison's 'Heirloom' design for Hornsea became a defining look of the 1960s and this was followed by his 'Saffron' and 'Bronte' patterns. 'Heirloom' was reminiscent of Islamic design and this referenced a new-found interest in tradition and religion as opposed to the future and science and technology. 'Bronte' also had a strong traditional design with echoes of medieval European styles; but with 'Saffron' we can see the arrival of the stylised flower symbol. Better than religion, flowers represented perfectly the peace, anti-war, pro-environment and civil rights values of the baby boomer generation as it passed out of college and began to form households.

The hedonism, mobility and political interests of the beat generation morphed into a more affluent and style-driven Mod culture whose values embraced the intoxicating music of Afro-American soul. At the centre of a late 1960s cultural melting pot, the Beatles opened new cultural fronts on civil liberties, the cultural conservatism of the nuclear family, Indian transcendentalism, industrial nostalgia, peace and the body. Flower power, hippy values and a more tolerant and curious worldview undermined the confident, style-led consumerism of the 1950s, ushering in an even more open-ended, experimental and differentiated design aesthetic. At this time, London began to swing and eclipse the style leadership of Scandinavia. London provided a more fertile medium for this experimentation, tolerance and pleasure seeking, since in truth it had always been a tolerant city of great cultural diversity, and its sheer size frustrated any possibility of surveillance and censorship. Although rigorously disciplined and well trained, the ceramics industry of Scandinavia was held back by its immersion within social democratic values, its standardisation and a prevailing suspicion of individual freedom, laissez faire, and particularly the hedonistic avant-garde that was growing in London. Set around the culture of pop, with inspiration from shops such as Biba and Heal's and the Design Award showrooms in Bond Street, Carnaby Street, Brewer Street Soho and the Kings Road, London formed an epicentre of 1960s civilisation that lasted well into the 1970s. This was a time when the demand for new shapes and designs coincided with the positive reappraisal of older traditions, particularly those of

47

48

49

50

the middle ages, and handcrafts and a slow pace of life were perceived to be appropriate to build back into modern lifestyles.

It was in the postmodern times of the late 1960s that the bone china industry also made an effort to modernise and fight off competition from the mug. Almost as soon as drinking from cups and saucers was declared old fashioned and stifling, it could inspire others to feel nostalgia for its quaint social formalities and ritualised nature. With the help of some ex-Midwinter designers like John Russell, Ridgway Potteries launched a new low-cost porcelain series called 'Hostess Tableware' in 1968. The designs have all the hallmarks of the Biba/mod years: a new fashionable silhouette decorated in the op-art style inspired by Bridget Riley and in the much-favoured colours of chocolate and lavender. Priced to sell in huge volumes, one imagines that this was aimed at the giftware market, particularly for weddings, and may not have entered into popular daily use as was hoped for. If eBay is anything to go by, 'Hostess' and other such bids for a reprieve for tea ups achieved some considerable success – but they never achieved anything like the sales for mugs. Design always has to follow *social* function as well as operational function, and apart from occasional use among a declining demographic, 'high tea' and the full tea service ritual was dead in the water by 1970. From then on, social meals became more flexible, fragmented and individualised and the manufacture, sales and marketing of tablewares had to follow this trend or perish. Woolworths in Britain had

51

52

47
Jenny Orchard tea set, Australia, c. 1985 Powerhouse Museum collection

48
Gill Pemberton 'Chevron' lidded marmalade pot for Denby, England, c. 1962

49
London swings: a stylised Beefeater pepper pot by Carlton Ware, England, c. 1969

50
John Clappison 'Springtime' butter dish for Hornsea Pottery, England, c. 1969

51
'Saga' jug, Figgjo-Flint, Norway, 1950s

52
John Russell 'Hostess' cup and saucer for Ridgway Potteries, England, 1968

53

54

55

56

57

58

53
Ellis Pottery planter,
Australia, c. 1970

54
Arabia ash tray.
Clever design that
mimics their low
crown trade mark,
Finland, c. 1965

55
Kaj Frank marmalade
pot for Arabia,
Finland, 1970

56
Tea time revival?
Hornsea Pottery
'Swan Lake' teapot
designed by Martin
Hunt and C.B.
Rawson, England,
1983

57
Kaj Frank 'Plums' jug
for Arabia, Finland,
c. 1970

58
Kaj Frank 'Cow' jug
for Arabia, Finland,
1970

sold tableware like Ridgway's iconic 'Homemaker' range on an individual item basis rather than by the set and this was how new retailers like Terence Conran's Habitat shops sold to this new flexible, casualised dining culture. Habitat opened in Chelsea, London in 1964, following Conran's successful Bazaar business. Like Herman Miller in the USA, Conran focused the business around high-design, affordable furniture for the young professional middle classes. On opening, his staff wore clothes by Mary Quant and 'hair design' by Vidal Sassoon, and very soon the shop succeeded by selling a lifestyle that hinged around kitchen life (his first successful business was Soup Kitchen). Conran has said that Habitat succeeded where other similar shops failed because his was the only place you could buy cheap containers for pasta just as the market for dried pasta took off in the UK. Very soon Habitat was the place to buy affordable, well designed tablewares too. By the 1970s his stores were opening everywhere and were being copied widely by others, in the UK and elsewhere.

Flower power, neo-traditional, psychedelia and Pythonesque: the 1970s

1970s table and kitchen wares were a lot of fun. Unlike taste in the 1950s, 1970s taste began to fragment into class, lifestyle and generational driven niche markets. Flower power extolled the virtues of peace and the metaphor of nature as a value to guide human societies. These were the early days of the environmental movement and followed closely on the heels of the anti-war, anti-nuclear bomb movements, and involved a large cross section of Christian, socialist and liberal cultures. We would recognise these today as an important element in the creative, intellectual and educator classes, so it is no surprise that their values became widely adopted generally.

Taunton Vale Pottery was a typical company that made and successfully marketed flower power to the masses. The three storage jars pictured

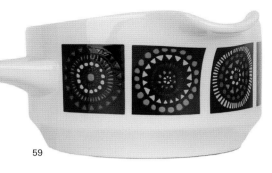

59

59
Nicholas Jenkins 'Madiera' psychedelic pouring vessel in the 'Fine' shape for Midwinter Pottery, England, 1965–74

60
'Barcarole' jug by Turi-design for Figgjo Fajanse, Norway, c. 1970

60

combine an honest, clunky shape (squares and spheres were something of a motif at the time) with the warm fuzzy feel of flowery loveliness. In elevated, bright colours and in dreamy, other-worldly stylisation, these referenced the successful TV show *The Magic Roundabout* that drew global audiences at this time. This aesthetic was embraced by the Norwegian company Figgjo Flint whose 'Annemarie' and 'Turi' designs remain among the 'best of class' for this period.

Portmeirion took this magical mystery period to new heights with their 'Magic City' and 'Magic Garden' designs, but it was 'Acapulco' from the Luxembourg/German based tableware company Villeroy & Boch that became the lasting icon from this period and possibly one of the most successful retro designs of all time. The design is so successful that Villeroy & Boch have recently updated it in their so-called 'New Wave Acapulco' range (that includes some extremely cool espresso cups and saucers).

Villeroy & Boch had beginnings in France when a factory was opened at Audun-le-Tiche in 1748. It opened its Luxembourg factory at Septfontaines in 1766 and a German factory at Mettlach in 1809. In the twentieth century it was inspired by the Bauhaus movement and became renowned for its avant garde designs and designers, including Luigi Colani, Christine Reuter, Helen von Boch and Paloma Picasso (Pablo's daughter).

'Acapulco' was designed by Christine Reuter and introduced in 1967, at the height of the psychedelic/flower power period. It was a time when western designers were taking inspiration from indigenous designs from around the world, and 'Acapulco' is based on stylised bird and flower designs from Mexico. It has vibrant colours and a magical arrangement that seems to put a smile on everyone's face. It is something that every child and every adult, regardless of age, will warm to instantly – and if you think about it, that is quite a feat. It is also somewhat surprising given that the psychedelic

63

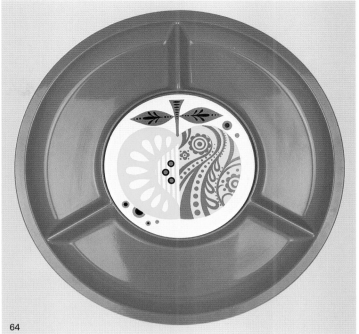

64

65

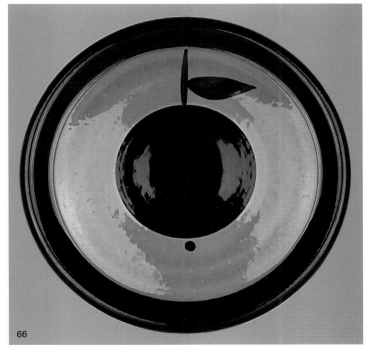

66

61
Flower power candle
stick, Japan, 1970

62
Three lidded storage
jars by Taunton Vale
Pottery, England,
c. 1969

63, 64
Two Japanese
cheese platters
(ceramic tiles on
plastic bases),
designers unknown,
c. 1970

65
Figgjo Flint lidded
pot, Norway, 1973

66
Apple platter by
Marianne Westman
for Rörstrand,
Sweden, c. 1969

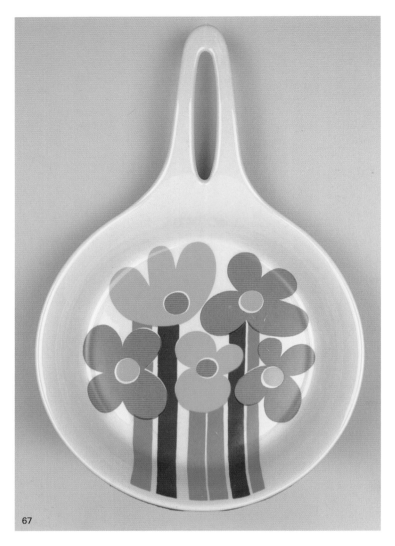

67

68

movement was hardly mainstream and much given to promoting mind-changing drug experiences. In fact the main psychedelic period was very brief indeed, perhaps no more than three to four years beginning around 1967. Musically, its legacy has lived on but it is quite hard to build a collection of objects that was inspired by it, because it was probably only bought by a very youthful middle class market in the first place; because it went out of fashion extremely quickly (and I think it was thrown away soon afterwards) and because not much was made in the first place.

'Acapulco' was almost immediately copied (roughly speaking) by the British company Lord Nelson Pottery, with their famous 'Gaytime' design. This is really worth looking out for and has a fanatical following. But you will find other examples of this type of design and another good company was Ridgway Potteries which promoted some very wild and experimental designs – in shape as well as pattern. A good example of this is their 'Indian Summer' design from around 1970. It's a fabulous product with the same vibrant contrasting, dreamlike colours

as 'Acapulco', but I chuckled to read its claim to be made from 'pure bone china' – it seems a bit old fashioned for hippy ware. Still, I would have to say that I think tea tastes far better from 'Indian Summer' than 'Acapulco'...

The Monty Python fascination with the Victorian and earlier periods of modern life found expression in Susan Williams-Ellis's use of original advertising plates for a range of products from the Victorian age, including dated-and-ludicrous products from Victorian chemist's shops, women's lingerie and more.

67, 68
Figgjo Flint
'Annemarie' skillet
and coffee pot,
Norway, 1971

69
Ridgway Potteries
'Indian Summer'
trio, England, c. 1971

70
Christine Reuter two
'Acapulco' mugs
for Villeroy & Boch,
Germany, 1967

71
Christine Reuter
'Acapulco' tray for
Villeroy & Boch,
Germany, 1967

71

72

73

74

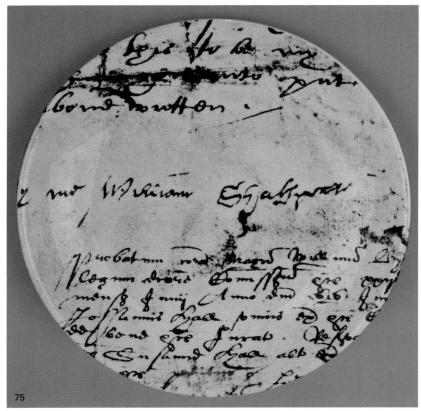

75

76

Vases and bowls

Throughout the retro period, as more and more household space was opened up to display one's taste, artistic sensibility and interior design talents, vases and bowls proliferated as they became the premier surface and form on which the decorative arts were expressed in a three-dimensional format. Within household spaces, modular storage systems, shelving units and systems, and shelving room dividers greatly increased the number of surfaces for the display of these objects. The idea was not so much to fill a new space created by furniture designers and architects, but to produce a display of art after the style of museums, galleries and exhibitions. Thus, the displays tended to have themes or showcased emerging collections. In this way we can understand why the vase, an object that was designed to enhance the display of flowers, lost its prime function and became purely, or mostly, decorative and sculptural in its own right.

This is very evident in the Henry

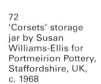

72
'Corsets' storage jar by Susan Williams-Ellis for Portmeirion Pottery, Staffordshire, UK, c. 1968

73
Psychedelic bull plate, designer unknown, Staffordshire Pottery Company, c. 1968

74
Ellgreave kitchen container, England 1960s

75
A detail from 'Shakespeare's Will' by Holkham, Lidor production for W.H. Smith & Son Ltd, England, Shakespeare Exhibition 1564, 1964

76
'Barry Humphries' earthenware bowl (potter: Tom Sanders; decorator: John Olsen), Cottlesbridge, Victoria, Australia, 1970

77
Upsala-Ekeby bowl by Ingrid Attenberg, Sweden, c. 1955

77

78

79

80

81

Moore–influenced 1950s holed vessel from Italy (most likely by Bitossi), the 1950s green Bornholm vase by Michael Andersen and the 1960s 'Bullseye' vase by Plankenhammer. Although Aldo Lundi produced a magnificent and playful range of textured and patterned bases for Bitossi in the 1950s and 1960s, culminating perhaps in the orange spot vase of the late 1960s, it was the Swedish designers who dominated the decorative art vase. Ingrid Atterberg imported many ethnic influences from African and Asian design as well as sgraffito-textured designs to produce tall and elegant centrepieces for domestic displays, and spectacular new

shapes such as the square bowl for her 'Grafika' series for Upsala-Ekeby. The 1950s desire to break the mould of the traditional style of pottery established by potters such as Leach also inspired the 'Triangla' design for Rörstrand as well as Olle Alberius's, 'Lavendel' vase (also for Rörstrand), with its atomic bomb-blast mushroom shape. Alan Compton also added bold new space-age shapes in his work for the British company Royal Norfolk. By the 1960s and 1970s, texture and shape and abstract decoration featured widely. Among the best exponents of this studio art look was Colin Melbourne for Royal Norfolk, whose work combined textured

surfaces and sculptured lines with abstract and nature-inspired themes.

Arguably, it was at Poole Pottery in Dorset, England that modern inspired ideas spread to the very manner in which the vases were produced and decorated. Under the guidance of Robert Jefferson, 'paintresses' the all-female group of ceramic painters (who had previously endlessly copied the house artists' designs) were now trained to paint their own designs onto an astonishing new modern art range called 'Delphis', made between 1966 and 1979. In bright reds, oranges, yellows and greens arranged in abstract juxtapositions, the 'Delphis' range

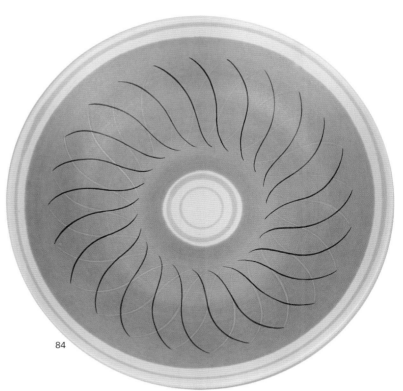

82

83

84

78
Japanese designer unknown, 'Hole' vase, c. 1956

79
Michael Andersen vase for Bornholm, Denmark, c. 1956

80
Axel Salto sculptural 'Le Noyau de la Force' stoneware vase for Royal Copenhagen Porcelain Manufactory, Denmark, c. 1956
Powerhouse Museum collection

81
'Bullseye' vase by Plankenhammer, Germany, 1960

82
Alan Crompton 'Comet' vase for Royal Norfolk, England, 1958

83
Bitossi horse vase, Italy, 1958

84
Poole Pottery 'Freeform' bowl (shape: John Adams; painter: Pat Dightam), England, 1955

85

86

87

88

89

90

80

91

92

93

85
Ingrid Atterberg
'spiral' vase for
Upsala-Ekeby,
Sweden, c. 1958

86, 87, 88
Bitossi cylinder
vases, Italy, 1969 and
Bitossi banded vase,
Italy, 1959

89
'Triangla' jug or vase,
Rörstrand, Sweden,
c. 1968

90
Ingrid Atterberg
'Vinga' vase for
Upsala-Ekeby,
Sweden, 1956

91
Nittjo hand-painted
vase, Sweden, 1950s

92
Mari Simmulson vase
for Upsala-Ekeby,
Sweden, 1960s

93
Bitossi orange and
black psychedelic
vase, Italy, c. 1975

94
Ingrid Atterberg
'Grafika' bowl for
Upsala-Ekeby,
Sweden, c. 1959

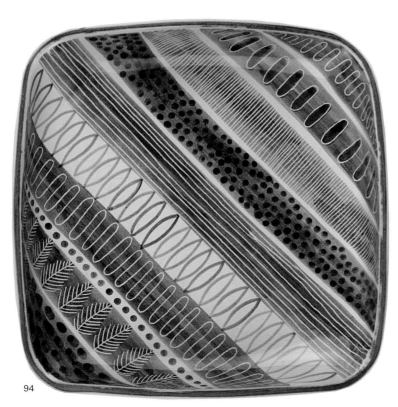

94

remains one of the high points of retro innovation and design, not least for its socially revolutionary achievements inside the factory. The output of its core designers, such as Tony Morris, comprised some of the very best and most adventurously decorated studio work. The huge charger Morris created in the late 1960s is iconic both in terms of its realisation of the mood and sensibility of late 1960s counter culture and also its aspirations for a new form of consciousness and apprehension of the world. Here there are no aspirations for a technology-led future, but a more introspective exploration of consciousness and possibly an early indication that nature and the environment require our attention.

95

96

97

98

99

100

95
Poole 'Delphis' vase,
painted by Carol
Cutler, England, 1967

96
Colin Melbourne
'Petra' vase for Royal
Norfolk, England,
c. 1972

97
Olle Alberius
'Lavendel' vase for
Rörstrand, Sweden,
c. 1965

98
Colin Melbourne
'Petra' vase for Royal
Norfolk, England,
c. 1969

99
Tony Morris
psychedelic
woodland landscape
charger for Poole
Studio, England,
c.1968

100
Poole 'Delphis' bowl
with white rim,
England, 1970

101
Poole 'Delphis'
bowl with blue rim,
England, c. 1970

102
Poole 'Delphis' plate,
painted by Carol
Cutler, England, 1967

103
Poole 'Delphis' vase,
painted by Carol
Cutler, England, 1968

101

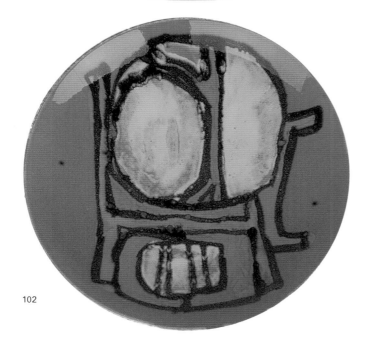

102

103

West German ceramics

Not very long ago those huge, garishly coloured pots, marked 'Germany' or 'West Germany' and produced after 1945, were left over at garage sales or passed in at auctions. Apart from arousing lingering national prejudices, they seemed so far over the top, so completely kitsch and in such bad taste that no right thinking person could possibly display them in their home. Not any longer.

Back then (I am thinking of the 1980s and 1990s), people like me who collected modern design wanted two things mainly. First, we wanted our things to be well designed. Second, we wanted *provenance*, in the form of a known company, clearly marked on the piece somewhere and preferably a designer's signature. Works by Poole Studio, Troika and Midwinter complied with these demands perfectly. Just a 'nation of origin' mark fuelled doubts and dismissal.

So how did West German pottery become desirable? First, the more established makes and designs from England and Scandinavia became prohibitively expensive. Second, the whole world of kitsch was reconsidered and found 'interesting' precisely because it was mocking 'real art' and because it was an expression of popular culture. Third, in the mid-1990s and early 2000s designers of domestic interiors began to experiment with the same colours as

those used in these works, especially oranges, bright reds and ochres. A pair of floor vases, for example, could be stunning in an interior of this era, and they were plentiful and easy to find. Fourth, and most important of all, a new generation of collectors discovered that, actually, West German/German pottery had a serious claim to be 'art' and *was* produced by talented designers and manufacturers. These collectors developed a way of reading the somewhat plain marks on the bottom of these pieces in order to decipher the manufacturer and become more familiar with the works of the ceramic artists working for them. So, what do you need to know in order to collect these works of art with confidence? Let's get behind the simplicity of the 'Germany' or 'West Germany' marks and start to recognise different manufacturers; and there are quite a few to know.

Recognising these pieces has become quite an art but we no longer operate in the dark. Some pieces have surviving paper labels on them from companies such as Bay, Dumler & Breiden, Scheurich, Carstens Tonnieshof, Jasba Keramik, Jopeko, Steuler, Strehla GDR, U-Keramik, and VEB Haldensleben – these are the principal names to remember.

Some of these – such as Bay, (some) Dumler & Breiden, and Jasba – have the

104

104
Gundars Lusis, West German inspired lava vase for Gunda Pottery, Australia, c. 1975

105
West German vase typical of the 1950s and now highly sought after, manufacturer unknown, c. 1953

106
Dumler & Breiden textured vase, West Germany, 1950s

107
West German vase, manufacturer unknown, c. 1969

108, 109
Bay Keramik vase and label, West Germany, c.1957

110
Bay Keramik planter, West Germany, 1960s–1970s

105

106

107

108

109

110

85

111

112

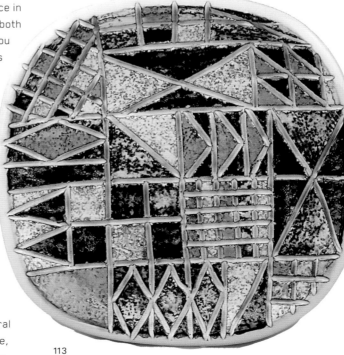

113

manufacturer's name moulded onto the base. Others – such as Steuler, (some) Dumler & Breiden, VEB Haldensleben and Scheurich – have symbols as part of the moulded stamp. Scheurich has a three circles mark, Dumler & Breiden has crossed swords and VEB Haldensleben has a capital H inside a circle.

Then there are even more refined ways of spotting different makes from the way their German origin is displayed; for example, Scheurich uses 'W.GERMANY' whereas Bay uses 'W.-GERMANY'. Sometimes there are numbers on the bottom of German ceramics and these can also help with provenance. With Bay, for example, the first two or three numbers are the 'form' or design numbers, whereas the second denotes their height in centimetres. The colour of the clay used can also help: Bay and Scheurich used white clay but Carstens Tonnieshof used reddish-coloured clay.

This information makes it far more exciting to go off on ceramic hunts, as well as providing greater confidence in buying. There are two new books, both published in 2009, that will make you even more knowledgeable. There is *An Introduction to West German Pottery* by Forrest Poston and *Collecting West German Ceramics* by Kevin Graham.

Many European-trained artists successfully established themselves in affluent ex-colonial places such as Australia and New Zealand and there a retro ceramic tradition flourished. Gunda Pottery, founded in Australia by Gundars Lusis, is emerging as one of the more outstanding examples of work that carried European modern aspirations into new cultural contexts. Lusis's work, for example, was inspired by, but did not copy or

114

115

111
Mari Simmulson,
small painted dish
for Upsala-Ekeby,
Sweden, c. 1957

112
Mari Simmulson,
small painted dish
for Upsala-Ekeby,
Sweden, c. 1960

113
Ingrid Atterberg
geometric bowl
for Upsala-Ekeby,
Sweden, c. 1965

114
'Pika' wall plate
by Stavangerflint,
Norway, c. 1951

115
Bjørn Wiinblad
'Saison Start'
plate for Nymolle,
Denmark

116
Mari Simmulson
'Fantastic Big
Bird' wall plaque
for Upsala-Ekeby,
Sweden, c. 1967

116

117
Unknown artist
(initials NH),
modernised
Crucifixion scene on
plaque, for Villeroy
& Boch, Germany,
c. 1965

118
Lisa Larsen 'Fantastic
Peacock' wall plaque
for Gustavsberg,
Sweden, c. 1967

119
Marianne Starck wall
plaque for Michael
Andersen, Denmark,
c. 1969

120
Margareta Hennix
floral wall plaque
for Gustavsberg,
Sweden, 1982

121
Esther Wallin
modernist wall
plaque for Upsala-
Ekeby, Sweden,
c. 1953

122
Dovecot Studio tile
with design taken
from an ancient
Scottish chair back,
Scotland, c. 1968

123
Heljä Liukko-
Sundström wall
plaque for Arabia's
Finnair in-flight gift
range, Finland, 1978

borrow, Aboriginal designs, and his output from the 1950s to the late 1970s has a freshness and originality that few European one-man potteries could match (see his small bowl on page 97).

Another concentration of talent emerged at Upsala-Ekeby in Sweden, lead by the Estonian-born Mari Simmulson. Her Picasso-inspired works on small bowls and dishes, often featuring youthful women's faces, became one of the defining looks of Scandinavian ceramics, but it was the pottery plaque where their ceramic art really shone the brightest.

The modestly sized pottery slab that forms the basis for most Scandinavian wall plaques is large enough for the narrative artworks and townscapes of Stig Lindberg (for Upsala-Ekeby), the abstract peacocks and other birds by Lisa Larsen (for Gustavsberg), the dreamlike gardens of Marianne Starck (for Michael Andersen), the geometric abstract designs of Esther Wallin (for Upsala-Ekeby) and the fantasy birds of Mari Simmulson (for Upsala-Ekeby).

In the right hands, even smaller sized wall plaques and tiles produced

c. 1978, for Arabia's Finnair in-flight gift range, and the strangely jarring Saracen guard by Elbogen of Denmark (designer unknown). Even the Crucifixion was modernised to great effect by an unknown artist for Villeroy & Boch.

From the 1950s onwards, almost every pottery produced decorative art tiles for the souvenir/gift trade. Hand painted tiles were a speciality of Poole Pottery which inherited a rich tradition of tile making from its predecessor Carter Tiles. These are acknowledged

123

124

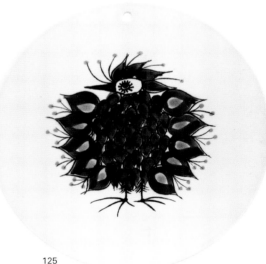

125

an intensity of design that suited the multiple spaces available for art in the modern home. Here we find the eccentric birds of Beth Breyen for Royal Copenhagen, the highly mannered 'Saison Start' series by Bjørn Wiinblad for Nymolle, Denmark, the naked girl by Stavangerflint, Norway, the haunting landscape of Finland by Heljä Liukko-Sundström,

handsomely in the Victoria and Albert Museum, as are the fabulous abstract 1960s tiles by Ann Wynn Reeves for Kenneth Clark Pottery, London. Among the best of the 1970s is a tile featuring a modern representation of an ancient Scottish design, a Scots thistle (taken from a chair back) by Dovecot Studios of Edinburgh. This was acknowledged with a Design Award in 1973.

124
Tony Morris, 'Poole Harbour' wall plate for Poole Pottery, 1951

125
Beth Breyen 'Eccentric Bird' plate for Royal Copenhagen, Denmark, c. 1974

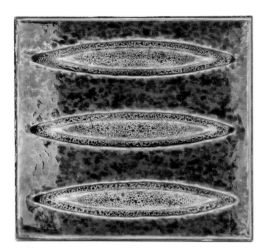

126

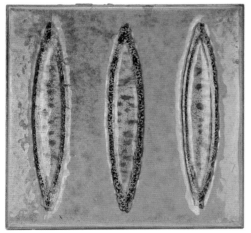

127

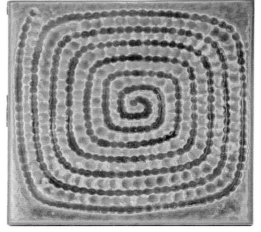

129

128

130

131

132

Animals

There is scarcely a human culture or civilisation that has not incorporated animals into its symbolic and emotional life, and this is always reflected in the decorative arts. Although the essentially modern nature of the retro years placed some considerable distance between humanity and nature, it was this very separation, alongside growing concerns for the environmental consequences of modernity that fuelled a great enthusiasm for animal figures in all media, especially perhaps in ceramics.

Animal figures provided yet another form for domestic display, and in the hands of modern artists and designers, these retro animals could be astonishingly abstract, kitsch or anthropomorphised. Certainly there was no felt need for the accurate, if sometimes romantic, representation of earlier traditions although here the exceptions include the iconic three flying ducks made by various companies (and something of a cliché in the hands of set designers wishing to establish a scene in the 1950s) but also Bossuns's fabulous seagulls. Here is an echo of the seaside and leisure theme we noted above in tablewares which, especially in the 1950s, was repeated in many forms and in many different ways (curtains, ornaments, wallpaper, prints and so on) around the house.

Collections of finely made porcelain animals, fish and birds were a mainstay for many potteries in England, especially Beswick and Poole, and also Royal Copenhagen in Denmark.

In Italy, Aldo Lundi produced some of the first examples of postmodern, almost carnivalesque, animal forms for Bitossi, and these remain one of the great achievements of the retro years. In the 1980s these could be seen in junk and charity shops with giveaway prices. By the early 2000s a strong interest had grown among serious collectors of this period and prices were quickly driven up, exposing the fact that these were not made in substantial numbers but, being largely handcrafted in moulds and hand finished with lines of impressed shapes, they were originally made for an upmarket demographic and sold through high-status department stores. Among the many exquisite designs, the triangular-headed cat, the fat-cat money box, the puffer fish, the cubist horse and the long sausage dog stand out. The point of these figures was to tease out the character and essence of these animals rather than reproduce their natural form. Character and essence communicate far more, of course, than form alone and this wanting to go deeper and to explore using the ceramic medium was a feature of the best retro design.

Bitossi is short for Ceramica Bitossi, a company set up in 1921 by Guido Bitossi in the Tuscan town of Montelupo Fiorentino. The town has an ancient ceramic tradition and was known as 'the kiln of Renaissance Florence'. Bitossi

126, 127, 130, 131
Malkin tiles,
England, 1968

128
Ann Wynn Reeves
tile for Kenneth
Clark Pottery,
England, 1967

129
Alan Wallwork tile,
England, 1970

132
Bossuns's seagulls
wall decoration,
England, c. 1957

133

134

135

136

137

138

139

140

141

142

143

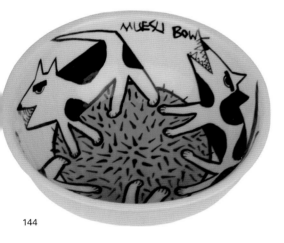

144

made a wide variety of ceramic objects, but what makes them especially groovy today are pieces by the great designer Aldo Lundi, from 1946 to the mid-1970s. In these designs Lundi seems to be saying: 'The modern world shall be bright and light-hearted. Life-like modelling is not necessarily more interesting than something that tries to capture character or mood. *Design* is better than mere representation. Somehow abstraction is more *inspiring* than figurative replication.'

Lundi's triangular-headed cat looks nothing like a cat and yet it is very *cat-like*: something a bit ruthless, but at the same time sensual. And his horse is very architectural but from different angles you can see its nobility, its strength and its beauty.

You can see how the strange, circus-like patterns are applied by hand with no particular attention to neatness or straight lines but the repetition of these symbols seems to act like a coded texture. It adds mystery somehow. At the same time, the broken texture it produces creates a range of colour densities as the glaze is spread thin in some places but pools in others. The lion and the cats were made using a two-piece mould, the clay pressed into the mould before being snapped together – you can see the mould line across the lion's back.

After a few years of collecting this stuff you can recognise it immediately, which is just as well because the marks are confusing! There is no definitive guide but this is what I have gleaned so far. From 1921 to the 1950s the only clue you get is the painted letter B, followed often by a design number. However, most older pieces often only have the word Italy and a number on them. Sometimes it is painted on but often it is only a paper label. The reason for this is that powerful importing companies like Raymor would request that manufacturers leave their names off the design so that consumers could only buy from them. Sometimes, the design was even owned by the importer. Either way, this pottery ended up in places like Bloomingdales in the USA, Harrods in the UK and David Jones in Sydney. Once that paper label is lost or removed, the piece is completely unmarked. But it is still fabulous, still valuable.

From the 1960s, an impressed stamp or a printed stamp with the word Bitossi plus Made in Italy was occasionally used. Then, around the mid-1970s, Bitossi was dropped and all the pieces were marked Flavia Montelupo, as on my lion. Finally, if you find a piece with an impressed stamp, usually the word Bitossi with the Bitossi family crest, then you will know it is a recent product from after 2001 or a reissued design.

133
Stylised bird, Japan, c. 1955

134
Kitten, by Dagmar and Miloslav Kratochvil for Ellis Pottery, Australia, c. 1964

135
Briglin Pottery owl, England, 1960s

136
Fish serving dish by Gabriel, Sweden, c. 1971

137
Psychedelic horse money box, Carlton Ware, England, 1973

138
Horse by Dagmar and Miloslav Kratochvil for Ellis Pottery, Australia, c. 1963

139
Novelty sea lion, Italy, c. 1960

140
Dartmouth Pottery 'Glug-Glug' water jug in shape of a fish. A pair were given to the Queen and Prince Philip on their visit to Britannia Naval College to present New Colours in 1958. Made from 1870–2002, England

141
Jaroslav Jezek 'Kocka' cat for Royal Dux, Czechoslovakia, 1960

142
Stylised polar bear, earthenware with white moonstone glaze, Wedgwood & Sons, England, c. 1950 Powerhouse Museum collection

143, 144
Dog mug and bowl by Pig Tail Pottery, Australia, 1985

145

146

148

147

149

150

Indigenous themes

The 1950s were unique in promoting a less voyeuristic view of indigenous peoples as exotic, sexual or savage. The 1920s and 1930s aroused a period of curiosity and excitement, particularly about black African peoples, that the writer Edward Said termed *Orientalism*. In the postwar period, European, American and other white colonial cultures, at least through their servicemen and women, had acquired a more first-hand experience of global peoples in the extensive theatres of the Second World War. Certainly in the case of the Pacific peoples, stretching from Polynesia to Micronesia, Melanesia and Australasia, this gave rise to a new aesthetic that was based on a cultural appreciation and particularly their material and ritual cultures. The craze for Tiki, a generic term for collectables that derive from a deity figure common (if not everywhere) across the Pacific region took off as major elements in popular culture in 1950s USA. In Australia a new-found curiosity for Aboriginal art and design was fostered, especially by new migrants from Europe. Many potters and potteries owned by European migrants were kept on a secure financial footing through their

Aboriginal-inspired ceramic souvenirs and decorative studio lines.

Brownie Downing, an Australian artist (1925–95), produced very sentimental but well meant paintings of Aboriginal children, mostly in natural settings and alongside native wildlife with whom they appeared to have a special affinity. Downing thought that this ability of children to make natural and magical connections with their environment was not confined to Aboriginal children and she painted similar themes with Majorcan, Mexican, Scottish and Romany gypsy peoples.

151

145–50
Aldo Lundi abstract cat, lion, horse, cat money box, fish and smug cat for Bitossi, Italy, c. 1955

151
Brownie Downing jug showing Mexican boy for J. H. Weatherby and Son, Hanley, England, c. 1958

152
Alexander Takacs, Aboriginal elder sitting, for Takacs Studio, Australia, 1960

152

153

154

155

156

157

153
'Nanja' earthenware
vase with modelled
Aboriginal figure
standing near a
sacred tree by
William Ricketts,
c. late 1930s
Powerhouse
Museum collection

154, 157
Ceramic sculpture
of an Aboriginal
elder and child
sitting on a boulder
by William Ricketts,
c. 1950 Powerhouse
Museum collection

155
'Mind thought,
beauty wrought'
ceramic sculpture
by William Ricketts,
c. late 1940s
Powerhouse
Museum collection

158

Some of Australia's leading potters
were inspired by the feeling that
Aboriginal people and art should be
brought into the canon of Australian arts
and crafts. A leading inspiration here
was William Ricketts, whose haunting
works from the 1950s celebrate the
close relationship that Aboriginal people
have with their land and nature.

Many Australian potteries themselves
produced huge quantities of really high
quality slip and other ceramic wares.
Many were unashamedly producing for
vacation destinations and labelling the
wares with the names of tourist cities
and villages. Others produced fine
studio wares and hybrids of Aboriginal
and western modern design. Gunda
Pottery from Melbourne is a leading
example of this and now has a huge
collector following, although it was widely
regarded as kitsch until very recently.
Still others sought to produce very
ethnographic pieces of the Aboriginal
everyday, avoiding all semblances
of the noble savage or other exotic
constructions.

159

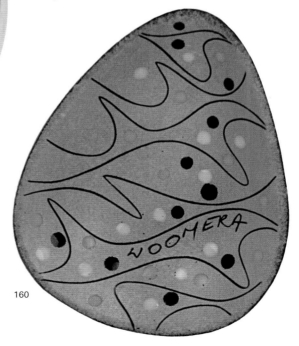

160

156
Earthenware
mug with the
modelled face of an
Aboriginal boy by
William Ricketts,
1955 Powerhouse
Museum collection

158
Brownie Downing
transfer print of an
Aboriginal girl on
porcelain pin dish,
Australia, c. 1954

159
Unknown designer,
wall plate souvenir
for Melbourne
showing an
Aboriginal hunter
and his hunting
equipment,
Australia, c. 1958

160
Gundars Lusis for
Gunda, small dish
with dots and stylised
lines, souvenir of
Woomera, Australia,
1956

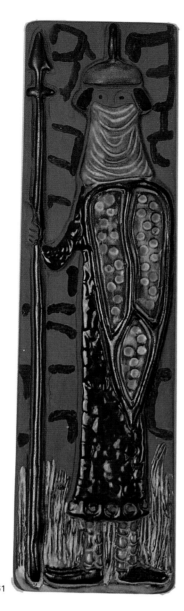

161

162

Medieval revival

I recently bought a wall plaque. It was not expensive but it was very intriguing. It depicts a rather splendid, tall Muslim foot soldier from the Crusades period, complete with his long lamellar armour garment (a Khayagh, if we are being technical), a beautifully decorated shield, spike-topped helmet and spear. He seems to be on guard outside a massive citadel, the stone details of which are sketched in by the artist with the minimum of strokes. At first I thought that it was a piece of modern Israeli pottery: it had what looked like *Elboyeh* hand written on the back, alongside the words HAND MADE and the initials MH. I imagined that this was a piece sold mostly to American and European visitors to the Holy Land, where, in the 1960s and 1970s, tours to the old Crusader-period castles (Christian and Muslim) were popular. Modern Israeli ceramics from the 1960s and 1970s have caught the eye of many collectors in the past five years.

What also drew me to this piece was the strong influence of Scandinavian ceramics from that period. The plaque was made of terracotta and decorated in those favourite yellow, blue and crimson Scandinavian glazes, and everything about it was similar to the work of top artists Lisa Larsen and Stig Lindberg. However, my research on the name Elboyeh, which was stamped on the back, came to nothing. I thought the mark might not be Elboyeh but maybe Elbogen. I was right: Elbogen was a small pottery in Malmo, Sweden and they turned out very nice pieces, in the style of Lisa Larsen who worked

for Gustavsberg. This made me think. This plaque was clearly not made for sale to tourists in the Holy Land but to modern-day Scandinavians, probably in the 1970s. And why would a technically advanced country like Sweden in the 1970s be remotely interested in the events or styles of the Middle Ages? Then again, this was not an isolated example of what we might call the *Medieval Revival* in the 1970s. Scandinavians generally have been obsessed with their own medieval past, especially the Viking and post-Viking period. It calls to mind Lisa Larsen's wonderful depiction of the one-eyed Viking god Odin or the strong Viking figure by Taisto Kaasinen for Upsala-Ekeby – and it's not just in ceramics. There also is that wonderful Viking ship–shaped teak fruit bowl by Jens Quistgaard for the Danish company Dansk.

The Brits also had a love affair with their own medieval past in the 1970s. There are the extraordinary pieces that Guy Sydenham did for Poole Pottery's (stoneware) 'Atlantis' range. The best is his 30 cm long design for a 'knight's helmet' lamp. With incredible glazes, he created an impression of the chain mail protecting a crusader's head, and this hooded head-shape formed a hollow vessel into which a candle could be placed. As the candle flickered, it illuminated the rugged features of a knight's face painted onto the inner back of the helmet. It cleverly re-creates the stony, candle-lit interior of castle life.

163

164

161
Elbogen Pottery,
Saracen guard, Malmo,
Sweden, c. 1970

162
Medieval-styled
hand thrown mug,
Canterbury Pottery,
England, 1968

163
Earthenware plate with
two lug handles, with
sgraffito decoration
inside of a potter at
a wheel, titled 'The
Potter's Craft', signed
John Olsen 70, Tom
Sanders, potter,
Cottlesbridge, Victoria,
Australia, 1970

164
Michael Andersen and
Son, pottery replica
of the Aakirkeby
baptismal font on
Bornholm, Denmark,
c. 1972

165
Bendigo Pottery
pitcher, Australia,
1970s

166
Bendigo Pottery
tankard, Australia,
1970s

167
Tony Morris 'October'
charger in the style of
a stained glass window
for Poole Studio,
England, c. 1967

165

166

167

168

169

170

171

172

173

174

175

176

In Australia *Medieval Revival* was a defining feature of Bendigo Pottery in the 1960s and 1970s. Beautifully executed, chunky stoneware wine goblets, jugs, wine coolers, bread crocks and lidded pots are still keenly sought after.

The reason for our periodic love affairs for this 'golden age' is simple enough. Modern life is constantly seeking the new and wiping out our past. We feel uneasy about heading constantly into unknown futures and find reassurance in our various pasts. If we don't always know where we are headed, as collectors at least, we know where we have come from.

Such is the case with the Cornish potteries of Troika, Carn, Tremaen and Tremar. While the first three succeeded as studio art potteries mostly, Tremar specialised in topical whimsy and sold great numbers of small pieces to passing tourists. Among these were a great many native animals such as badgers, farm animals (their sheep were magnificent) and fantasy animals (their fish is a real winner). Even in the central London pottery of Briglin that also sold its wares through the top design store Heal's, sales to the tourist trade must have been important judging by the numbers of small animal pieces they produced.

These potteries tended to stick with a narrow range of creatures with great character, and in this they were following Aldo Lundi. Key among their animals was a shaggy sheep dog, an odd

looking cat, a stylised owl, and some tiny robins that absolutely burst with personality and energy. Briglin Pottery was very near Harley Street, so it is surprising that there was not a medical theme to their output! Not so the beautiful Chelsea Pottery which specialised in all the city professions around them, including some amazing surgical and legal designs.

Thus the world of retro ceramics traces a somewhat circular route. First it pulled away from older traditions and sought a 'new' industrial look that was fun and inspired by the new leisured society. This look was followed by a cooler aesthetic that was as much modern art as tableware. Popular culture then became mirrored in its profoundly new and experimental shapes and patterns, a sure sign that a new generation was growing to adulthood and setting up home. The counter

culture was also briefly in the cultural ascendant and many ceramic companies cashed in on changing tastes. But in addition to its experimental and psychedelic aesthetic it also ushered in influences from other cultures and past times. It seemed as though we had as much to learn from the past as we did from our aspiration for new futures. Thus, by the 1970s and 1980s we had come full circle and embraced hand made pottery alongside the strange contortions of postmodern design.

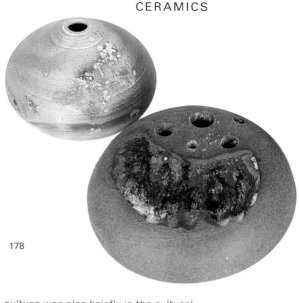

177

178

179

168
John Beusmans, three abstract vases, Carn Pottery, England, c. 1972

169, 174, 175, 176
Roger Birkett and Doreen Birkett, sheep 1970, fish (yellow wrasse) 1975, pub money box 1970, 'Teenage Girl' c. 1967, Tremar, England

170, 171, 172
Brigitte Goldschmidt and Eileen Lewenstein, robin, lidded pot, coffeepot, milk jug and sugar bowl, for Briglin Pottery, London, c. 1972

173
Peter Ellery pebble vase for Tremaen Pottery, Cornwall, England, c. 1970

177
David Rawnsley 'Surgeon' tankard for Chelsea Pottery, London, c. 1968

178
Two pebble vases by unknown studio potteries

179
Postmodern Memphis: 'Sepik' earthenware teapot by Marco Zannini for Memphis, Italy, 1983–86
Powerhouse Museum collection

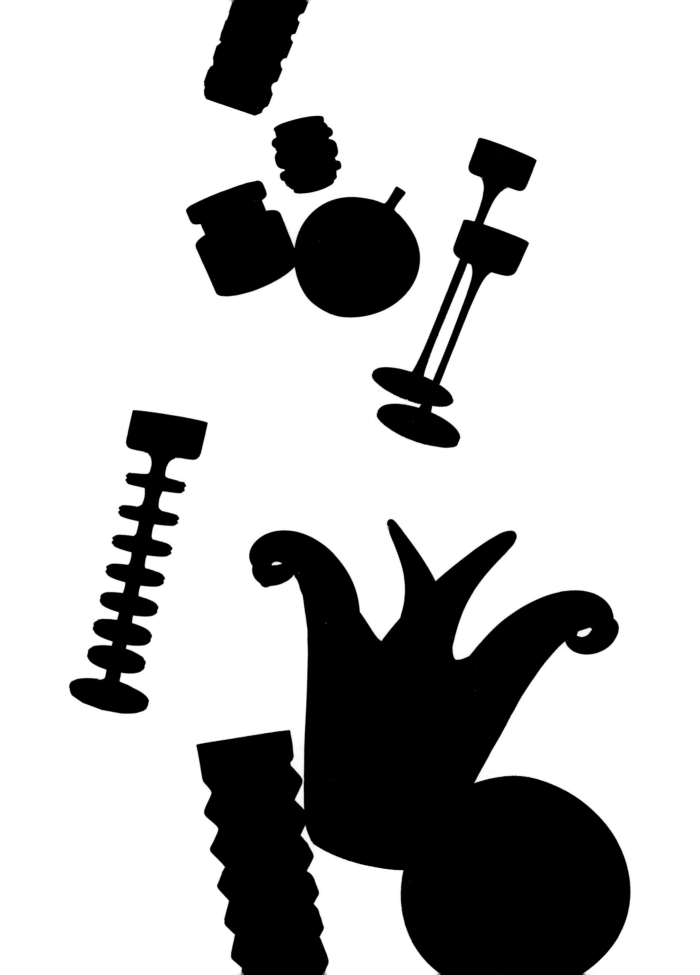

GLASS

GLASS IS A WONDER MATERIAL
OF THE TWENTIETH CENTURY

PAUL RENNIE TWENTIETH CENTURY DESIGN 2003:140

HISTORICALLY GLASS WAS ALWAYS EXPENSIVE to produce and not therefore an everyday object. Modernity changed this. Although made from the most basic materials – soda, sand, lead and so on – great temperatures were required to produce the molten material and to keep the furnaces going on any kind of permanent basis meant it was monumentally expensive. Glass was never made on the same scale as steel in blast furnaces because making fine glass was laborious as well as being a very highly skilled craft. By definition, it was slow going and made only in small daily batches. In most cases, whether in the UK or Italy, it was part of the guild craft sector rather than an industry. Hence, until the twentieth century when efficient furnaces, factories and even glass blowing and pressing machinery was invented (and more affluent markets arose), all glass was a high status and prohibitively expensive *luxury* good.

In the early twentieth century, popular forms of glassware were made possible though new techniques of production, such as pressing and moulding, and even bottles could be blown by machines. Fittingly perhaps, the first bottle blowing machine was patented in 1899 and in production by 1903. Pressed 'Depression glass' appeared as a cheap, dime store product and as free gifts (for an oil change at a garage or in detergent or cereal packets) from the late 1920s to the 1940s. Most of this would not be regarded as 'retro' precisely because of its unimaginative design, its association with poverty (rather than affluence and a leisure-rich lifestyle), its poor quality and its dull colour schemes.

Depression glass was not merely functional, it was almost a form of charitable aid for consumers and, while historically interesting is largely *joyless*. It is a reminder of hard times rather than good times. After 1945, with growing affluence, growing markets and an acceleration in social mobility and aspiration, glass production and consumption was set on a steep, upward production curve. Resource-poor Scandinavian countries needed to exploit their massive reserves of fuel from wood, as well as reserves of the basic ingredients of glass and so it was from them and other traditional glass manufacturing centres in Murano in Italy and in Czechoslovakia that the push for a more export-driven and democratised market in modern decorative glass emerged.

Despite all the costs involved in producing high-grade glass, designed and blown by skilled designers and artisans,

1

2

their ambition was to produce large quantities for the burgeoning luxury gift industries. This was where almost all quality retro glass was first sold, and because it was not something that most householders could afford routinely, the amount produced was strictly limited. This is also why it is comparatively rarer than say, ceramic tablewares or even many ceramic vases.

Until the late 1950s, English glass houses such as Stevens and Williams, alongside other Stourbridge companies and Whitefriars on the edge of London, remained tied to their traditional high-status wares and markets, and it was pioneers such as Ronald Stennett-Willson who translated European aesthetics onto a broader and global basis.

Ronald Stennett-Willson not only designed beautiful modern glass and established King's Lynn Glass, a forerunner in British modern glass production, he *personally* persuaded a reluctant and conservative public to let go of their Regency revivalism, with its emphasis on 'pretty' cut glass 'crystal' and go wild with colour, organic shape and bold design influences from Scandinavia and Europe.

Despite the suggestion of a privileged background given by his double-barrel name, Stennett-Willson was from a rather modest Cheshire home; he attended state schools and left school to become a junior at Rydbeck & Norström, a company specialising in the importation of Swedish glass into the UK. During the war he fought in North Africa and led a special tank force in the D-Day landings. After the war he became sales

manager for the bespoke company Wuidart, which imported Scandinavian decorative arts; and then began to design for Wuidart himself. British glass factories were not interested in making these designs so he had them made in Sweden. In 1959 he won several commissions to design for Lemington Glass Works and one set of vases he designed for the P&O liner *Canberra* won a Duke of Edinburgh's Design Centre Award.

In the early 1960s he was appointed head of glass design at the Royal College of Art in London, where he influenced that group of designers who would later make London swing. These included David Queensberry in ceramics, Robert Gooden in metalwork, Robin Pye in furniture and Frank Thrower in glass (he founded Dartington Glass). Not content just to teach and publish books on modern glass, Stennett-Willson promoted modern design through the extravagant avant-garde shop Choses that he ran with his wife Elizabeth in Hampstead. But the ultimate ambition, to start his own factory, required leaving London for King's Lynn in Norfolk, where he set up King's Lynn Glass in 1967.

Design ideas came easily and some great European glass makers came to join his enterprise but he needed to wean the British public away from the thought that the only good glass is cut crystal, made by one of the 'Stourbridge four': Webb Corbett, Thomas Webb, Stuart and Royal Brierley. As is often the case, great people will not leave anything to chance or mere talent. One by one he personally persuaded the buyers from the main stores to try

1, 2
Joyful modern glass: Peter Wheeler Studio vase for Whitefriars Glass, England, 1969

3
Gunnel Nyman 'Serpentiini' vase, for Nuutäjarvi Notsjö, Finland, c. 1952 Powerhouse Museum collection

4
Dino Martens 'jester's hat' vase, blown glass with aventurina (golden) patches, 'Oriente' series, for Aureliano Toso, Italy, 1952 Powerhouse Museum collection

5
Scandinavian modern glass brought colour and elegance to war-torn Europe: green glass vase, c. 1950

6
Ronald Stennett-Willson abstract elephant and hedgehog for Wedgwood Glass, England, c. 1966

7
Ronald Stennett-Willson (L) 'Brancaster' and (R) 'Sheringham' candlesticks for Wedgwood Glass, England, 1960s

CROWN CORNING 1970s–80s DOMESTIC GLASSWARE

PAUL DONNELLY = CURATOR, DESIGN AND SOCIETY, POWERHOUSE MUSEUM

The Powerhouse Museum recently acquired a selection of glassware produced in Sydney during the 1970s to 80s by Crown Corning Glass. Donated by Denise Larcombe, senior designer at Crown Corning from 1970 to 1989, the collection highlights her pioneering work, which led to a number of award-winning designs – many of which would be familiar to people today the world over.

In the early 1960s the company installed a Hartford 28 automatic glass-blowing machine, which was the latest technology at the time. This allowed blown glassware to be industrially produced without a seam, but was initially limited to making prosaic containers such as bottles. Charles Furey, Crown Crystal's designer in the early 1960s, saw the machine's potential for domestic ware but this wasn't realised until 1969 in

the enormously successful 'Regis' range designed by Ted Kayser. Its success formed the basis for a whole new series of designs which have won seven Australian Design Awards and secured export business in over twenty countries. Hand operation at Crown Crystal Glass ceased in 1968.

Denise Larcombe's designs from 1970 to 1989 pushed the capability of the machinery and responded to the requirements of informal dining in the period. Wine glasses became shorter and sturdier, and most ranges such as 'Haama' included a bowl variant for dessert or the inevitable prawn cocktail! Because the output of the machinery outstripped local demand, a healthy export business saw these products sold in over twenty countries. Marketing demanded names that conjured a Scandinavian association but over time these became more

Australian or cosmic related. 'Koenig' (1970), 'Haama' (1972), 'Oslo' (1975) and 'Bergen' (1976) were followed by 'Hunter' (1976), 'Nova', 'Galaxy' and 'Clare' (1978) among many others, finishing with 'Moon Glass' (1987).

The ability to identify the origins of an item is attractive to collectors and useful for building a 'retro' market. Marked ceramics, for example, are much easier to recognise than commercial glassware, which is usually labelled with removable stickers – if at all. For Crown Corning this has changed thanks to the presentation of this collection on the museum's website, along with drawings, blueprints and brochures from Australia and other countries. This unique resource will assist in taking these beautiful, high quality objects to a wider audience.

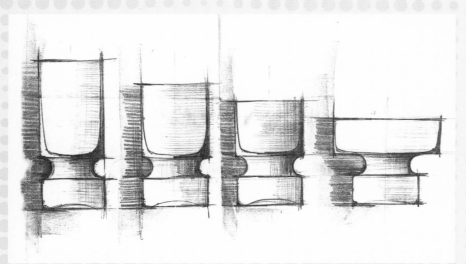

Original sketches by Denise Larcombe for 'Haama' (1972) and 'Oslo' (1975)
Powerhouse Museum collection

Six finely crafted Hunter sweet/seafood dishes.

CRAFTED IN AUSTRALIA
CROWN CORNING GLASS

To celebrate the 100th year of glassmaking in Australia Crown proudly announces the newest and most exciting shape in glass—

HAAMA

CROWN GLASS
OVER 250 BEAUTIFUL GIFTS

AN EXCITING NEW SHAPE IN GLASS: 'HAAMA'

'Haama' is a bold, simple design.
It is a heavy glass with a cracked off and polished rim.
Beautiful to hold. Beautiful to look at — the contents contrast sharply with 'Haama's solid glass base.
'Haama' is the result of extensive research. In test it proved as popular as 'Regis'. Consumers acclaimed it:
"Good looking enough for formal entertaining". "Robust enough and reasonably priced enough for everyday use . . ." "Nice to hold". "Comfortable and easy to hold". "It's versatile". (You can use it for more than one drink.) "Nice to drink from . . ."
In short, 'Haama' is everything the consumer looks for in a glass. It's going to be a winner!

WOMEN'S WEEKLY	ISSUE DATE	
	21.6.72	DIAGONAL SPREAD MONO 'Regis'
	5.7.72	DIAGONAL SPREAD COLOUR 'Regis' Punch Set, 'Regis' Salad Set, 'Regis' Decanter Set, 'Regis' Water Set
	19.7.72	DIAGONAL SPREAD COLOUR 'Olympus', 'Espada', 'Seadrift', 'Empire' table
	2.8.72	DIAGONAL SPREAD MONO 'Haama'
	9.8.72	DIAGONAL SPREAD ½ COLOUR/½ MONO 'President' Range
	23.8.72	DIAGONAL SPREAD MONO
	6.9.72	DIAGONAL SPREAD COLOUR
	20.9.72	DIAGONAL SPREAD MONO
	18.10.72	DIAGONAL SPREAD COLOUR
	1.11.72	DIAGONAL SPREAD ½ COLOUR/½ MONO
	22.11.72	DIAGONAL SPREAD ½ COLOUR/½ MONO
	29.11.72	DIAGONAL SPREAD COLOUR
	6.12.72	DIAGONAL SPREAD COLOUR
	13.12.72	DIAGONAL SPREAD ½ COLOUR/½ MONO
	21.2.73	DIAGONAL SPREAD MONO
	28.2.73	DIAGONAL SPREAD MONO
	14.3.73	DIAGONAL SPREAD COLOUR
	21.3.73	DIAGONAL SPREAD ½ COLOUR/½ MONO

We'll be doing other things in other media, too!
'Haama', for instance, will be launched through press as well as magazines. Crown will appear in other magazines but, at the time this brochure goes to press, the details are not yet finalised. We will advise as soon as we can.

HAAMA

'Haama' is a bold, striking design. Beautiful to hold. Beautiful to look at—any drink is greatly enhanced by Haama's heavy solid glass base.

CROWN GLASS
OVER 250 BEAUTIFUL GIFTS

ᐯ Product development, not released, about 1980 Powerhouse Museum collection

ᐯ 'Hunter', designed by Denise Larcombe, 1986 Powerhouse Museum collection

ᐱ > 'Hunter' and 'Haama' marketing materials, 1972–86 Powerhouse Museum collection

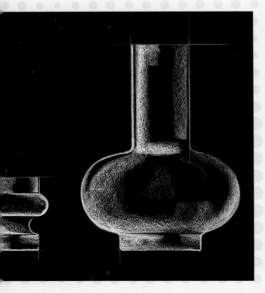

8

9

out his modern designs, to give people something new and fresh. This story is important to know if you are trying to understand retro because what we take for granted as the look of the period was not inevitable; it was definitely not merely the evolution of one thing from another. At some points along the way, some things had to be made to happen. The point where the British stopped making purely cut crystal glassware and began to design modern, hand-blown colourful glass is where the retro period begins, at least in the UK, and possibly the Anglophone world.

This is why one seldom ever sees reference to cut crystal glass and the like in retro books even when it

was made well into the period. It was just not the look; it was conservative and safe, as opposed to being daring and new. It continued in production for a long while into the retro period precisely because many, especially older people, resisted modern design very vigorously. However, as younger and affluent generations came through and made their presence felt in the market, some glass companies saw the need for change. As we will see, Whitefriars was about the only other exception to the conservatism of British glass, and their risky strategy of appointing Geoff Baxter, newly graduated from art college in the 1950s, also paid dividends.

Stennett-Willson's promotion of modern glass worked and sixties Britain loved it. King's Lynn Glass even got into exporting, and within just two years had attracted the curiosity of one of the best names in the decorative arts: Wedgwood, the ceramics and tableware giant. With their take-over, the factory carried on with better backing and expanded its range of designs and workers (they had over 100 by 1969).

Stennett-Willson remained their managing director and chief designer and produced some amazing new looks for glass. It was the 'Sheringham' candlestick design that became something of a signature piece, winning the Queen's Award for Industry

11

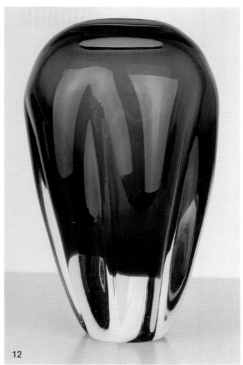

12

13

8
Geoff Baxter
textured vase in
Meadow Green for
Whitefriars Glass,
England, 1969–72

9
Space-age designs
for the 1950s:
Geoff Baxter ruby-
coloured vessels for
Whitefriars Glass,
England, c. 1958

10
Geoff Baxter organic
modern vase for
Whitefriars, England,
c. 1959

11
Geoff Baxter, an
early Scandinavian-
influenced vase in
Ocean Green for
Whitefriars Glass,
England, c. 1957

12
Influential Swede:
Tom Moller grey
vase for Reijmyre,
Sweden, 1960

13
Jim Dyer vase for
Liskeard Glass
England, c.1972

14
Glass icon: Paul
Kedelv 'Coquille'
bowl for Flygfors,
Sweden, 1952

15

16

17

18

19

15
Geoff Baxter organic modern 'molar' vase for Whitefriars, England, c. 1959

16
Geoff Baxter 'drunken bricklayer' vase for Whitefriars Glass, England, c. 1967

17
Geoff Baxter 'mobile phone' vase for Whitefriars Glass, England, c. 1971

18
Geoff Baxter 'stitch' vase for Whitefriars Glass, England, c. 1973

19
Geoff Baxter 'zig zag' vase for Whitefriars Glass, England, c. 1970

and making massive sales. It required two glass makers to construct these architectural pieces, and they were made in a range of sizes. The late 1960s re-introduced the joy of candle light back into modern life and Stennett-Willson's candlestick designs were essential to this. His 'Brancaster' design shows how far he would go to achieve something worthwhile. Their long hollow stems (the one pictured is almost 30 cm tall) required the specialist skills of Austrian glass blowers, but he thought nothing of finding them and persuading them to work for him.

Stennett-Willson also produced fantastic textured bowls and vases, as well as astonishing new paperweights that are seriously underrated by collectors and can be bought for very modest sums today. On the other hand, the abstract animals and birds series produced by Wedgwood were an instant hit and collected to display – in place of all that cut crystal (that was beginning to go out of fashion). Even after he left Wedgwood, Stennett-Willson couldn't stop, founding yet another studio glass company (Langham Glass) that is still in operation today.

At Whitefriars, a similar story emerged. Whitefriars was a very old company formerly called James Powell and Sons which was first recorded in a central London site in 1720. Originally their glass works were located in a City of London factory on the corner of Whitefriars and Temple Streets, in an area between Fleet Street and the River Thames. They were there from at least the 1720s and only moved to a new, bigger factory at Wealdenstone, near Harrow, in 1923. They remained there until 1980 when they finally (and very sadly) closed, but not before they amassed an amazing catalogue of glass designs.

The most intense Whitefriars collector-focus is on the much later work of Geoff Baxter in the 1960s and 1970s, especially when he broke free from the direct influence of Scandinavian 'cool modern' and developed his own style of astonishing shapes and textures that used both industrial and natural surfaces – often in the same piece.

Baxter also innovated a range of colours that were directly in line with 'swinging London's' love affair with the psychedelic. He came up with mind-blowing colours such as tangerine (orange), kingfisher blue, meadow (green), aubergine, pewter, willow (green), cinnamon and twilight (both browns).

Despite being youthful and trendy – shocking even – Whitefriars was a commercial success, even if one of the mainstays of their output was in the more conservative ruby colour. Orders from department stores for ruby glass were always strong at the gift fairs and this actually annoyed the youthful Baxter. Ruby glass was considered to be more tasteful by a largely conservative public but in any case it was the most often purchased gift for ruby wedding anniversaries. Presumably, with lengthening lifespans in the modern world, more and more married couples reached their fortieth anniversary, an accomplishment that was assisted by the relative difficulty of obtaining a divorce until the 1970s. It was the new generation of affluent and fashionable people who bought his colours to wash away the drabness of postwar austerity. Baxter's glass was received very well by the art and design world and won several design awards. His pieces might be seen alongside other works of modern art by Bridget Riley and sculptures by Barbara Hepworth.

Cut to the 1980s and 1990s and Baxter's pieces began to turn up as discarded bits of kitsch in op-shops and garage sales everywhere. Modern people move with the times and even the best crafted works have their day and are replaced or sold off. This is the point where Whitefriars Glass began a new life as a *collectable*. At first, people like me kept quiet about these amazing works and bought them up for just the change in your pocket. Then the inevitable happened. A curator from the Manchester City Art Galleries caught onto to this new enthusiasm and realised that this unsung company and its output from the mid-century was historically very significant. An exhibition was staged which then moved to London and was a smash hit. Suddenly prices rose as everyone wanted to buy this glass. A casually-placed glass ashtray (actually a 'Tooth' vase) in a front cover photo on an Oasis album (*Definitely Maybe*) just happened to be by Geoff Baxter.

By 2001, the market for Whitefriars switched from shops and markets to eBay. Here is a good illustration of the impact of the internet on collecting: whereas before, prices were dictated by *local* conditions of supply and demand, suddenly buyers from remote, outer areas had access to a global market. What happened?

The internet did two things simultaneously. First, it produced a larger collecting population that could go shopping more often and in more places. When this happened in 2001 it had an impact on a limited supply of Whitefriars coming onto what was still a smallish and specialised market. This caused prices to skyrocket, especially for the rarer, larger pieces. A good example is the outrageous 'Hooped' vase (30 cm) of 1967. In 2000, the average price for a 'tangerine' piece was $210 but by 2002 with the market in warp-drive, it rose to $450 and by

2004 it was $1225. The Holy Grail is of course the massive 'Banjo' vase. In tangerine, it rose from $1750 to $2125 in three years but the rarer colour 'sage' reached $12 500 and 'meadow' $4500!

Second, these rising prices meant that suddenly, dealers were trying to source it and sell it. Soon the more common patterns became super plentiful and after 2005 prices began to drop. As a result, collectors' tastes shifted and changed. Tip: Whitefriars' super rare 'architectural slabs' are now worth looking out for. I have been collecting Whitefriars glass since the late 1980s and I can tell you that almost everything has come into fashion over that time. But then again, some designs

have mysteriously gone out of fashion too…

On the back of a massive interest in collecting modern glass, another collecting culture built up around Murano glass from Italy. Here the problem was that most of the glass turning up in the USA, UK or Australia, for example, was of their 'tourist wares'. Cheaper and less artistic, they often had fish, dog, clown and other whimsical themes, although many minor pieces of sommerso layered glass forms made their way out too. Harder to find were the outputs of designers such as Dino Martens and Aldo Nason. These are extraordinarily complex pieces to make and hence were rarely copied elsewhere.

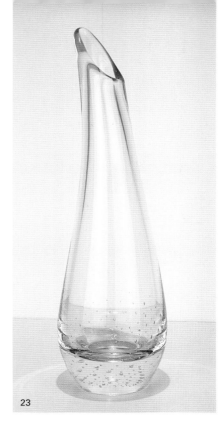

21

22

23

Retro glass form

Organic freeform

If I can generalise somewhat, it might be possible to argue that prior to the arrival of the modern forms of glass we associate with retro, glass makers tended towards a highly ornamental look, finding ways of embellishing the natural beauty of glass through numerous techniques of adding glass to blown vessels. Murano glass of the nineteenth and early twentieth centuries was extremely finely ornamented, achieving a gothic look, with piped streams of hot glass, sometimes in different colours, applied to the main glass body. Highly elaborate concoctions of delicate threads

and twists of glass, often in candy stripes and cased coloured strands, these fragile pieces were certainly impressive and were widely copied – by Whitefriars London factory, notably, in the nineteenth century. Otherwise, the British manner of ornamentation was mostly through skilled techniques of cutting and engraving in heavy-bodied flint (ie uncoloured) crystal works. Whitefriars was inspired, as were many others, by 'glasses with histories' and in the nineteenth century designers travelled the length and breadth of Europe to study classical works of art in order to copy or at least be inspired by classical and renaissance glass design. In this way, their designs did

not look forward to a new modern age but were resolutely set on resurrecting a golden past. Whitefriars was even inspired by Roman glass and produced some excellent reproductions of Roman designs.

By the early 1950s sales were less than brimming and the Powel family who owned Whitefriars decided they needed new blood, specifically a designer who could bring their range up to date. Geoff Baxter was appointed and he rapidly began to design radically new shapes and colourways. He was very clearly inspired by Scandinavian glass design, both in terms of their flowing organic aesthetic and their love of landscape colours. Tom Moller's silky-grey design

24

25

26

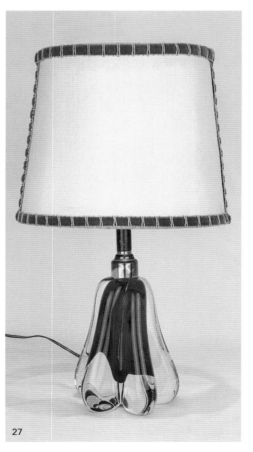

27

28

for Reijmyre was prototypical, with every line being formed by glass's natural tendencies to stretch and flow. This liquid quality of glass was especially relevant when deployed metaphorically in the form of a droplet for such objects as decanters. The Orrefors droplet decanter with a glass stopper that simply extends the design is something of a classic in this tradition.

Nature was clearly the new big idea and Baxter set about exploiting the natural qualities of glass to achieve softer tones and generous, curvaceous lines. His early 1950s take on the familiar beak vase, much liked by Swedish firms such as Orrefors, was substantial and original. The vessel was begun much like Moller's but then it was held at the narrow end and swung to stretch and elongate it. A closer look at the base shows the inclusion of one of Whitefriars signature techniques: very fine, controlled bubbles.

Baxter's 'molar' vases, his triangular stem vases, and his 'nipple' vases are all natural inspirations from the sensual forms of human and animal bodies. At the same time a series of vases that deployed the cutting skills at Whitefriars showcased simple botanic specimens, of grasses and sprays of dill flowers. The colourways of arctic blue and green were soothing and refreshingly new to the British scene. Before long, other glass companies, including the new firm, Liskeard Glass in Cornwall, followed in the same path.

Soon, the organic style dominated most glass design in Europe. Murano designers in Italy produced exquisite globular vessels that were then cut at the top to form beaks and other

24
As seen on an Oasis cover (*Definitely Maybe*): Geoff Baxter's 'molar' vase for Whitefriars Glass, England, c. 1965

25
Jim Dyer vase for Liskeard Glass, England, c. 1970

26
'Apple' vase, designed by Ingeborg Lundin, made by Orrefors Glasbruk, Sweden, 1957 Powerhouse Museum collection

27
Whitefriars lobed ruby lamp base, c. 1965

28
William Wilson and Harry Dyer for Whitefriars brown streaky knobbly vase, c. 1969

29
'Sommerso' glass vase by Luciano Gaspari for Salviati, Italy, c. 1958 Powerhouse Museum collection

29

32

33

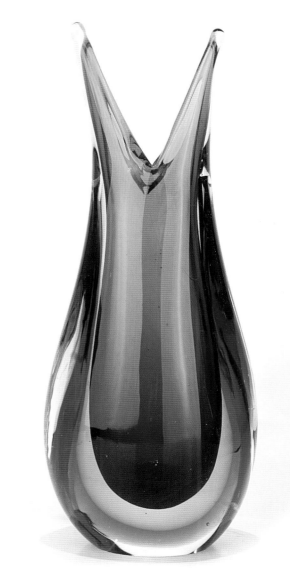

34

cascading shapes. Murano was particularly good at designing its watery totems, large impressive fish and even eels.

At Bohemia in Czechoslovakia, glass was twisted to give it a dancing movement and rhythm. New ways of combining and casing coloured glass were developed at Murano and Bohemia but it was in Scandinavia that very complex techniques were innovated.

Despite the obvious cleverness and complexity, few Swedish glass makers went past Paul Kedelv's 1952 'Coquille' bowl for Flygfors. Even today, when this much copied shape has become something of a glass cliché, to suddenly come across his 'Coquille' bowl lit with natural light is nothing short of exquisite. I particularly like the way its three-coloured glass forms a coloured shadow underneath.

30
Vase from 'Piume' series with engraved feathers between layers of coloured glass, by Archimede Seguso, Italy, 1955 Powerhouse Museum collection

31
Murano, eel in cased pink glass, Italy, c. 1958

32
Twisted vase from the 'Andromeda' range by Jan Beranek for Skrdlovice, Czechoslovakia, c. 1964; escorted by two 'Scruf' vases, Sweden, c. 1959

33
Murano Glass 'jester's hat' vase, by Flavio Poli for Seguso Vetri d'Arte, Italy, c. 1965

34
Murano sommerso 'beak' vase by Flavio Poli for Seguso Vetri d'Arte, Italy, c. 1965

35

Pop art

Glass was not only suited to mimicking nature, its natural spangle and plasticity made it one of the favourite mediums for pop art – in the right hands.

A simple, heavy sphere of purple attached to a tube – all in thick, full-lead crystal – was a winning shape and colour for the Finnish company Riihimäen Lasi. At Orrefors a large green apple chimed well with late Beatlemania, while Michael Bang at Holmegaard created a range of acid-coloured vessels and containers in hot yellow, hot orange and hot red. However, it was Geoff Baxter at Whitefriars who took most of the 1960s honours. Nothing quite captured pop better than his range of sculptural pieces from this period. His coffin vases in a range of spangled colours, cased in a brilliant flint crystal, were small but powerful statements of their time, but

his (now-called) mobile phone vases, drunken brick-layer vases, hoop vases and banjo and TV vases are possibly the most sought-after pieces of 1960s retro glass. And it is easy to see why. They were unique, they were somehow witty and fun, they were audacious, and they were at the same time convincing as works of art. Although having great street appeal among young consumers, they also had a studio feel that the great glass blower Ronnie Wilkinson gave great consistency to.

Animals were a favourite pop motif and these appeared in the manufacturers' catalogues as whimsies and novelties at this time; Whitefriars and Wedgwood being typical, and ever alert to what might be gifted and collected in series. Whitefriars swans have a fluidity and grace that really captures the beauty of the living swans they represent. I was curious

35
Michael Bang containers and vase for Holmegaard Glass, Denmark, c. 1969

36
Pyrex 2½ quart Flower Power casserole, USA, 1972

37
Murano Glass leaping fish, Italy, c. 1965

38
Stevens and Williams acid-coloured glass bowl, Stourbridge, England, c. 1968

39
Orrefors 'Eternell' tea-light holders, Sweden, c. 1978

40
Fiesta Glass 'Beefeater' dish in 'Carnaby Street' style, England, c. 1967

41
'Zebra' vase designed by Ingeborg Lundin, made with 'Ariel' technique, Orrefors, Sweden, 1975
Powerhouse Museum collection

42
Two-tone orange bowl by Orrefors, Sweden, c. 1985

43
Unknown designer, pop art orange platter, USA, c. 1966

44
Ann and Goran Warff plate in sand-blasted, coloured glass for Kosta Glass, Sweden, 1971 Powerhouse Museum collection

45
Peter Wheeler striped orange studio vase for Whitefriars, England, 1969

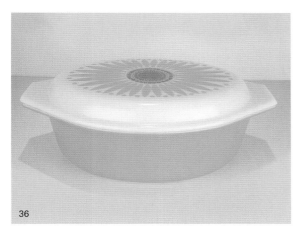

36

37

38

41

39

40

42

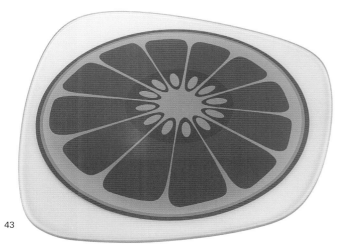

43

44

45

119

to know when they first appeared and was surprised to learn that it was in the 1940 catalogue. This was one of their more successful designs and it last appeared in their 1969 catalogue when their more pop-styled ducks and penguins put in an appearance. However, if you ever see glass swans that look just like Whitefriars but deviate a bit in their size and finish, then don't despair because they are probably 'friggers', the much rarer unofficial pieces that the blowers made with spare glass left over at the end of a day's production run. Although not sanctioned by the company, I think they were tolerated as a perk of the trade for the blowers, who took them home and sold them off privately.

According to the Whitefriars catalogue of 1940, the swans (model number 9167) came in three sizes: 14 cm, 20.5 cm and 25 cm and ranged in price from seven shillings to eleven shillings each. These were princely sums in their day, because Whitefriars glass, even novelty items like these

swans, was made from very high quality, full-lead crystal. The catalogue also tells the collector what colours they were made in (sea green, gold amber, emerald, sapphire, amethyst and sanctuary blue), so they will know when they have amassed a complete set! And they do look very good all together.

The other design, a smoky-coloured glass form, reminiscent of Frank Lloyd Wright's Johnson Wax building in Racine, Wisconsin, that has taken off among collectors recently may only have been produced over a very small period because catalogues for it were not saved in the factory archive. But I think they are magnificent designs for the early 1960s and they feature that characteristic pedestal base and those slinky, smoky colours. Although only small specimen vases (20 cm high), they are obviously genuine Whitefriars pieces because you can see the factory labels very clearly and these are specific to the period 1950–63.

46

46
Assortment of Christmas tree lights, Hong Kong, 1950s

47, 49, 50
Ronald Stennett-Willson glass animals for Wedgwood, Kings Lynn, England, c. 1967

48
William Wilson 'nipple' vase for Whitefriars Glass, England, 1940

51
Bristol Blue Glass, Concorde commemorative disc, 1969–2003, England, 2003

52
Whitefriars swans, England, c. 1940s–70s

53
Futuristic vessels in smoky glass, Whitefriars Glass, England, 1967

47

48

49

2

53

50

51

54

55

56

57

58

59

54
Geoff Baxter textured decanter for Whitefriars Glass, England, c. 1967

55
Frank Thrower 'Sunflower' salad bowl for Dartington Glass, England, c. 1973

56
Textured amethyst glass arrangement featuring Geoff Baxter's 'TV' vase, c. 1970; Riihimäen Lasi long-necked vessel, Finland, c. 1958; Thomas Webb wavy ribbed and textured vase, England; and Geoff Baxter 'Onion' vase, England, 1965–72

57
Tapio Wirkkala 'Ultima Thule' cocktail glass for Iittala, Finland, 1968; and Bunny Club cocktail stirrers

58
Timo Sarpaneva dessert glasses for Iittala, Finland, c. 1968

59
Frank Thrower 'Sunflower' dessert bowls for Dartington Glass, England, c. 1973

Texture

Geoff Baxter's designs of the time show that the late 1960s and early 1970s was a very distinctive period in itself. The smooth, organic surfaces favoured in the 1950s and early 1960s gave way to more textured, craggy and humanoid, sculptured looks. A range of bright colours (hot orange, kingfisher blue, meadow green) gave way to more muted, natural colours that included browns (cinnamon), greens (willow and blue/violet) amethyst and pewter. Baxter used innovative moulds with natural tree bark and ancient medieval surfaces to inject historical and environmental themes into his work, rather as brutalist architects did with concrete.

Texture was to be found dominating the outputs of Iitalla – particularly the vases and glassware by Timo Sarpaneva (eg his 'Atomic Bomb' vase) and Tapio Wirkkala (eg his *Thule* tumblers) – and the 'Eden' range of tableware from Orrefors. In these, the Scandinavian inspiration came from the impressions that nature provided for glass in the form of leaves and the various manifestations of ice. This aesthetic was not limited to studio glass but extended to entire ranges of wares and even the more commercial glass manufacturers such as Ravenscroft Glass and Dartington Glass's designer Frank Thrower.

Rising affluence and social mobility created the conditions for the extension of the 'cocktail party' to more and more sections of society. Whereas modest budgets in previous eras may have extended to beer and perhaps sherry, by the 1950s a wider choice of drink became normative, both in public drinking cultures and at private functions and parties. As the retro TV shows *Madmen, Life on Mars* and *Ashes to Ashes* amply demonstrate, alcohol consumption required tumblers for spirits such as whisky, longer cocktail glasses for mixed drinks, as well as beer schooners and a range of wine and liquor glasses.

Sets of glasses as well as decanters were offered to an enthusiastic public to give as wedding and Christmas presents. One notable design from the late 1960s and early 1970s is the decanter and glass sets designed by the great Domhnall O'Broin for the Scottish company Caithness. These capture very well the mood and colour aesthetic of the period, as well as its enthusiasm for the past. O'Broin's goblet forms are among the best drinking vessels produced at this point, though the goblet found favour else-where; at Bendigo Pottery, for example.

When the modern home was opened up for better lit interiors, the conditions were ripe for glass manufacturers to design and sell coloured glass vessels that exploited light better than any other decorative medium. Even small coloured glass objects produce dramatic effects when backlit against windows. The translucent and iridescent qualities of coloured glass, particularly when distorted by interior structure or exterior texture, were particularly apt for a culture that was interested in perception, mystery and complexity. In this sense, retro glass was a form of pop art that most could afford. Along with other objects with special optical effects, such as lava lamps and disco lamps, glass added a very distinctive light and mood to this period, which speaks of a more experimental, mind-expanding and social sensibility. Glass was also a vital component in the consumption of the retro drug of choice: alcohol.

Drinking alcohol, particularly the more expensive forms, had been a luxury that only the few could afford until this period. In addition to the specific occasion, the new enthusiasm for cocktails and cocktail parties was at the same time a celebration of rising fortunes and perhaps the realisation of greater equality. This theme seems to be suggested by the iconic 'jazz' glasses that were very popular at this time. It shows freer expression in dance, a youth culture predicated on its own music and the end of racial segregation in public spaces.

Glassware for alcohol, as well as glass designs for desert dishes, containers, vases and figurines was a radical improvement that was largely taken for granted as part of modern life. However, nothing provides quite the same register for this improved lifestyle as a material that was in relatively short supply in earlier times and confined largely to a social elite. When people could begin to throw away hand-blown, art designed glass by Geoff Baxter in favour of newer fashions in domestic interiors, they had come a long way indeed!

60

61

62

63

64

65

66

67

68

Communist glass

Everything featured so far in this chapter was produced by the capitalist west but in the Soviet bloc, particularly in Czechoslovakia, modern glass was produced in a dazzling variety of forms and using a wide variety of techniques. It is different, fresh and becoming very collectable.

Arguably one of the greatest achievements of these factories was the use of pressed glass techniques, particularly by the Sklo Union factories. Formed in 1965, a number of factories (including Rosice Glassworks, Hermanova Hut, zavod Libochovice and Rudolfova Hut) used a centrally directed design organisation as well as the designs of an emerging group of star designers.

Most of the traditional glass industry of Czechoslovakia was nationalised after the Second World War and the return from exile of the Benes Government. This occurred in order to centrally reconstruct Czechoslovakia's industries but also to take control of these German-owned factories as part of war reparations and enact the policy of expelling many ethnic Germans. Historically, the Czech glass industry had been largely owned and controlled by ethnic Germans.

So how did Communism influence the designs and output from these factories? Although an organising principle was to produce good design for the masses, it seems that the national design organisation was less influential among the Sklo Union factories than their own Centre for Pressed Glass Design Technology. Here a group of

designers produced a startling diversity of abstract designs using pressed glass technologies. Besides Rudolf Jurnikl, other key designers include Frantisek Peceny, Vladislav Urban, Jiri Brabec, Adolf Matura, Jiri Zejmon and Pavel Panek. Officially, the art policy of Communist Czechoslovakia was social realism but these designers used optical effects and surface texturing to suggest more abstract ideas. In this, they followed their western counterparts, but their abstract expression reflected more the social reality of state socialism. The Czech glass industry was a very valuable export to the government and the government gave these designers great licence to compete on the international design stage – which they did at Expo 58 in Brussels and at the Osaka World Expo in 1970.

Whereas western glass designers were inspired by organic and natural metaphors as well as historic and environmental textures, much of the Czech output seemed to focus on the life and organisation of Communist societies. Many of the pieces seem to be inspired by the social–industrial project of modern Communist Europe, with its emphasis on production, social organisation, democratisation and a politically centralised machine age.

Typical is the machine-like, and complex block design jardinière produced by Vladislav Urban for Rosice Glassworks. It is extremely solid and heavy, and its amethyst colour seems to glorify this man-made, synthetic world. Meanwhile, Rudolf Jurnikl's very architectural vase

69

70

71

for Rudolfova Hut seems to celebrate standardised social housing, where equality and repetition are valued. The optimistic, bright blue glass seems to positively endorse these concepts and values. These pieces were widely sold into the Communist bloc countries and they were also very successfully exported to many destinations in the west.

Jiri Zejmon's iridescent vase, built of textured blocks, forms a monolithic brick that is also reminiscent of huge buildings, perhaps factories or scientific foundations. Either way, it also seems to be a comment about life in Czechoslovakia, but it might be taken a number of ways. Is it saying we are overwhelmed or dwarfed by these huge structures or is it suggesting we are safely supported by them?

The 'Osaka' pattern candle holder and jardinière in clear glass are also by Rudolf Jurnikl, from 1969. Sculptural and intriguing, these use optical effects (a very common feature of Sklo Union glass) and radiating lines to create an object that appears to be both transparent and distorted. Perhaps this is a metaphor for

life in Communist Czechoslovakia at the time or in modern times generally. One is tempted to interpret the radiating, expanding lines and central focal point as inspired by the highly organised and ambitious nature of these societies.

There are also reasons to think that some (dissident?) designers were also influenced by western freedom, particularly its experimentations with freedom from the late 1960s and 1970s. The bubble vase in bright green glass seems particularly utopian, or at least a projection beyond familiar forms and structures; and perhaps the fluid nature of glass gave these designers much greater freedom of expression than other art disciplines.

Czech glass designers also modernised cut glass designs to great effect (the key factory names here are Exbor and Borské Sklo and the key designers include Jiri Harcuba and Pavel Hlava), as well as older techniques using enamelling and metallic applications – the best in my opinion were made at Borské Sklo, though I have yet to discover who the main designers were.

69
Vladislav Urban
vase for Rosice
Glassworks/
Sklo Union,
Czechoslovakia, 1967

70
Lime green bubble
vase, designer
and manufacturer
unknown, attributed
to Sklo Union,
Czechoslovakia,
c. 1968

71
Frantisek Vizner
vase for Rosice
Glassworks/
Sklo Union,
Czechoslovakia, 1965

72
'Osaka' jardinière
by Rudolf Jurnikl for
Zavod Libochovice/
Sklo Union,
Czechoslovakia, 1969

73
Flint glass
'candlewax' vase
by Frantisek Peceny
for Hermanova
Hut/Sklo Union,
Czechoslovakia,
pattern no. 20245,
c. 1972

74
'Osaka' candle
holder by Rudolf
Jurnikl for Zavod
Libochovice/
Sklo Union,
Czechoslovakia, 1969

75
Blue architectural
vase by Rudolf
Jurnikl for Rudolfova
Hut/Sklo Union,
Czechoslovakia, 1963

76
Amethyst jardinière
by Vladislav
Urban for Rosice
Glassworks/
Sklo Union,
Czechoslovakia,
pattern no. 619/19,
1967

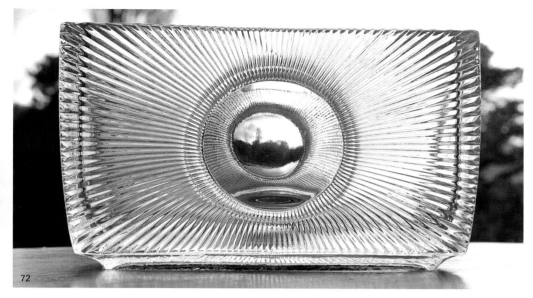

72

73

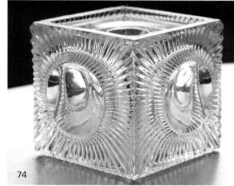

74

75

76

MODERN METAL

AS ROBERT WELCH SAYS, 'THE
PHILOSOPHY OF THE SCANDINAVIANS,
SO POPULAR AT THE TIME, WAS
DESIGNING SIMPLE, EVERYDAY OBJECTS
THAT WERE FUNCTIONAL AND BEAUTIFUL
AND WHICH MOST PEOPLE COULD
AFFORD, GREATLY APPEALED'.

ANNAMARIE STAPLETON SILVER AND METALWORK 2001

IF ANTIQUE METALS CAN BE THOUGHT of as brass, silver, silver plate, bronze and gold, then retro metals can be thought of as aluminium, tin, stainless steel and iron (wrought and cast), even if the 'older' metals were still favoured and used by some artists and designers. The Danes, for example, continued to produce some really lovely silver and gilded silver designs through this period. The textured cufflinks (pictured on page 180) from the late 1960s have that understated but strong style that we see from the Danish designers of this period.

This transformation from older to new metals was a mixture of innovation born of necessity, a more plentiful supply of (therefore cheaper) existing materials and the arrival of new materials. Mild steel was in great abundance following the end of the iron-rich Second World War, and this contrasted with the relatively short supply of materials such as wood. Thus, we begin to see things made from wrought iron that had previously been made from wood: everything, from garden gates, coat hooks, pot plant holders, candlesticks, magazine racks, fruit bowls and other minor elements of furnishing (such as stools, shelf brackets, the new telephone tables, patio chairs and so on).

The postwar period saw a great rise in hydro-electricity supply, and this new abundance of high power electricity made aluminium, a very expensive and semi-precious metal in the 1920s, extremely cheap and available for mass produced homewares that had the added advantage of being hard-wearing and cheap to transport. One of the great stories here is of the Bialetti 'Moka' espresso coffee makers.

Many years ago, Alberto Alessi's two grandfathers were none other than Alfonso Bialetti (who invented, designed and manufactured the original octagonal Bialetti aluminium coffee maker) and Giovanni Alessi (who started Alessi, one of the world's great design companies). Alberto, who is now the Co-Chairman of Alessi, talks about how the two companies in the Strona Valley of Italy defined clear and different strategies so as to avoid competition: Alfonso Bialetti decided to produce good designs that could be made cheaply in factories so as to reach as many people as possible, while Giovanni Alessi opted for the arts and crafts market, producing beautifully designed and handcrafted pieces for a smaller, elite market. Two coffee makers, one the classic Bialetti 'Moka' and the other, architect Richard Sapper's '9090' design for Alessi, illustrate how

1
Modern metal in the contemporary home: Bialetti 'Moka' espresso maker in aluminium and plastic, Italy, 1950; Richard Sapper's '9090' espresso maker in stainless steel, copper and titanium for Alessi, Italy; Philippe Starck's 'Juicy Salif' lemon squeezer in alloy for Alessi, Italy; and Innoplan Design corkscrew, Switzerland, 1979

both strategies worked to benefit the consumer.

The Bialetti 'Moka' is one of the most successful designs of all time; indeed it is so successful that to this day it is the only product they need to produce! They currently sell around four million pieces per year but they reckon they need to reach two-thirds of the Italian market in order to stay afloat.

With a very large proportion of the European population already owning the long-lived 'Moka', it was not at all easy for other companies to break into the domestic coffee maker market. Arguably, the most successful and stylish venture was the 'Atomic' that not only produced espresso coffee, it also converted water into steam for the heating and frothing of milk – a must for the cappuccino and other hot milky coffee recipes. Its clever space-age design and use of bold plastic

elements meant it won the prize for 1960s coffee makers. Its Achilles heel was its use of aluminium, which became so associated with the 1950s and 1960s that by the 1970s designers were looking for something new and in tune with their more radical times. When Alessi was commissioning Richard Sapper to produce a new coffee maker in the late 1970s, they realised that his exquisite design would be expensive, with its mirror polished stainless steel and magnetic steel base, alongside its technically sophisticated detailing, including the audacious use of titanium for its handle. Stainless steel was gradually becoming the most fashionable material for a wide range of kitchen and tableware products but it was still very expensive to produce. So with the '9090' it was the opposite economics of the 'Moka': they

needed to charge far more per item and therefore needed to capture only a tiny fraction of the market. In fact, it was going to be the most expensive espresso maker ever. They had to make sure that they would capture two per cent of the Italian market (or 100 000 pieces) if the venture was to succeed. They need not have worried. It captured the imagination of the *world*, won prizes and was placed in the permanent collection of the MOMA in New York.

All this is not to say that aluminium was now a completely outmoded material; far from it, but to succeed again it needed to be associated with new ideas to which it was suited. Again, it was the thinking company Alessi, and one of its favourite designers Philippe Starck, who came up with such an idea: the very 'un-1950s' 'Juicy Salif' lemon squeezer circa 1989.

2
Candle holder by Turner of Melbourne, Australia, c.1958

3
Philippe Starck's 'Juicy Salif' lemon squeezer in alloy for Alessi, Italy, c. 1989

4
Telephone table and chair in iron rod, vinyl and wood, Australia, c. 1952

5
Candelabra in wrought iron with unusual plastic liners, USA, 1960s

6, 7
Alessandro Mendini, 'Anna G' corkscrew for Alessi, Italy, 1994

8
Viking ship model in cast metal: a symbol of Scandinavia's continuing excellence in design and craft production, 1964

9
'Arden Candlestick' by Robert Welch, chromed stainless steel, c. 2008

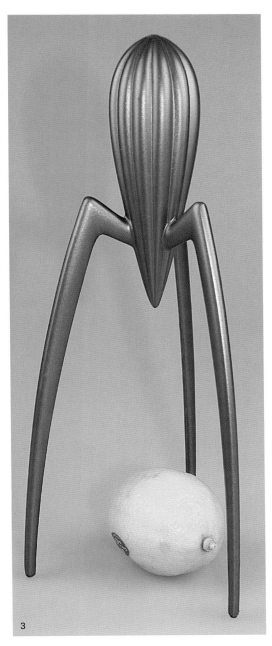

3

4

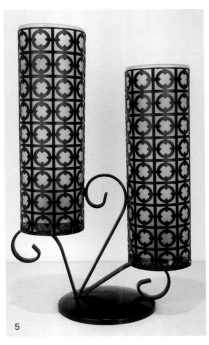

5

6

7

8

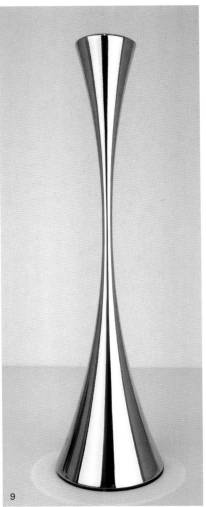

9

131

THE 'RITE-LITE' TV LAMP DEBBIE RUDDER = CURATOR, SCIENCE AND INDUSTRY, POWERHOUSE MUSEUM

This lamp was made in Melbourne in 1957 and purchased by the Powerhouse Museum, on eBay, in 2005. It created appropriate ambience as a prop in the 2006–07 exhibition *On the Box: Great Moments in Australian Television*.

Designed to fulfil a need – created by advertising and 'expert' opinion – this set-top lamp was one of millions installed in homes when TV became the new centre of attention. The so-called 'experts' deemed that TV should not be watched in the dark; who knew what damage this could do to impressionable young eyes?

Many TV lamps are now traded online, with most featuring kitsch ceramic figurines. By contrast, this lamp is made of anodised aluminium and is an adaptation of its maker's own elegant desk lamp, with the conical shade removed from its stem and inverted so the light points upwards. An adjustable shade above the cone allows some brightness control. A cheeky touch is provided by a further adaptation: the perforations around the cone's rim repeatedly spell TV.

Anodised aluminium was an excellent choice of material and helped ensure the lamp's longevity. Made to hold an incandescent globe (which produces a lot more heat than light), the lamp is heat-resistant and corrosion-proof, and its colour is still vibrant. As anodised aluminium products are experiencing resurgence in popularity, this lamp (retro-fitted with a compact fluorescent globe) would not be out of place in a modern home. Just don't try to perch it on top of a modern slimline TV set!

This 'Rite-Lite' TV lamp, Melbourne, Australia, 1957, was purchased for display in the museum's retrospective exhibition *On the Box*. It was later acquired into the permanent collection
Powerhouse Museum collection

Aluminium

Just prior to the retro period, aluminium had enjoyed great fame and favour as a new and truly remarkable material. It was light, mouldable, strong, would not tarnish through contact with air or water, it was heat resistant and could be spun and welded. For many of these reasons it had become the most high-tech material and would eventually come to be associated with the sophistication and glamour of aeroplane construction and air travel. So, for its first few decades, it was associated with relatively high status goods, such as jewellery and even vases. Russell Wright deployed spun aluminium to produce a range of aluminium flared vases that were the very height of New York sophistication in the 1930s. These designs have now been reissued but it is remarkable how well the originals have survived the past eighty years.

By the 1950s, with the sudden arrival of large supplies of cheap aluminium thanks to hydro-electric schemes in the USA, Australia, Scandinavia and elsewhere, it was used for a great many applications and this is why it is so symbolic of the 1950s.

Aluminium appeared widely as the modern look for electric lamps, lamp shades and TV lights, often deploying the streamlined looks of contemporary ships and motor cars. It was a favoured uplight material and was used extensively by architects of the period such as Harry Seidler. Its appearance in the racy machine look of the 1950s gave it a certain glamour that was

10

10
Russel Wright, spun aluminium vase, USA, c. 1939

extended to other areas of design and consumption.

Since aluminium was light and very durable it was extensively used to make cheap water beakers and drinks tumblers. It could be found in

schools and works canteens as well as in restaurants and resorts but also in giftware. One prominent gift often given to men has survived in plentiful numbers and seems to be championed by retro collectors: the travelling drinks

11

12

13

set. Typically housed in an attractive vinyl case and complete with a can opener and sometimes a corkscrew, the set normally comprises four well made anodised aluminium tumblers in different colours. A good idea in theory; I have yet to see many that seem to have been used much. I suspect they were kept in a secure place and just treasured.

Some companies attempted to make aluminium vases that echoed Russell Wright's spun aluminium vases but this idea never succeeded in the anodised form, perhaps because bright metals and flowers were not a winning association.

Anodised aluminium was, however, very strongly associated with cocktail culture and there are some magnificent cocktail shakers to be found from the 1950s. However, the most iconic object has to be the Sparklets 'Hostmaster' soda siphon in gloriously coloured anodised aluminium. Here is yet another object that is still in use and manufactured today. Its gush of frothy water was a key expression of the new affluent leisure culture and one could be seen on every bar across the world.

14

11
Anodised aluminium vase, Conrah, Wales, c. 1958

12
Caffe Rapid aluminium espresso maker with twin outputs by Brevettato, Italy, c.1968

13
Anodised aluminium tumbler set by Vermont, Australia, c. 1955

14
Making aluminium possible: Hydro-electric schemes like 'Norsk Hydro Rjukan' at Rjukan, Norway, could produce power supplies for many new, modern products such as aluminium and fertilisers, built 1911

ANODISED ALUMINIUM TUMBLERS
DEBBIE RUDDER = CURATOR, SCIENCE AND INDUSTRY, POWERHOUSE MUSEUM

From the 1930s to the 1960s, milk bars flourished in Australia, just as juice bars do today, using youth-oriented advertising and ambience to sell a 'healthy' product. These milkshake tumblers remind us of the heyday of the milk bar as a hang-out and a focus of youth culture, in a way that the fast-paced takeaway juice bar faintly mimics. Made of durable, anodised aluminium, the tumblers were strictly for use within a main-street milk bar; they were washed and re-used as customers lingered and listened to music they selected from juke-boxes.

These tumblers were acquired in 1991, along with other objects from Keary's Strathfield milk bar. They were first displayed in the museum's Recent Acquisitions Showcase; then in the modest *Milkbar Music* exhibition at the Powerhouse Discovery Centre; and most recently as part of a recreated milk bar in the 2008 exhibition *Modern Times: The Untold Story of Modernism in Australia*.

While these museum objects have been favoured by curators of the 'baby boom' generation, there is also a roaring trade in aluminium tumblers online. To boomers they are objects of nostalgia. To later generations, they are lightweight, unbreakable and colourful, all virtues more commonly associated with plastic; but they are not made of that ubiquitous material and they don't lose their sheen through constant use. All of these features fit with current notions of a sustainable lifestyle, making them attractive to those who also proudly take re-usable containers to their favourite barista for filling.

These anodised aluminium milkshake tumblers were used in a Sydney milk bar and purchased by the museum in 1991. They have led a more colourful life in the museum than many older and more venerable objects. Powerhouse Museum collection

It seemed that the natural place for aluminium was the kitchen, and here it found applications in almost every function and was produced in some very new designs. The Bialetti 'Moka' was a very extrovert design, deliberately decorative and somehow fun. Its design seems to suggest a carousel; it makes an arresting noise as the coffee comes through and it has a stove-to-table, one-piece function, making the need for a separate coffee jug redundant. However, even more exuberant than that, and perhaps a little *too* exuberant was its Polish rival from Kawa (which means coffee in Polish). Its excessive rarity today is, sadly, a result of very poor sales and one can understand why: it has all the looks of a parasitic worm or a dastardly surgical instrument. Still, it has a place in my collection.

These coffee makers contrast with the aesthetically pleasing tea

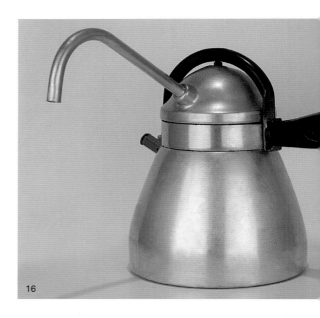

16

and coffee wares made by Piquot in the 1950s. Made with sycamore handles and rare white hornbeam lids, overall the Piquots have the lines of interesting cars of the 1950s and 1960s such as Bristols or Citroëns. They are slightly portly designs and perhaps had the most appeal to an affluent middle-aged demographic. Although French sounding, they were a Northampton-based English company (originally Burrage and Boyd) which formed in 1932 to produce non-electric vacuum cleaners using aluminium cast components. They branched out to design high class tea wares but their vacuum cleaner, launched in 1938, halted progress and the other products did not roll out until the late 1940s and 1950s – hence their rather 1930s look. Piquot are particularly interesting because not only are they still in business, they are still making the same successful designs, albeit now in an alloy metal. On their web site they ask if you have any of their original designs – they show illustrations of them all – and say that they offer a refurbishment service to restore them. This enduring design life is a key feature of many retro objects, as we have seen with furniture especially.

15

17

18

19

20

Iron ware

Wrought iron and iron rod–built products were a strong feature of 1950s design aesthetics. One of the most recognised and treasured retro objects in mild steel is the atomic-themed coat hook; and while the eye is drawn first to the coloured wooden balls, the zigzag of black (always black) connecting ironwork is just as important to the overall design. The magazine rack was another painted mild steel favourite and

with the one pictured overleaf, the ironwork is the main decorative feature and the eye only subsequently catches the red wooden atomic balls used on its base. These days this simple and cheap design would be appreciated in its own right. I for one would never spoil it with a pile of magazines.

Clement Meadmore, the great twentieth century sculptor who began his creative life designing and building furniture in Sydney, Australia, quickly realised the aesthetic potential of painted

mild steel – in really very simple designs. His stool (see page 30) could not be more elementary, yet its impact is surprisingly pleasing. Meadmore also produced white iron chairs for patios and pool sides, and a range of very well engineered coffee tables.

The same can be said of the 1950s fruit bowl, which, like many of Meadmore's designs of the period, deployed a strung material to complement a very engineered look. In this case the strung material is cheap plastic twine, pale

21

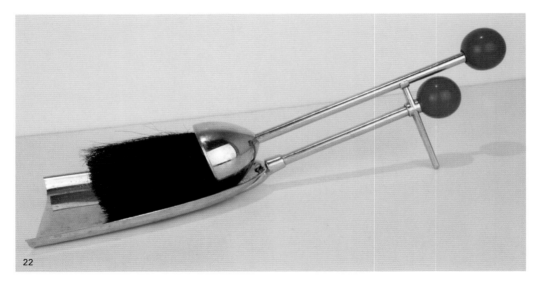

22

23

24

against the black painted iron, with matching plastic 'caps' for feet. Its winning look was surely one of the reasons why it stands out as a defining feature of the 1950s, especially when it was combined with other new materials of the age like formica and textured plastic with bright painted highlights. While mostly substituting for other materials then in poor supply and too expensive for household furnishing

goods, a few new objects were made exclusively in this way: the telephone table/chair (see page 131) is a case in point.

This innovation related to the dramatic expansion of telephone ownership and use in the 1950s, a time that seemingly required the telephone to be confined to the semi-private space of the ground floor hall, where individuals could sit alone

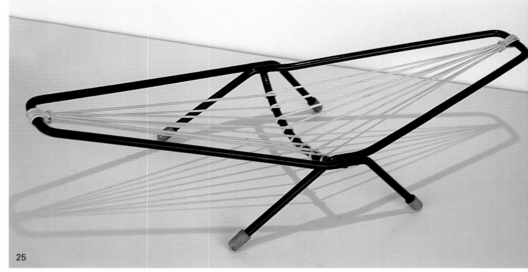

25

22
'Atomic' fireside
equipment, England,
1950s

23
Unknown designer,
tripod table (petrol)
lighter, Japan,
c. 1955

24
'Atomic' magazine
rack, England, 1950s

25
Strung fruit bowl,
USA, 1950s

26
Michael Lax skillet
for Copco, Denmark,
c. 1970

27
Cinzano tray, France,
c. 1958

28
VW car badge as
purloined by Beastie
Boys fans in the
1980s

26

27

28

29

30

and talk to friends or relatives while the rest of the family were occupied elsewhere. Looking remarkably like the structures that shoes salespeople used to assist shoppers to try on shoes, its diminutive size was well matched to the narrow dimensions of the modern hallway. Retro collectors like them not because of the original function, since phones are now mobile and multiple, but because there is still a call for temporary seating in hallways and entrance halls: in my family's case it is used for those annoying waits while someone else takes longer than expected to get ready to go out.

Open fires might have been superseded but they have never gone out of fashion completely, particularly in cottage or villa styled homes. This is where one normally expects to see some form of fireside equipment and these too were given a makeover in the 1950s. The small chromed set pictured is a very rare brush and pan for ashes that features the ubiquitous red atomic balls. It's an object that juxtaposed one of the oldest technologies (fire) with one of the newer technologies (atomic energy) making it quite comic, or at least, ironic.

The atomic magazine rack is still curiously commonplace in markets and collectable shops and is testament to the many companies that cashed in on these simple-to-make designs, and the desire of war-weary people to modernise and brighten up their homes.

Being cheap and cheerful was something of a watchword back in the 1950s and Worcester Ware, the manufacturers of tin waste bins and

29
Candlesticks
by Turners of
Melbourne,
Australia, 1965

30
Worcester Ware
waste bin, England,
c. 1955

139

other products, hit on a winner. Many of their bins have lasted surprisingly well, perhaps due to being more decorative than functional, and these have an extremely keen retro following, especially in the UK. They did a very broad range of designs, from large flouncy rose designs popular in the 1950s to the more abstract (now far more popular). Cheaply pressed metal trays were also proliferating, and getting a substantial design input as companies, such as Cinzano, built market share after the Second World War.

Aside from its universal use in modern gates, wrought iron was also used in the modern home for a variety or purposes, not least as combination pot plant holders and candlesticks. In theory, the modern world had dispensed with candles, experimenting with electric lighting instead. You see very few 50s candelabras but, in the late 60s they had second thoughts about losing the past altogether, and the candle made a comeback.

The Australian company Turners of Melbourne was particularly successful in cornering a national market in modern candlesticks and achieving more than just a perfunctory design. Many of them were very upbeat and

31

were clearly designed for a younger, perhaps newly married demographic – and like so many other retro objects, the candlestick was designed first and foremost for the gift industry. Turners of Melbourne was also a relatively long-lived company whose wares clearly began in the 1950s but extended into the 1970s. Their 1950s candlesticks and candelabra were in relatively simple, Spanish-styled swirls of flat iron which had

pleasantly contrasting candle holders in electroplated gilt. In the 1960s a more sculptural look emerged and the pair of candlesticks pictured on page 139 has a lively almost dancing movement to them. The more sophisticated candelabra of the later period, perhaps stretching into the early 1970s, featured playful modern designs with more finely made perforated screens, teak legs and handles, and even plastic shades to mute the light.

Cast iron cooking pans, lost to British, American and Australian kitchens since the 1930s, made a substantial comeback from the 1960s and 70s onwards as a result of increasing travel to France. Prior to the entry of French manufacturers such as Le Creuset, there were some very good Scandinavian designs that were sold through Habitat and similar stores. A case in point is Michael Lax's skillet for the Danish company Copco, so named because of its heat-efficient copper-bottomed designs. This is a superbly balanced and beautiful design, far more than a skillet properly needs, and it cooks omelettes like a dream.

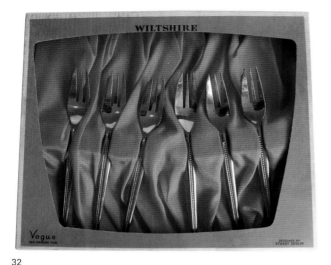

32

33

34

35

36

Stainless steel

It fell to stainless steel to truly embody the spirit of metal for the retro period. It was not only a new material; it was a new material that offered huge improvements on the past. Being rust-proof, it did not have to be coated with other materials such as chrome or silver and it required less care to keep it looking as it should. On top of this, it had none of the toxic properties and risks associated with aluminium and enamel in cookware.

Also in its favour was its somewhat basic, honest and matt appearance, which made it on a par with another, favoured material of the 1960s and 1970s: concrete. Concrete and stainless steel had magical properties but were not flashy. They could be quietly involved in the production of new industrial designs without taking away anything from the design itself. Gold and silver, chrome and glass always vied with design but not so stainless steel.

It was for this reason perhaps that it was included among those materials favoured by the new arts and crafts of the late 1960s and early 1970s. In the hands of Stuart Devlin, Robert Welch, Gerald Benney and Richard Sapper, stainless steel became a substitute for silver and made appearances as up-market teapots, candelabra, toast racks, wine goblets, martini glasses and champagne flutes, as well as flatwares, jewellery, bowls and tumblers.

31
Abstract design tin ice bucket, Hong Kong, c. 1969

32
Stuart Devlin 'Vogue' cake forks for Wiltshire, Australia, c. 1964

33
Max und Moritz salt and pepper in stainless steel and glass by Wilhelm Wagenfeld for Württembergische Metallwarenfabrik Cromargan, Germany, 1952–53

34
Stuart Devlin 'Asfodel' canapé forks for Wiltshire, Australia, c. 1963

35
Lundtofte salad servers, Denmark, c. 1956

36
Stuart Devlin 'Scintilla' serving spoons for Wiltshire, Australia, c. 1962

In the world of retro stainless steel collecting, three names loom very large indeed: Robert Welch, Gerald Benney and Stuart Devlin. All of them are master craftsmen, trained as silversmiths who created major works in silver and gold. However, the really important pieces tended to be commissions for major corporations that don't come onto the market, while the pieces in precious metals are not only more expensive, they are comparatively rarer than the pieces they designed in stainless steel. To many people stainless steel often looks more beautiful than silver and, as the name suggests, is less prone to tarnishing and staining. In fact, it is impressive in the way it maintains that straight-out-of-the-factory look that retro collectors really like (it is where they differ strongly from patina-loving antique collectors).

All three designers came under the influence of Scandinavian design and designers and none are quite as prominent as Arne Jacobsen, the Danish architect and designer. His 'Cylinda Line' coffeepot (as pictured on page 240) and other tableware items established a very strong reputation for stainless steel as an arts and crafts material.

Stuart Devlin was a graduate of RMIT in Melbourne in the late 1950s and took several very early commissions for Wiltshire, where the influence of Danish design is very evident. His 'Scintilla' serving spoons show great design flair using a minimum of manipulations;

the lines are contoured and organic and the broad profile bowls are very typically Scandinavian as you can see in comparison with the Danish salad servers by Lundtofte. In the most beautiful manner, one of the spoons is given fish-fin-like prongs to grip food more efficiently.

Stuart Devlin became a darling of the swinging London scene in the late 1960s, where his designs for boxes and richly textured goblets in silver chimed very well with the aspiring 'brutalist' modern architecture of London. In 1972 he designed a set of vessels for Viners (also produced in sterling silver), including a martini goblet, a wine goblet, a tumbler, a potpourri bowl, a textured bon bon or nut dish and a candlestick.

Devlin had very modern aspirations and values that guided his work. He once said: 'I hope that my work reflects four maxims: that the future is much more important than the past; that creativity is paramount; that skill is fundamental; and that the justification for being a goldsmith is to enrich the way people live and work'. Looking back over his design biography one is left feeling that these maxims were put into practice very consistently and prolifically. This is well illustrated by his place in a great many kitchens through his clever and commercially successful 'Staysharp' knife and sharpener design for Wiltshire. It never made him a household name but nothing

enriches kitchen life better than a knife that won't lose its edge…

Robert Welch was born one year earlier than Stuart Devlin, in 1929, and trained at the Birmingham College of Art in the early 1950s. He won a travelling scholarship to Sweden and then he studied with the Norwegian silversmith Theodor Olsen. In Scandinavia he became aware of the potential of stainless steel, which he put to good practice in 1955 when he became a design consultant to J & J Wiggin Ltd, whose products were marketed under the name Old Hall.

One of Welch's most celebrated designs was the tea and coffee set he designed for the 'Oriana' range for use on P&O ships. These stainless steel pieces are beautifully designed, and made with as much care and craftsmanship as any lavished on sterling silver. Not surprisingly, his 'Oriana' range won a Design Centre Award in 1963. Those made for the P&O ships have 'Shipco' marked on them (and they did occasionally wander off these ships…) but they were also made for sale under the Old Hall badge and are marked 'Old Hall/Oriana'.

His candleholders, also designed for Old Hall, were designed in 1957 in stainless steel with lovely little teak feet. These fluted candleholders are set at three vertical levels and joined together with stainless steel struts that establish three horizontal levels. I always think they suggest something futuristic, perhaps a high-rise tower

37
Robert Welch
'Oriana' teapot for
P&O and Old Hall,
England, 1963

38
Stuart Devlin nut
dish for Viners,
Sheffield, England,
1972

39
Stuart Devlin
candlestick for
Viners, Sheffield,
England, 1972

40
Sparklets soda
siphon in stainless
steel, British Oxygen
Company, 1958

41
Stuart Devlin martini
goblet for Viners,
Sheffield, England,
1972

42
Robert Welch
teapot for Old Hall,
England, c. 1958

43
Wiltshire 'Staysharp'
MKI metal knife and
plastic scabbard,
designed by
Stuart Devlin,
made by Wiltshire
Cutlery Company,
Melbourne, 1969
Powerhouse
Museum collection

37

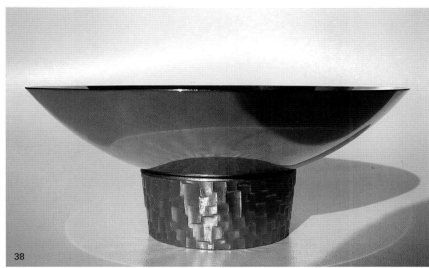

38

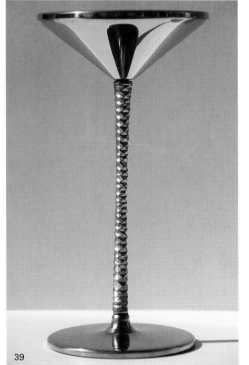

39

40

41

42

43

development. Perhaps they may yet inspire such a thing. I was lucky enough to find a pair and I remember the look of bewilderment on the face of the market stall holder; he seemed to be thinking, 'Why on earth would he want those?' As you can see, I wanted them because they are very cool.

This candlestick design was recognised and rendered more collectable when it was included in a major retrospective of Welch's work, *Robert Welch Designer/Craftsman: A Retrospective Exhibition 1955–1995* in Cheltenham, England in 1995 – which contributed to his desirability among retro collectors.

Gerald Benney came from a solid arts and crafts training at the Brighton College of Art under Dunstan Pruden, who was in turn a member of the prestigious Guild of St Joseph and St Dominic, founded by Eric Gill. Benney also turned his attention to the mass market. His early work was influenced strongly by Scandinavian design, and from 1957 to 1969 he designed some astonishing stainless steel cutlery for Viners, notably a range called 'Studio'.

Into the 1970s, stainless steel took an even tighter grip on kitchen- and tablewares. In part, this was due to concern over the previous incumbent: aluminium. Aluminium cooking wares were ubiquitous across the world but, used constantly, carried serious health risks. Given its durability and longevity, this was a valid concern. Those who could make the expensive transition to stainless steel did so. Ole Palsby's 1975 design 'Eva-Trio' for a saucepan and lid was an aesthetic breakthrough as well as being functionally ingenious.

By 1975 kitchens were no longer hidden-away places where cooking pans and implements need only have functional look. Open-plan homes plus the fashion to inhabit spaces adjacent to food preparation areas restructured aesthetically the design of kitchens and everything in them. Palsby's pan had a loop of stainless steel for a handle, giving it strength and efficient heat dispersing qualities. It replaced the need for other, less durable materials for a handle. The pan lid, which had a matching loop of stainless steel, fitted tightly into the top of the pan but had a rim at the top to allow other items to be placed there to keep warm.

By the 1980s the fear of aluminium was undermining a gathering love affair with the aluminium 'Moka' coffee maker by Bialetti and others. This fear ushered in a new generation of stainless steel coffee makers and the prohibitive cost of production, as we saw above with Richard Sapper's design for Alessi, meant that the cost could be justified by making them extremely well designed or architecturally splendid. Sapper's designs were both these things, and others followed suit. Notable among them was the space-age espresso maker by the Italian company Vov. This design took out the need for an expensive handle assembly (which in Sapper's had been made of titanium) by constructing tough plastic ribbing around the lower end of the jug section – away from the heat and the pouring end: very clever. Then added to that, it made incredibly good coffee while looking as good as an architect's model.

Like P&O, airlines were also quick to exploit the hygienic easy-care

44

45

46

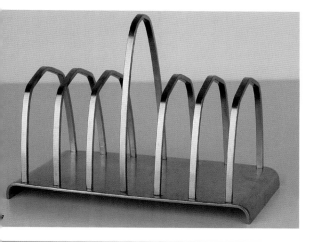

VINERS·STUDIO

50

51

44
Robert Welch candleholders for Old Hall, England, 1957

45
'Murmansk' silver plated brass fruit stand, designed by Ettore Sottsass for Memphis, made by Rossi & Arcandi, Italy, 1982–86 Powerhouse Museum collection

46
Ole Palsby 'Eva-Trio' saucepan and lid for Erik Mangor, Denmark, 1975

47
Robert Welch toast rack for Old Hall, England, c. 1959

48
Stainless steel and brass 'Kettle with a Singing Whistle', with heat-resistant plastic handle, designed by Richard Sapper in Germany, made by Alessi, Italy, 1980–83 Powerhouse Museum collection

49
Terence Conran flatware for British Airways' Concordes (notice the Concorde shape in the handles), London, c. 1968

50
Set of 'Studio' forks by Gerald Benney for Viners, Sheffield, England, c. 1963

51
Vov espresso maker, Italy, c. 1989

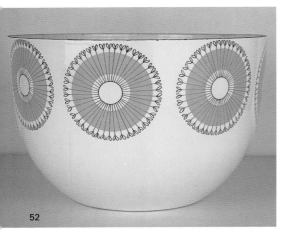

52

55

53

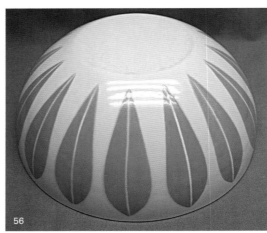

56

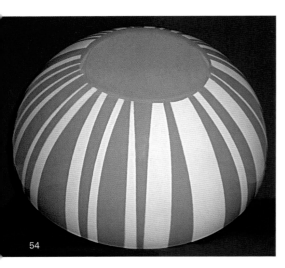

54

57

advantages of stainless steel. Marc Newson was not required to design a fine metalware knife owing to new security risks after 9/11 for his contemporary Alessi set for Qantas. You can, however, collect the amazing Concorde-shaped knives and forks that Terence Conran designed for the British Airways' Concordes.

Even more outstanding was an Alessi project under the direction of people like Alessandro Mendini and Ettore Sottsass. They established the perfect space for world-class designers and architects like Michael Graves, Charles Jencks, Robert Venturi, Philippe Starck and Aldo Rossi. In the 1980s Alessi invited thirteen architects to design their own tea and coffee services. It was an audacious move but it worked and it launched a new brand of sophisticated, high-end products – 'Officina Alessi' – that was not limited by the constraints of industrial production and the needs of mass markets. Sapper also produced one of the memorable kettles from this period. It was in stainless steel with a singing whistle (it has three lovely haunting notes like an organ). Tea drinkers can get their morning high from it and it will be admired by all.

Alessi designs breed ever more beautiful offspring. Sapper inspired Michael Graves to design the now famous 'Kettle with Bird-Shaped Whistle', perhaps a high point in stainless steel design.

52–58
Kaj Franck designs
for enamelled
copper bowls for
Finel/Arabia, Finland,
c. 1965–70

Copperware

Copper was very evident in the craft scene from the late 1960s onwards, though these pieces are rarely considered as serious design contenders. However, there is at least one exception. These are the outputs of a Finnish company called Finel and their designs are properly designs of enamel on copper, rather than copper per se. Aside from his ceramic wares for Arabia, Kaj Franck also designed enamelled copper bowls, coffee pots, kettles and even mugs for Finel, a sister company of Arabia. Franck designed the form and shapes, and the artwork was done by various artists such as Esteri Tomula. There is a large range of these, and their designs place them all squarely in the mid-1960s. Not quite as sentimental as flower power (with the exception of the kettle and some saucepans) they are nonetheless stylised and botanical, although the designs are distinctively Scandinavian. Famous among these are mushroom designs, abstract citrus designs, medieval scenes and leaf patterns.

59
Enamelled coffee percolator, Kaj Franck design for Finel/Arabia, Finland, c. 1965–70

60
Kitchen thermometer, Japan, c. 1962

Tin

Tin was especially important to the postwar toy industry and toys from this period capture the retro imagination more than any other items. Their cheerful demeanour, their initial cheapness and their ability to create good first impressions, combined with some very clever innovations and technical mastery have ensured a global and affluent fan base. Initially dominated by the established German tin toy industry, production soon spread to Japan and Hong Kong in particular.

61
Two tin cars and a clockwork coach, designer unknown, West Germany, c. 1955

62
Beijing Toy No 1 Factory battery operated 'Univers Car', China, early 1970s Photo courtesy of Claudia Chan Shaw

63
Masudaya battery operated moon rocket, Japan, 1962 Photo courtesy of Claudia Chan Shaw

64
Disney-themed child's tin beach bucket by Willow, Australia, c. 1940s–50s Courtesy Peter Kelly

65
Noguchi wind-up 'Mighty Robot', Japan, 1960s Photo courtesy of Claudia Chan Shaw

66
Horikawa battery operated robot, Japan, 1960s Photo courtesy of Claudia Chan Shaw

67
Two dancing chicks in a bucket, unknown manufacturer, Japan, c. 1954

68

71

72

69

70

73

Silver

In the aftermath of World War Two silver was in great shortage and according to Bevis Hillier 'there was no originality to be found' within British silversmithing by which he meant that it was stuck in the past mostly making antique reproductions or art deco pastiche. Hence it is largely true that we do not see much of a modern aesthetic developing until well into the 1960s though it blossomed in the 1970s. In Scandinavia it was different and their simple modernism mixed in with sharp viking lines was the key influence internationally. We see this simple elegance in the Titus watch

shown here which also has a distinctly rule-breaking 1960s feel to it. Stuart Devlin emerged as one of the leading modern silversmiths with his own style that chimed well with late 1960s and 1970s: it combined texture and natural shapes with elements of gothic fantasy. Aside from designing coinage for around thirty countries he also did commissions for major ecclesiastical, academic and corporate bodies. By the 1970s sterling silver was both abundant and popular as we can see by the lavish etching on silver by Sir Russell Drysdale for the emerging 'affordable art' collecting market .

74

68
Titus sterling silver watch with Biba-style band. Marked '925 A*D', West Germany, c. 1968

69
Two Stuart Devlin sterling silver wine goblets with textured stems, England, 1970s

70
Stuart Devlin, textured bud vase, England, c. 1977

71
Stuart Devlin, silver-gilt tumbler with architectural relief pattern, England, c.1972

72
N.E From, silver abstract leaf design brooch, Denmark, 1966

73
Silver gilt medallion with sunburst and floral pattern with a couplet from the Romantic poet Per Daniel Amadeus Atterbom on the reverse. Hallmarked 1976 with makers mark, Sweden

74
Russel Drysdale etching on sterling silver plate 'The Old Timers', produced by Stokes of Melbourne, 1974

PLASTIC

THUS WE HAVE, AT ONE AND THE
SAME TIME, A RAW MATERIAL UPON
WHICH THE WORLD DEPENDS BUT WHICH
IS ALSO USED TO PRODUCE HIDEOUS,
OUTRAGEOUS TRIVIA REGARDED BY
MOST PEOPLE AS A WASTE OF THE
EARTH'S LIMITED RESOURCES

PERCY REBOUL, PLASTICS HISTORICAL SOCIETY 1997

RECENTLY I VOLUNTEERED TO BECOME a custodian of a complete set of *Plastiquarian*, the journal of the Plastics Historical Society. OK, it's not for everyone, but it made me realise how much we take plastic for granted. For example, if you asked people when plastic was invented, what would they say? Most would place plastic unequivocally as a retro period material that appeared immediately beforehand in the form of Bakelite but which then branched out into significant forms of material and application. What they probably would not say, unless they were experts or *Plastiquarian* subscribers, is the year 1530. But this is when the first plastic, stuff called casein, was made: from cheese. It was discovered by the German alchemist Bartholomäus Schobinger and was used to replace horn in marquetry work.

Interesting trivia is a stock in trade of *Plastiquarian*. For instance, the Scotsman Charles Macintosh was the inventor of the Mac, in 1823. Nothing amazing about that, until you realise that its waterproofing agent came from a plastic compound made from a base of natural rubber. It's just not something we would expect to see in a nineteenth-century costume drama.

So Bakelite was not the first plastic. It appeared in 1907, and before that there was nitrocellulose, Parkesine (renamed Xylonite and famous for the combs made from it and its limited colour range of yellow and beige), celluloid (first used for billiard balls) which saved many elephants since it was a good substitute for ivory, and galalith (made from milk and used to waterproof cardboard, making the milk carton possible).

Plastic has been evolving ever since, and it is used so widely and in so many applications that the modern world and its economies would cease to exist without it.

In the pages of the *Plastiquarian* there are articles on path-breaking designs and objects that became household names. My favourite is the 'GPO 162', a 'hand combination set' aka a telephone, and the classic heavy Bakelite phone that was widely used from 1929–60. The 'GPO 162' made the telephone sound in every British film from that era, with its distinctively cheerful ring and its modulated dialling sound. It was made by only two companies: Siemens Bros whose model was called 'Neophone' and General Electric Co who called theirs 'Geophone'.

My last bit of trivia concerns the connection between plastics, the materials they replaced and the guild that was based on the latter but came to adopt and even promote the former. Whatever was once made of horn (which is a natural

BAKELITE DOMESTIC WARES

ERIKA TAYLOR = ASSISTANT CURATOR, SCIENCE AND INDUSTRY, POWERHOUSE MUSEUM

Bakelite jewellery and household items of the 1930s have soared in popularity in recent years. Celebrity collectors Whoopi Goldberg and Lily Tomlin are leading the trend by snapping up retro pieces, and Michelle Obama has been observed wearing Bakelite jewellery to compliment her vintage style. Prices keep rising, and what once was produced as a cheap alternative to materials like jade and pearl is now almost as expensive as the real thing.

Perhaps the high prices of authentic Bakelite pieces can be partly attributed to Andy Warhol, who was an obsessive collector of the plastic in the 1970s and 80s. He eventually amassed one of the world's largest collections, which sold for record prices at Sotheby's after his death.

Although Bakelite was invented in 1909, it did not find its first wave of popularity until about 1927, when it became available in a wide array of colours. During the Great Depression of the 1930s, handcrafted Bakelite jewellery and homewares became widely popular, and the versatile and cheap plastic readily available. After the Second World War, Bakelite's popularity slowly subsided, as the market showed a preference for cheaper, more advanced, mass-produced plastics. It was during these years that the Powerhouse Museum collected most of its Bakelite pieces, including radios, telephones, homewares and jewellery.

Despite its celebrity following, the revival of Bakelite is perhaps indicative of a revolt against the worldwide glut of mass-produced plastic objects. The Museum recognised this trend with its 2007 exhibition *Smart Works: Design and the Handmade,* and you only have to look at the incredible popularity of websites such as etsy.com (the 'eBay' of the handmade) to see that there is growing appreciation for the time and effort that goes into making handcrafted objects.

Collection of
Bakelite homewares
Powerhouse
Museum collection

1

The 1950s

Plastic was even more vital to postwar recovery than it was as a new introduced 'wonder' material in the 1930s and 1940s. After 1945 it dominated the bodies of electrical goods, it replaced glass and ceramics in a range of cosmetics and other containers and it also made an appearance in many personal items such as combs, sunglasses, beauty aids and kitchen implements.

Invented by Earl Tupper (who also invented the fish-powered boat and a dripless ice-cream cone), Tupperware became one of the best and most successful products in the world. The secret of Tupperware is the unsurpassed and indestructible seal. I have a large collection of Tupperware from the 1950s still in daily use and the seals on all of them work as well as the day they were made. The same cannot

thermoplastic protein with similar properties to synthetic polymers) by the Worshipful Company of Horners (first established in England in 1284), gradually came to be made from plastic. I like the way plastic was embraced rather than rejected by these traditional craft workers because this ensured that plastic remained a material for *designers* and that, despite criticism of its synthetic nature, we can look back on an impressive design record spanning the retro years. There is no country or designer who seems to have eschewed plastic as a medium for design. It is liked as much by architects as by industrial designers and craft workers. There are also a lot of artists who have consistently used plastic as a medium for sculpture.

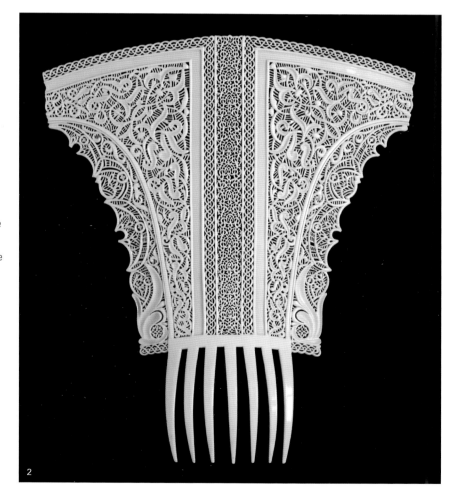

2

1
Bendigo Bank piggy bank, Australia, c. 1973

2
Hair comb (cellulose acetate) by Auguste Bonaz, France, 1950 Powerhouse Museum collection

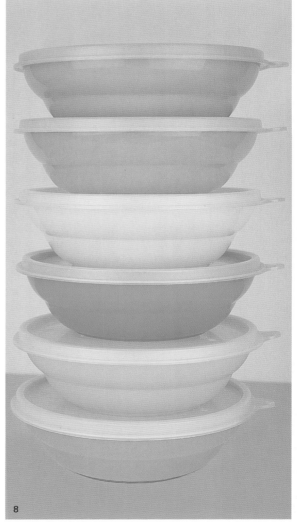

3
Rouge container
by 'Muriel Astor',
Australia, 1925–55
Powerhouse
Museum collection

4
'Ericofon' for
Ericsson, Sweden,
1958–65

5
Cyber-man money
box, USA, c. 1962

6
Shell bowser
ornament, England,
1956 Powerhouse
Museum collection

7
Tupperware
stackable egg cups,
USA, c. 1978

8
Tupperware
containers, USA,
1958

9
Santa's helper, USA,
c. 1956

9

be said of all the 'sealable' containers I have bought. The new 1950s kitchen was more sophisticated than the kitchen of the 1930s and earlier, and needed good organisation and storage, so a lot of Tupperware production was based on 'the container'. Despite this, they were highly innovative in extending this basic idea to masses of new applications such as a portable milk jug that has an outer layer that can be filled with iced water.

By the postwar period, the chemistry required to colour plastic brightly was solved and this replaced the need for paint on a lot of goods. It gave postwar industrial output a colourful, glossy finish for goods which had hitherto been lacklustre. Radios and telephones emerged in bright new colours and with new shapes such as the 'Ericofon' from Sweden; it really changed the look of the period.

Plastic also made some luxury goods more affordable and thus more popular. The best example of this is the success story of Kodak's 'Brownie 127' camera which sold in the millions around the world between 1952 and 1967 and was responsible for a dramatic growth in the photographic history of modern society (see page 237). It had very alluring art deco lines, it was simple to use, was very comfortable to hold, and was light and practically failsafe. I can remember entire family groups assembling on beaches and at weddings to grin into its tiny aperture.

Plastic made its way into practically everything in the 1950s and I recall being struck by the strange plastic smell of new mini cars that

were designed in 1959. Up until then, cars smelled of leather and engine oil, but leather upholstery had become a luxury, while plastic vinyl covers were an element that reduced the costs of production considerably.

Christmas in the 1950s was a time when plastic became noticeably more present in material culture. This was a period when plastic toys vied with the tin toys of the early 1950s and although die-cast metal held on for a very long time in such things as toy cars, plastic was soon the material of choice for electric railway sets and 'Minic', the accompanying scale-modelled cars by Tri-ang, the new Scalectric racing sets and many others. Plastic also revolutionised toy figures and dolls, making these far more accessible to lower income families. By the mid-1960s Topper dolls from the USA produced a racier version of the Barbie doll, which showed off high-street teenage fashions.

The 1950s also ushered in a staple product that has remained with us ever since: the snow dome. It is hard not to want to pick one up and create a blizzard, and they have certainly added an element of playfulness to souvenir creation. The presence of a snow storm over Cairns or Brisbane or underwater on the Great Barrier Reef gets a laugh every time. Ditto the snow that was falling inside the Jenolan Caves (in Australia) snow domes of the 1960s. When you shook the Jenolan Caves snow dome, hundreds of tiny bats flew about. I read recently that Wayne Golding, the art director of Mambo clothing, has a huge collection, including some that prove how eye-catching placing objects and people in a snow storm can be. His collection includes one of the Pope and one of Nelson Mandela, but I have seen crucifixion scenes in a snow dome and 'political' snow domes produced by the Green Party in West Germany featuring dirty, polluted snow falling in Berlin. I have also seen English police constables in a dome, surrounded by a dirty swirling snow that was intended to resemble London smog.

The first snow *globe* was actually produced as a souvenir of the Paris Exposition of 1889, and featured that other object made for the exhibition, the Eiffel Tower. The snow globes were a runaway success and were widely

copied, but they were expensive and thus there are not a huge number from this era left for the collector. Cheaper glass globes were produced in the USA when Joseph Garaja discovered a way of mass producing them in 1927. From then on they were a common souvenir item. But the big breakthrough came with the invention of plastic *domes* by a German manufacturer in the 1950s. It is reported that the reason why they were dome- rather than globe-shaped was because he was inspired by snow scenes he saw through the curved back window of his Volkswagen beetle. These domes were so cheap to produce that every place in the world could have its own snow dome souvenirs.

10

11

12

13

10
'Miss Mixer', bar toy,
USA, 1957

11, 12, 13, 17, 18
Topper dolls from
the 1960s. The blue
discoloration on the
doll's face in Figure
11 is a common fault
with the plastic used
or it may be reacting
to the metal used
in its construction.
This is more or
less accepted by
collectors. USA, late
1960s

14
1960s snow dome
showing the nativity,
designer unknown,
Hong Kong

15
1960s snow dome
of Sydney Harbour
with a back-lit
feature showing the
red entrance of the
Luna Park funfair on
Sydney Harbour

16
Teenager's rocket
radio set, USA, 1959

16

14

15

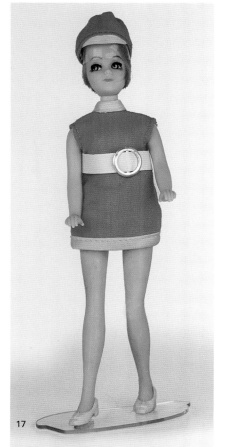

17

18

THE 'PILLOLA' LAMP SET, 1969

MELANIE PITKIN = ASSISTANT CURATOR, ARTS AND DESIGN, POWERHOUSE MUSEUM

In 1972, the Museum of Modern Art in New York held a landmark exhibition on the achievements and problems of Italian design, titled *Italy: The New Domestic Landscape*. Dubbed 'avant-garde' by its critics, this historical survey of contemporary Italian design, told through more than 150 objects, was the first of its kind, anticipating an ensuing spike in interest in Italian design – with particular regard to collectability – and the celebrity status that many of the featured designers would later assume.

Among the objects selected for the 1972 exhibition was the 'Pillola' lamp set. Designed by Cesare Casati and Emanuele Ponzio in 1968, and produced by Ponteur in 1969, the lamp set is a take on the everyday pharmaceutical gelatin capsule, inspired by the 1960s Pop Art movement. The weighted base of each lamp gives them a playful twist by enabling them to be re-configured at various angles; embodying both the adventurous spirit and fresh aesthetic of postwar Italian design.

When the Powerhouse Museum was developing a design collection for the 1988 opening of its new Ultimo site, the 'Pillola' lamp set and a number of other Italian design pieces displayed in the MoMA exhibition were actively pursued and acquired into the collection. This broadened the international scope of the museum's design collection and brought about a renewed interest in mid-late twentieth century Italian design. The lamp set has featured in two retrospective exhibitions held at the Powerhouse Museum – *Mod to Memphis: Design in Colour 1960s–1980s* and *Inspired: Design Across Time*. In both cases, the influence of the earlier 1972 exhibition was acknowledged.

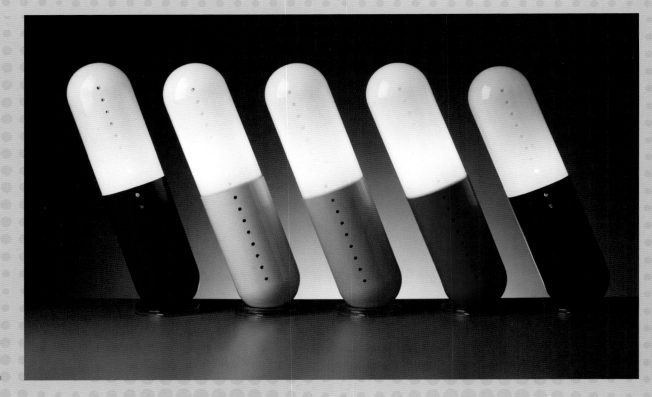

'Pillola' lamp set, designed by Cesare Casati and Emanuele Ponzio in 1968, produced by Ponteur, Italy, in 1969 Powerhouse Museum collection

The 1960s

In the 1960s plastic became considerably more acceptable and desirable across a range of products but it had become notably more fashionable among leading designers. Thus while maybe not every household bought their dramatic new designs, they remain iconic visions for a new age. The classic revolutionary design was the 'Panton' chair but, as we saw in the furniture section, plastic became a dominant medium in the hands of leading makers such as Joe Colombo and Pierre Paulin.

Plastic also vied strongly with products normally made of metal and wood; clocks being a case in point. Smiths were able to usher in plastic clocks during this time, but they did so by choosing themes where plastic seemed more appropriate. This can be seen clearly in their 'Timecal' wall clock from 1965, with its highly developed space-age theme.

Plastic soon became acceptable and then desirable for a vast range of household goods in the 1960s. For obvious reasons, it could compete very easily with ceramic and metal in terms of cost of production and durability. You could drop a plastic cup a million times and it would not break, making it the only choice for children below a certain age. Seeking to extend the children's market, plastic manufacturers used tough and brightly coloured melamine plastic. This was not only extremely tough; it could be moulded into high quality designs that mimicked ceramic slipwares. It found its niche market in picnic and outdoor settings and sold like hot cakes in southern USA, Australia and other places with warm climates.

The new plastics were also excellent for model making and other moulding production processes. From simple but luxurious goods such as the cocktail stirrers in London's Bunny Club (see page 122) to advertising figures for basic products such as Homepride flour, plastic was literally pressed into service. It was particularly successful in the freebie toy market, especially such things as cereal toys, BBC merchandising, ashtrays, and the Italian 'Kinder' egg toys (released in 1972) – all of which have a huge retro collector following.

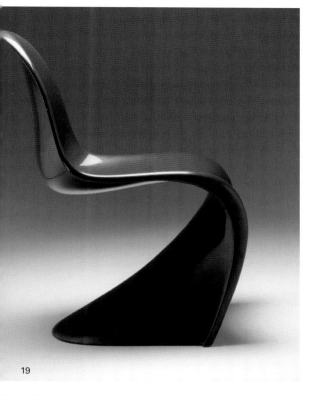

19

20

21

19
'Panton' polyurethane hard foam chair designed by Verner Panton, Denmark, 1960, made by Herman Miller/Vitra, Germany, 1968–70
Powerhouse Museum collection

20
Space-age 'Timecal' electric clock by Smiths, England, 1965

21
Ashtray advertising Moët Champagne from the Lido, Paris, 1967

22
Topper doll mirror,
USA, 1969

23
Melamine souvenir
ash tray of the P&O
ship *SS Himalaya*,
Ornamin Swift, UK,
1960s

24
Melaware melamine
cup and saucer,
Australia, 1965

25
'Bashful' plastic
figure on powder
compact,
manufacturer
unknown, USA
1950s-1960s

26
Homepride flour
men, Homepride,
England, 1966

27
Barometer, designer
unknown, West
Germany, c. 1967

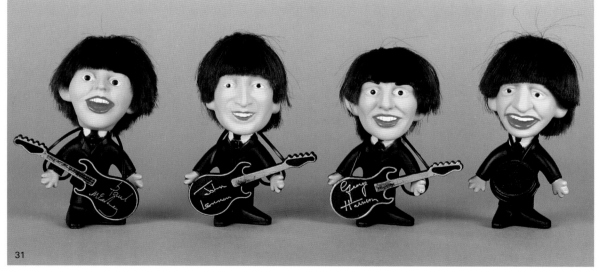

28
Toy Tardis and Dalek
from *Doctor Who* for
BBC, England, 1966

29
Espresso cups
and saucers in
melamine, Italy, 1966

30
Toy American Indian
totem pole, USA,
1966

31
Beatles figures,
England, c. 1965
Powerhouse
Museum collection

32
Hippie on a Barrel
water toy, Hong
Kong, 1968

161

The 1970s

We remember the 1970s for its very bright and vivid colourways and this was largely the result of plastic's capability to represent the loud, flower power and acid-influenced visual dimensions of 1970s popular culture. Favoured colours were hot orange, acid yellow, deep blood red and apple green. These displaced the pastel beiges and mushrooms of the 1960s and gave everything sharp definition and a bold presence. In a way, this reflected the aesthetic of industrial design to give everything a sense of beauty, regardless of its function. I see this in many emerging design forms from the 1970s. It is there in Rosti's kitchen implements, in Tupperware's bright storage containers and colanders; it is there in office equipment (most famously in Olivetti's 'Valentine' typewriter) in the 'Café-Bar' by Neilsen, in the humble office fan by Marco Zanuso and the 'Dolphin' torch by Paul Cockburn.

33
National Bank 'Minibank' money box, Australia, 1970s

34
Spaghetti server by Magis, Italy, 1976

35
'Ariante' electric fan by Marco Zanuso for Vortice, Italy, 1976

36
Seiko jump-hour clock, 1976

THE CAFÉ-BAR
ANGELIQUE HUTCHISON = CURATOR, PRODUCT DESIGN, POWERHOUSE MUSEUM

Café-Bars replaced a lot of tea ladies in the 1960s and 1970s ('tea gentlemen' being quite rare). In 1963 the company patented a 'butterfly' valve that delivered the exact amount of instant coffee, powdered tea, milk, soup, chocolate or sugar, keeping ingredient costs low and reducing mess.

The first blue-painted metal models were designed for the factory floor. But by the 1970s, Café-Bar wanted to expand its market into offices and waiting rooms. This plastic 'Compact' model was the first to be designed by a professional industrial designer, David Wood of Nielsen Design Associates in Sydney. It was released in 1974 and featured futuristic styling to fit the contemporary office aesthetic: round corners, large simple knobs and plastic housing. It came in avocado green, beige, blue and burnt-orange, colours that suited the fashion of the times.

Increased sales of the 'Compact' took the company into new markets, from the Netherlands to New Zealand. Café-Bar also created a new demand for tea, coffee and biscuits, the supply of which eventually generated more profits than the machines themselves.

The Powerhouse Museum acquired this Café-Bar in the early 1990s for display in the *Success and Innovation* exhibition. Its inclusion in the museum's collection endorsed its status as a 'benchmark' for Australian design; it received numerous design awards in the 1970s and 80s, including the Australian Classic Design Award. The Café-Bar was once again revived

for display in the *Sydney Designers Unplugged* exhibition at the museum in 2005. This retrospective featured some of Sydney's leading industrial design firms, including one of the first, Nielsen Design Associates.

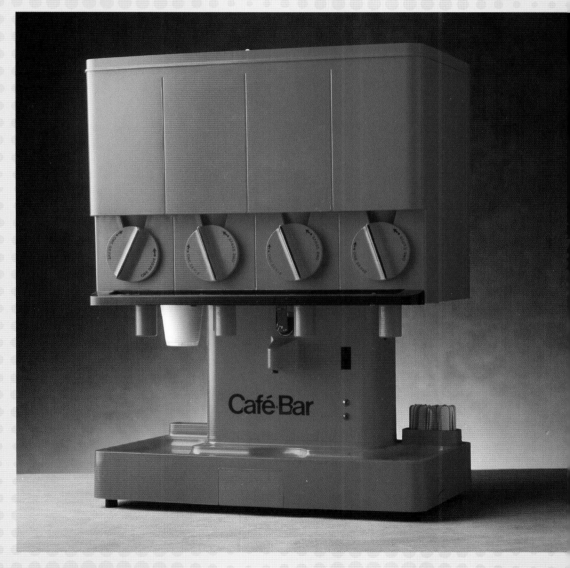

'Café Bar Compact' beverage dispensing machine, designed by Nielsen Design Associates and Café Bar International, 1974 Powerhouse Museum collection

37

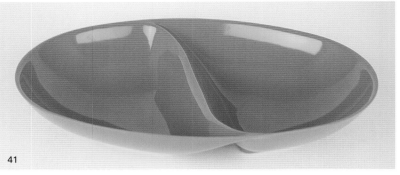

41

38

42

39

40

43

44

45

46

By the 1970s most of the older cast iron and ceramic baths and sinks were being replaced in homes and it was the relative cost of plastic that made this renovation of the bathroom so affordable and commonplace. Everything in the bathroom could now be made of a reliable form of plastic.

Another domestic object that needed a makeover in the 1970s was the conventional kitchen scales. Up until then, their form was always dictated by their function. Fair enough. But by the 1970s the kitchen had become a more decorative and social space and everything was being designed to look good as well as function well. The other thing about kitchen scales is that they do not just weigh things. They are involved in the operation of baking cakes and pastries and here a designer could

make a few improvements to their overall function. The Salter 0850 scales, in their striking orange and black livery, have a very pleasing and simple design. They combine a 'car instrument' dial feature, which is very refined, with a tough housing and two practical bowls that replace the rather redundant pan in conventional scales. The selling point of this design is the two large-capacity bowls, which have an internal measuring scale for measuring liquids. I don't know much about cake making but I do know that you divide the operation into the preparation of dry and wet ingredients, so by having two bowls you can complete your preparation without having to wash and dry the pan. The bowls have a well-designed pouring spout too, so no more spills and mess.

47

37
Salter kitchen scales, USA, 1973

38, 42, 43, 46, 47
Rosti kitchen bowls, kitchen implements, jugs and mugs, Denmark, 1977

39
Besserware canapé dish, Australia, 1973

40
Tupperware colander, USA, 1972

41
Divided serving dish, Ornamin, England, 1970s

44
Melamine in-flight dishes for BOAC, England, 1970–74

45
Tupperware containers, USA, c. 1970.

48
Tupperware condiment cruet, USA, 1974

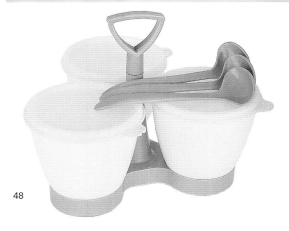

48

49

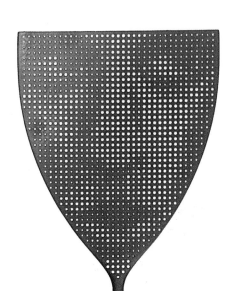

51

50

49
'Dolphin Mk2'
plastic torch by
Paul Cockburn of
Design Field for
Eveready, Australia,
1972 Powerhouse
Museum collection

50
'Kiss' phone, USA,
1975

51
Fly swat by
Philippe Starck for
Alessi, Italy,
c. 1990

52
Zyliss bottle opener,
Switzerland, c. 1985

53
Massimo Giacon's
'Mr Suicide' for
Alessi, Italy, 1994

54
IKEA waste bin,
Sweden, 1989

The 1980s +

Generalising, we can say that the history of plastic shows that the materials have become more efficient and durable and that once introduced to new types of product, it is rarely ever substituted by anything other than better plastics. Of course, fashions change. In the 1970s and 1980s, pine furniture was very popular and plastic lost some ground here and there, but generally it has held its own, particularly in the domain of small products. Again, in the 1970s handmade pottery dented its empire at the edges but into the 1980s it was still as commonplace and loved as it had been in the 1970s. Again, in the plastic age, colourways can be and typically were bright and cheerful and the 1980s gave up on the hot and acid colour schemes of the 1970s and went in for playful, naïve, primary colours that were fun and childlike.

In the 1980s one thinks of the massive takeover of yet another hitherto non-plastic commodity, the watch; most

famously the 'Swatch'. I can remember my first Swatch and I am not too proud to admit it was an exciting moment of my life. Mine was a very stylish but elegantly simple design: it had a black case and band and classic 'gents watch' looks – and yet it was plastic. It had largish Arabic numerals on a plain white background and an elegant, sweeping second hand. I also remember how suddenly *everyone* had to have one, and could because they were very cheap. Swatches became one of the defining 'looks' of the eighties, and one of the most collected things from that decade.

Swatch was a revolutionary idea, and it needed to be. The Swiss watch industry faced certain doom after their market in mechanical watches was flooded with ultra cheap Japanese digital watches – made in stainless steel mostly. The Swatch concept was very clever and contained a big dollop of humour. Instead of trying to compete with the digital monsters (which were

boring once you had got over their technical genius) they decided that watches could be ironic, fun and works of art. So, one idea was to repackage the classical mechanical timepieces *in plastic*, give them a contemporary designer look and make them every bit as accurate as their boring geekish rivals.

The second great idea was to challenge established watch-wearing habits. In the new quartz watch era, most people had continued in the habit of owning just one watch. Swatch had the audacity to suggest we all have several watches, to suit our mood, style of dress or whim … a bit like shoes or jewellery. The name Swatch is actually a contraction of 'Second Watch'.

Swatch was launched in 1983 and the marketing for it was spectacular: it included stunts like building a giant 162-metre-long, 13-ton *yellow* 'Swatch' and mounting it on the side of a bank headquarters in Germany. Before you knew it, they were putting out new

52

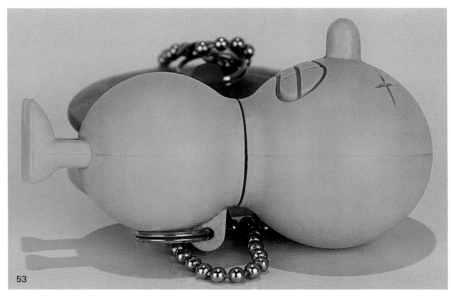

53

54

designs in a wide range of single block colours, including the defining primary colours of the decade but also moodier, quirkier and crazier, rock'n'roll patterns. All this aligned them very nicely with the fashion and art worlds that were becoming steadily less serious and a little more 'bonkers'.

So it was not long before punk-fashion queen Vivienne Westwood was invited to design a Swatch. Her 'art special' followed hot on the tracks of other art specials by the French artist Kiki Picasso (Christian Chapiron) in 1985, Andrew Logan (who designed the see-through 'Jelly Fish' special) in 1985, and the four art specials by

Keith Haring in 1986. Who else do you want? Yoko Ono? The designer Piero Fornasetti? The architect Renzo Piano? Yes, they have all designed for Swatch.

In sociological and cultural terms, Swatch was also important. It was a major influence on that eighties revolution where individual forms of self-expression became more important, and standardised forms of consumption, product design and production became more flexible. Swatch were among the first to release small numbers of a single design, to aim designs at specific markets and to release large numbers of new designs to keep pace with fashion and events.

Swatches have thus become one of the most vibrant collectibles in history. Around 100 million of them have been made but, due to clever marketing many are rare and sought after. Are we talking small-beer collecting here? Well, no. At a recent Christie's auction in London a Kiki Picasso went for over $US28 000 and a 'Blow Your Time Away' (face obscured by tufts of hair) had an estimate of $17 000.

For those who think Swatches are infra dig, Swatch has been so successful that they now own most of the top Swiss brands, including Omega, Longines, Breguet, Tiffany & Co, Blancpain and many more.

55

56

57

55
Innoplan Design
bottle opener,
Switzerland, 1979

56
'Dish Doctor' by
Marc Newson for
Magis, Italy, 1998

57
Pepper grinder by
Chef'n, USA, 1985

58
Bart Simpson figure,
Twentieth Century
Fox, USA, 1990

59
Wine cask cooler
(plastic and foam) by
Décor Corporation,
Australia, 1987
Powerhouse
Museum collection

60
Wine carrier with
wine chiller in
white plastic by
Décor Corporation,
Australia, 1986
Powerhouse
Museum collection

61
Alessi plastic
'Cohndom' boxes
for two condoms by
Susan Cohn, Italy,
1999 Photo Greg
Harris

62
Swatch watch,
Switzerland, 2008

Swatch also had a profoundly important impact on industrial design. Eventually the great design house Alessi began to see the potential of plastic (having been until the 1980s a company still dominated by designs in metal). Through designers such as Massimo Giacon and Mattia Di Rosa, Alessi began to populate (or is it enchant) the everyday world of the kitchen, bathroom and study with a colourful range of creatures (eg the 'Anna-G' corkscrew) which do something useful. Massimo Giacon's 'Mr Suicide' (this drowned plastic man floats above the bath plug to guide one's hand to it) is perhaps the best known, but so too is Philippe Starck's girl hiding in the plastic fly swat. There are men hanging from the lids of pasta jars, little ghosts who dispense tooth floss, little devils that open beer bottles and small pigs who hold and sharpen pencils (Giacon again).

Arguably, the best design in plastic to be inspired from the Alessi initiative 'Family Follows Fiction', went to Susan Cohn's ingenious 'Cohndom' box for two condoms. She noticed that a member of her family kept condoms in their wallet,

and, fearing the worst, she looked to buy this person a discrete container and found none on the market. Another product of more recent times that owes some credit to this retro period in the 1980s is Marc Newson's 'Dish Doctor'. Manufactured in a range of clean, bright colours and almost impossible to pick as a dish drainer on first inspection, this ingenious design combines a space-age aesthetic with functional cleverness and social awareness (after all, by the late 1990s many single people were buying apartments with minimial kitchen spaces.)

Less playfully perhaps, the 1980s also became the most design-conscious decade and, as this occurred, the functional designs and traditions of earlier periods became fashionable once more. Danish designs such as Erik Magnussen's vacuum jug were hugely successful. IKEA released many plastic lines whose designs had been commissioned from among Scandinavia's legion of new young designers – all yearning to have their name moulded on the bottom of their IKEA product.

61

62

FASHION

THE REVOLUTIONARY FASHION WAS
TURNING EVERY WOMAN INTO AN
EXHIBITIONIST. AT THE SAME TIME, THE
MEN AT THE EXCHEQUER TORE THEIR HAIR
IN FRUSTRATION. THE TAX ON CLOTHING
STIPULATED THAT A WOMAN'S SKIRT HAD
TO BE AT LEAST 24 INCHES FROM WAIST TO
HEM; ANYTHING SHORTER WAS A CHILD'S
SKIRT, AND CHILDREN'S CLOTHING WAS
NOT TAXED.

GERARD DEGROOT COMMENTING ON THE BUSINESS GENIUS OF MARY
QUANT, INVENTOR OF THE MINI SKIRT, IN THE SIXTIES UNPLUGGED 2008

NOTHING CHARTS THE RETRO PERIOD quite like fashion. This is partly because nobody in the modern world can truly opt out of fashion; instead there are merely *fashions* and if you understand this fashion diversity you understand the retro era in all its complexity. While we can easily identify looks that belong to different decades, and even periods within them, we must also be sensitive to very considerable divisions that describe differences according to gender, age, ethnicity, nationality and class, particularly class subcultures. However, until quite recently, a very particular middle American youth fashion from the 1950s has dominated the retro fashion world. This is curious. In part, this rockabilly look has been maintained as a living, unchanging fashion by the various biker, Teddy Boy and 'rocker' subcultures, which began as youth cultures back in the 1950s and early 1960s but somehow failed to ever grow up. At various stages it was also immortalised by key Hollywood films and TV series, not least James Dean's *Rebel Without a Cause* (1955), *Grease* (1978) and *Happy Days* (1974–84). Many other youth culture styles achieved a semi-permanent retroid presence, including Mods, skinheads, heavy metal and so on, preserved by revivals and retrospective appreciation of their associated music. However, none of these have quite the popular base of rockabilly modes or such an extensive geographical (global) coverage. Last year I discovered that the youth of northern Sweden, for example, are undergoing a major rockabilly revival, requiring the compulsory acquisition of extrovert 1950s cars and a complete adherence to 1950s fashion and looks. No supermarket car park is without a Dodge, a Cadillac or a Pontiac and jiving classes no doubt take place in every village hall.

Over the past twenty years, however, the enthusiasm for retro fashions generally has come into its own. All kinds of looks have (re)appeared: the zoot suit revival in the early 1980s championed by Kid Creole; the mid-1960s Mod chic look championed by bands and musicians such as The Jam and Paul Weller; the high street 1970s look worn in the TV series *Life on Mars* (2006–07) and its 1980s follow-up *Ashes to Ashes* (2008–09); the slick corporate American look of the 1950s and 1960s in the TV series *Madmen*; and the endless repeats of *Absolutely Fabulous* (1992–96) is surely behind the current love affair with 1990s high fashion.

Retrospective bids have also been commercially

successful in the fashion world itself with, for example, Ben Sherman repeating the Mod–Carnaby Street–Swinging London vibe, while the UK department store House of Fraser was alone among retail winners during Christmas 2010 with its reissue of classic Biba designs from the late 1960s and early 1970s. Equally, we have seen emerge what has been described as The Gentleman look; that extremely classically well-dressed man in bespoke suits and hand-made shoes, with a fine umbrella and perhaps a bowler hat. In a similar vein, some women have discovered and like the pre–New Look designs and body discipline of 1940s fashions. Whatever, all of the above signals the rather fuzzy and much hybridised lines of contemporary taste in fashion, which has seen more and more people take to shopping in vintage fashion stores, charity shops and markets.

Twenty years ago, vintage fashion was a minority obsession. However, that minority were about to become the most influential people in the world and turn the rest of us onto a new thing. Bored with the predictable and standardised look of 'current fashions', they tried to find something that gave them an exciting edge. One of these was Kylie Minogue's stylist, Will Baker. He bought her career-changing gold hotpants from a London Oxfam shop for 50p.

Eyes have been on Nicole Kidman for some time and they have noticed her shopping (rather frequently) at Decades Inc. in LA and Jim Smiley Vintage Clothing in Manhattan. When Julia Roberts wore vintage Valentino at an Oscars ceremony a few years ago, it started a

1
Chrysler Royal
Sedan, USA, 1957

2
Hood ornament from
Pontiac Torpedo 8
Fast Back, USA, 1950

3
The author in a
1970s Mod outfit

VINTAGE FASHION

GLYNIS JONES = CURATOR, FASHION, POWERHOUSE MUSEUM

At the 2001 Academy Awards ceremony, Hollywood sweetheart Julia Roberts surprised everyone when she accepted the leading actress Oscar wearing an elegant, black and white evening gown by Italian couturier Valentino – the gown was nine years old. The Academy Awards traditionally sees the world's most beautiful and celebrated women in garments from the latest designer collections, in a cosy arrangement that benefits both stars and designers. What was Julia thinking when she bucked this synergistic relationship and chose to wear what was dubbed by an over-enthusiastic press as 'vintage'?

She was actually on trend with her 'anti-fashion' statement. The 1990s saw a growing consumer backlash against globalisation, big luxury brands and mass market fashion, and an increasing passion for retro and vintage fashions. By 2001, celebrities were taking the trend upmarket, recognising the value of searching designers' archives and vintage boutiques for couture garments that would make them appear unique, with the added allure of classic Hollywood glamour.

The Powerhouse Museum also picked up on this vintage trend for its 2001 *Fashion of the Year* selection. This annual program brings together leading Australian fashion commentators to nominate acquisitions of international and Australian designers' work to update the museum's fashion and dress collection. A representative example of vintage couture was sought through Lorraine Foster, a retailer of fine vintage clothing and textiles at The Vintage Clothing Shop in Sydney's CBD, and this coat by Givenchy was acquired from the vintage couture archive of Patti Edwards. Made over thirty years ago, the coat has a classic style that could be comfortably worn today.

The popularity of vintage and retro has lasted more than a decade; its various permutations stimulated by popular culture, including the American TV series *Mad Men*, rock–n–roll dancing and burlesque performers.

Givenchy coat of silk velvet and gauze with diamante clasp fastenings, made in France, c. 1970 Powerhouse Museum collection

rush that has become a stampede. That stampede could be heard in the streets of London (where Oxfam opened a vintage shop on Bond Street) and Milan, as well as Manchester and Seattle. But now the buzz is all over Asia. It started in Japan and has overwhelmed China. Even Victoria Beckham was recently snapped wearing a black and white Courrèges original from the 1960s.

But here's the acid test. Within the last year, in-flight magazines for Qantas, BA, and Virgin have all featured stories about the newly emerging global hubs of vintage clothing emporia in London, NY, LA, Milan and Paris; and the features are carefully plotted to sell overseas destination holidays to their core demographic.

But just look at that age range and its champions. We have Barbara Streisand at one end, and she has given wealthy American women everywhere the confidence to wear vintage since the late 1990s. They are all having fun with the clothes from their youth, plus, they all look so much better in it; either

mixed with contemporary fashions or on their own. Then at the other end we have Drew Barrymore who stunned everyone with the 1980s dress she wore on David Letterman's show, and a whole load of celebs whose passion for vintage is all based on getting an edge and being almost *impossible* to copy (here we can include Beyonce, Nicole Richie, Ashley Olsen, Kate Moss, Mandy Moore and Lily Allen). In sum, the beauty of retro fashion is that any boy or girl can get a slice of that action.

Unlike the iconic shifts and innovations in say, furniture, silver smithing and sculpture that often occurred beyond most people's style radar, there is something about the affordability of modern fashion that has made it very inclusive, democratic and popular. In fact, fashion has connected people from very different classes and social groups owing to the ease with which one group's style could be emulated by others. Only recently, when Kate Middleton announced who designed the dress she wore at her

engagement to Prince William, global stocks of Issy sold out from London, New York, Italy, to China and Japan. But we can point to many other such emulations, including men's: from their slavish adherence to the royal males' DBS (double-breasted suit), to David Bowie's gender-bending in the early 1970s and the all-over punk look in the late 1970s, even to the habit of having unlaced sneakers in the 1990s (copying the look of Black men in US jails).

It would be impossible, therefore, to cover this rich fashion diversity in one chapter, so what follows is highly selective but hopefully it describes some key trends and looks. As always, there is design overlap from one period to another and even a certain degree of revival of previous looks. In the twenty-first century, we could almost say that every style is simultaneously in or potentially in, or in 'in combination' with other styles. Maybe all fashions are hybrids of some kind but during the retro years fashion did its level best to be audacious and new and preferably as shocking as modern art.

The 1950s

Coming out of the war years, the key influences on fashion were the legacy of tailored uniforms, the emergence of confident and affluent youth cultures, the cultural dominance of the USA and the appearance of the 'New Look' which gave Paris a new lease of life in the fashion world and gave women more unrestricted and more naturally fitting garments.

A large number of men were ex-servicemen and the 1940s tailored styles lingered on all the way through the 1950s, although the DBS, amply-cut trousers and turn-ups gave way to slimmer profiles, narrower cuts for trousers and a great deal more colour too. No matter which class or subculture, the suit standardised the masculine look as uniforms had done before.

There were quite a few role models who established dominant looks. The sons of the aging George V were among the most eligible men of the day and they championed the DBS and its variations. A classic look for this period was produced by Crombie, which made suits by appointment to the Prince of Wales. My lovely Crombie jacket from this period is in that characteristic soft brown with a cream pinstripe and made in the most comfortable cashmere wool. Interestingly, it is also cut very long, coming down a long way on the thighs, and this made it extremely warm in the colder seasons – and remember, cars were not as effectively heated back then and few homes had central heating. It is surprising how well it fits into contemporary fashion, because it really is very different. The eyes are mostly

4
Dance outfits at the Rose Seidler Fifties Fair

5
Dance outfits at the Rose Seidler Fifties Fair Photo Jody Pachniuk

6
Copy of linen skirt worn by Her Majesty Queen Elizabeth II (then HRH Princess Elizabeth) on the royal tour of Canada in 1951, Australia, c. 1951–60 Powerhouse Museum collection

7
The author models his 1940s cashmere Crombie jacket, England

8
The author in a 1950s German hat and aviator sunglasses from USA Courtesy Claudia Chan Shaw

9
Romance and glamour at Rose Seidler 1950s Fair Courtesy Historic Houses Trust; photo Jody Pachniuk

drawn to the architecture of the lapels and these have been included on most designer's collections for several years.

During the war and through the early 1950s, King George VI and his family enjoyed unrivalled popularity. Princess Elizabeth, soon to be Queen, was a fashion icon for teenagers at the time and the skirt she wore on their Canadian tour of 1951 was widely copied.

The other key role model, one for the more popular and youth markets, was Elvis Presley, and his rockabilly look, with its biker associations, brilliantine shininess and show-biz glamour made the well-made DBS look dowdy and conservative.

The colours favoured by tourists, musicians and film stars became generic, so we start to see a lot of light-coloured suits and sports jackets as well as single block colours, often extremely bright. This reflected the fact that people were more affluent, they travelled, they spent a lot of money on entertainment and they were pioneers

12

13

10
Cotton/synthetic fabric and velvet suit, used by Johnny O'Keefe, made by Thelma O'Keefe, Australia, 1956–58
Powerhouse Museum collection

11
Women's cotton swimsuit, worn by Australian star athlete Annette Kellerman, 1950s
Powerhouse Museum collection

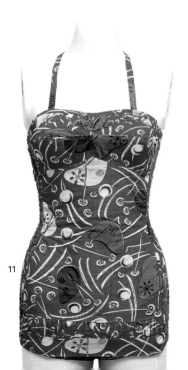

11

15

16

of what became known as the 'leisure society'.

Older associations and identities based on work or trades gave way to social identities based on leisures, styles, cultures and consumption. Nothing makes this point better than the poodle skirts, the pedal pushers and playful dance dresses of women's high street fashions or indeed, the amazing home knitted 'film title' pullover (see page 194).

So dominant were these popular middle American looks that the more extravagant and revolutionary designs from the couture houses were cast into something of a shadow. Nonetheless, Christian Dior's 'New Look' remains the most important innovation of the decade.

Though few would suggest Dior was a feminist, we can at least say he was interested in liberating women's bodies from a long period of restriction,

12
1950s summer dress, USA Photo courtesy of Darnell Collection

13
No ordinary look this: inspirations for men came from the military, silver screen and top 10

14
Women's ivory silk evening dress by Christian Dior, Paris, 1957 Powerhouse Museum collection

15
Women's cocktail dress by Christian Dior for House of Youth, Australia, c. 1955 Powerhouse Museum collection

16
Women's silk cocktail dress and jacket designed by Cristobal Balenciaga, Paris, 1954 Powerhouse Museum collection

discipline and obscurity. Dior said 'I wanted my dresses to be constructed, moulded upon the curves of the feminine body, whose sweep they would stylize'. In wearing these styles, women experienced a new freedom that would, in time, extend beyond even Dior's imagination. As you can see from the ivory silk evening dress illustrated, the 'New Look' involved a very pinched-in waist, an abundance of cloth that highlighted and embellished a woman's natural curves and gorgeous materials that were only just becoming more available after the lean war years. In the true spirit of the democratising postwar years, Dior introduced a licensing system so that his ready-to-wear designs were available to more and more women around the world. And, prescient as ever, Dior knew that future success in the modern world depended on media savviness, and his excellent relationship with the fashion press

secured a leading position for his company and for French couture generally. The evening dress and jacket in silk by Cristobal Balenciaga is a stunning example of the triumph of 1950s curvaceousness and poise. Although the form of the dress follows nature's lines, there is no corresponding absence of dignity, poise or sophistication.

While wild youth fashions dominate one of our views of the 1950s, with the likes of Dior, Crombie and Balenciaga dominating the other, it is nonetheless true that many people, perhaps the majority, dressed like neither. The photo below shows a group of retro enthusiasts dressed in a wide and more representative range of garments. You can see that 'ordinary' men and women did wear versions of the more elaborate and showy forms, proving that there was both a degree of emulation and trickle down.

17

17
A cotton summer
dress by McDowells
Fashions,
Australia, 1956–62
Powerhouse
Museum collection

18
Retro fashion
enthusiasts at
Rose Seidler Fair
Courtesy Historic
Houses Trust; photo
Jody Pachniuk

19
Man's sports jacket
(Gowing Bros Ltd,
Australia, 1956), hat
and tie Powerhouse
Museum collection

20
Men's leather
'Toledo' winkle-
picker shoes by
William Cook,
Australia, 1950–60
Powerhouse
Museum collection

21
Satin, leather and
wood 'Kabuki'
shoes, designed
by Beth Levine,
labelled Saks, USA,
c. 1964 Powerhouse
Museum collection

19

The 1960s

There was a lot of overlap between the 1950s and 1960s, so much so that it is difficult to begin to identify entirely new looks emerging much before the middle of the decade, after which the older styles were mangled and discarded, while previously unimagined audacity was unleashed on an unsuspecting and largely very conservative public.

While the 1950s were populated by demobbed military personnel, the 1960s began to fill up with graduates from art schools and universities. Where the ex-military had learned how to follow orders, the baby boomers had learned how to criticise, re-design, revolutionise and change. It was hardly likely that fashion would remain immune to their churning ways and experimental habits.

It is not surprising that a new 1960s subculture emerged to challenge those inspired by the 1950s. Mod culture grew in the fashionable coffee bars of London and was made up by students

initially, many of whom were from art schools. Infected with revolutionary ideas that spanned the political, the personal, the sexual and the familial, as well the arts, architecture and design, this was a generation impatient to make their mark.

Their first marks were made through their music but also through their own 'look'. Dominating the turning points of the 1960s were The Rolling Stones and The Beatles. Back in the 1960s, you were either a Stones or a Beatles person: the Stones provided a cultural home for the wilder element, the rebels and the misfits, while the Beatles, at least in their initial manifestation, were the face of the cultural mainstream now daring to cast off the chains of 1950s conformity and be a bit more 'with it'.

In truth, the Beatles and the Stones had very similar musical tastes, both being strongly influenced by the blues traditions that were finding their way

20

21

out of African-American culture into white America and Europe, mostly to the beatnik-inspired art school scene, initially.

By the time these bands had become successful, they were also coming under the spell of Mod-styled London. In early press photos and album sleeves they were to be seen in the sharp suit-and-tie look of the 'art school' café crowd. You may remember those strange but distinctive Pierre Cardin-inspired suits with cut down collars that the 'Fab Four' wore. If you look carefully at The Rolling Stones first album cover, the one with the rebellious title *The Rolling Stones*, you will see them lined up looking straight into the lens of the camera and all wearing suits and ties (OK, one is down to a waistcoat). At the time (the early to mid-1960s), both bands wore those clean, neat, slightly long Mod haircuts, they were clean-shaven and had polished shoes.

These were of course rebellious men from largely middle class, affluent homes. Student grants supplemented with parental help resulted in healthy sales for young men's fashions and a new crop of boutiques cropped up along Kings Road and in Soho, London, with analogous zones in most other 'with it' cities around the world. This is why so many of the more upmarket labels became involved in the new men's look. The snappy Burberry jacket was a hit among the Mod crowd well before the scene was captured by the cheaper Harrington jackets and excellent shirts by Ben Sherman. Ben Sherman was famously captured for 'uniform' by the skinhead offshoot from Mod England, as was the Crombie classic gents coat

22
Stylish women wore Chanel in the early to mid-1960s: women's wool suit, designed by Gabrielle Chanel for Chanel, Paris, 1965 Powerhouse Museum collection

23
1960s Burberry jacket, England; Ben Sherman trousers, England; shoes by Lloyd, Germany Photo Di Quick

24
1960s cufflinks in silver-gilt, Denmark

25
1960s brown corduroy jacket by Strads, brown turtle-neck sweater, shoes by Barker, trousers by Jack Wills, England, c. 1966 Photo Di Quick

26
Ben Sherman 1970s shirt label reissued as 'vintage' in the 1990s, England

27
Carnaby Street street sign, London, England

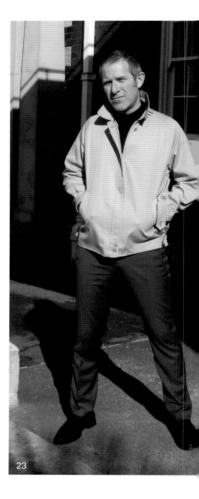

23

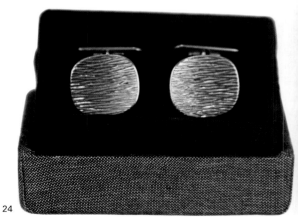

24

(go figure!), although in the 2000s Ben Sherman succeeded in producing a Mod revival with more mainstream appeal.

In my view, the ultimate Mod photo of this era was from the Beatles album *With the Beatles*, from 1963. The suits these guys wore were intended not to look conventional but the opposite, to be new, daring, 'pushing the envelope' as we would say today. Back then, my grandmother would have said 'Shocking!' On this album cover they also wore another standard 'new look' Mod garment: the roll-neck sweater; and this was shocking because it replaced the shirt and tie under a suit. (And, it was a black and white photo in the days of technicolour. Outrageous!) The roll-neck (or turtle-neck) seemed to frame the face and focus all attention on the expression, which in this case was unsmiling, dispassionate and neutral. Not smiling in a photo? Another act of rebellion, another unconventional move.

If you were a girlfriend of the Fab Four at the time, the ultimate style expression was captured by André Courrèges. Again, the shock tactics encompassed bold colours, spacey shapes and clunky architecture, with an ultra-short hemline. From their increasing number of trips to the USA, a sumptuous pair of Beth Levine boots might be given an outing from time to time.

In Paris you were spoiled for choice: the mini dress by Louis Féraud exploited the new love of black and white and used wool to produce that stiffer architectural shape.

On the other hand, London was now vying for a share of the fashion action,

the charge led by designers such as Mary Quant. In London, her miniskirts and new darker colour schemes set the style that everyone followed.

As the 1960s proceeded, these unconventional moves became bolder and bolder: facial hair appeared on men, then very long hair, strange glasses, velvet trousers and baggy tops and then we are into the drugs, trips to India and ethnic clothing styles: the kaftan, the Afghan coat, the parka and in the USA, inspiration

from the Apache. How fitting that The Beatles' last public performance was on the roof-top of a Savile Row tailor.

There were so many directions one could head in that the fashion world was for once in a kind of freeform. Some went in for the space-age look that was being translated into all kinds of household goods and furniture. Beril Jents designed a silver vinyl evening dress which is a great example, as is the space-age hostess uniform worn in the Australia Pavilion at Expo 67 in Montreal. Here in the space-age architecture of Roy Grounds and an

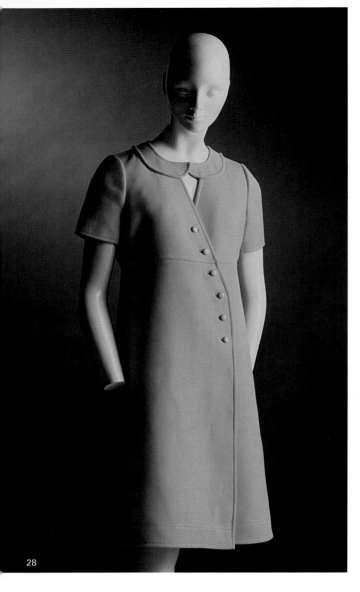

equally futuristic interior by Robin Boyd, hostesses were pictured in futuristic dresses for publicity in Grant and Mary Featherston's Expo 'Sound Chairs'. Not to be outdone, men's shirts soon included space-age themes: not so much the rocket or sputnik themes of the 1950s as the dreamier futuristic fantasy. Disposability was another trend, and with it came the ultimate fashion statement: the disposable paper dress. The example on page 184 is excessively rare. The transcendental hippy look,

with its emphasis on florals, psychedelic colours and patterns, and free flowing lines became another dominant look. Some fashions, like the range from Laura Ashley, referenced medieval and pre-Raphaelite themes. Others were more experimental, more moody and brooding, suggestive, in the case of women's fashion, of complex, thoughtful and revolutionary women. Such women wore chocolate-coloured eye shadow and lipstick. And they shopped at Biba in Kensington High Street.

Most shops did not have great Christmas sales in 2010. There were few exceptions, but one in the UK was the department store chain House of Fraser. This made the news, and I listened with great interest to their director saying how one of their fashion lines, reproduction designs by the famous 1960s company Biba, practically saved their bacon.

I have been a fan of Biba ever since I used to visit their Kensington shop with girlfriends back in the

28
Wool mini dress, designed and made by André Courrèges, France, c. 1967
Powerhouse Museum collection

29
Wool mini dress with snap fasteners, concealed zipper and black plastic Courrèges logo beneath neckline; designed and made by André Courrèges, France, c. 1967
Powerhouse Museum collection

30
Wool mini dress, vinyl belt and wool-acrylic coat, designed and made by André Courrèges in Paris and sold through Harrods, London, 1965 Powerhouse Museum collection

31
Black linen dress with white reversed collar, front zip fastening and full circular short skirt by Mary Quant of London for her 'Ginger Group' range, c. 1966
Powerhouse Museum collection

32
Hostess uniform from Expo 67 in Montreal, made by Val Gordon and others, Canada, 1967
Powerhouse Museum collection

33
Louis Féraud wool mini dress, Paris, France, c. 1967
Powerhouse Museum collection

34
Boots by Beth Levine for 'Beth's Bootery', in silk, satin, velvet and leather, USA, 1965–69
Powerhouse Museum collection

35

1960s and 1970s. The *Sunday Times* described Biba as 'The most beautiful store in the world' and I have yet to see it surpassed. Biba started out the brainchild of a Polish émigré to London, Barbara Hulanicki. She arrived in London in 1948 with her glamorous mother and sisters Beatrice and Biba. Her father was a well-known Polish Olympic athlete and then a diplomat working in Palestine before being assassinated in 1948, hence the family move.

Barbara went to good schools and then art school (art schools in the 1950s were extremely vibrant and radical) and eventually moved to London where she worked as a fashion illustrator. In 1961 she married Stephen Fitz-Simon and began to design dresses that she sold by mail order in the *Daily Express* under the name of Biba's Postal Boutique. Her work became steadily more and more recognised by the people who mattered; but when Cathy McGowan, presenter of the pop music program *Ready Steady Go*, became a firm fan, there was no turning back. McGowan, the 'Mod Queen' could not have been a better champion because she embodied the direction modern liberated women were heading.

Modern, Biba certainly were, but their secret, rather like The Beatles, was not to *exclude* tradition or the past out of the modern world but to *include it* and mix it with new ideas. So the bright and garish colours of the 1950s were muted and darkened. Biba's colours were darkish browns, prune colours, rust, ancient emerald greens and rich Tudor oranges. It has been said that these colours suited London and were

36

37

184

35
Paper 'Flower Modes' dress, USA, 1967 Powerhouse Museum collection

36
Men might have found a girlfriend dressed in Mary Quant difficult to dress for. This black and white fine hounds tooth jacket by Burtons would have been perfect, London, c. 1966 Photo Di Quick

37
Author's pop-art ice-cream disco shirt by Opus I, USA, 1973

38
The author in a 1970s French shirt by Chemise et Cie and red pants by the contemporary Swedish company Whyred (the pants were inspired by a publicity shot of Ray Davies from The Kinks in almost exactly the same cut and colour) Photo Di Quick

39
A space-age 1960s shirt by K-Mart, USA, c. 1974

40, 41
The author's daughter Brooke models a Barbara Hulanicki velvet skirt for Biba, c. 1968

part of what made it swing: they stood out and gave it the very boldest face lift that suited its old world charm.

Through the 1960s Biba was the look that defined swinging London and the Mod culture I loved. Julie Christie wore it, Twiggy wore it, Sonny and Cher dressed in it, and then into the 1970s we saw Yoko Ono in it, Mia Farrow in it, Barbara Streisand in it. What could the French fashion industry have felt when *their* Brigitte Bardot wore it?

As they grew bigger and bigger, their shop in Kensington High Street grew into a department store extraordinaire. They were among the first to start selling lifestyle goods alongside fashion and you just never knew what they would revamp next: there were Biba baked beans, purple nappies for Mod babies, Biba soap flakes, shampoo, posters, biscuit tins, food label stickers, pin-up playing cards and masses of the dark and especially brown shades of make-up that gave women the look of their age.

I used to reckon I could tell if a woman was wearing Biba: it was so distinctive and it seemed to bring out a greater confidence that combined seriousness with a playful, artistic sensibility. I have been on the Biba

collecting trail for some time. It is lean pickings for men (though what there is is revolutionary) but there is more women's stuff around. The skirt I bought for my daughter the other day is amazing. It is Biba personified, with its moody silhouette, its colour scheme and its trad/modern mix. In the vintage fashion store where I bought it, it was considered something of a Cinderella item: for months practically every woman who came in wanted it but when they tried it on it was too small for them. I imagine that the person who originally bought it may have dieted rigorously prior to a London shopping spree. However, I also imagine that soon after that, they put on more weight and could never wear it again. But, I also imagine that this was one of their favourite ever pieces; that it reminded them of their fabulous weekend in swinging London and that it was kept as a memento of one of the high points of their youth, which is why it is in mint condition. So, for many reasons, buying it for my daughter was an amazing thing to be able do. She loved it immediately and her mother looked on with a 'loving spoonful' of envy. She had been one of those who had tried it on, but alas, had been disappointed…

Biba's London colleague was Mary Quant, and although her designs were more Mod than hippie, they shared an experimental edginess with Biba. The brilliant plastic red shoes pictured are a clear example. London dominated the 1960s, but not completely. Pucci's dreamy designs on lightweight, figure-hugging fabrics were hugely successful as were the more mannered creations by Patou.

Men in the late 1960s began to blossom, literally. They burst out of the more bland colourways of the 1950s and early 1960s into a colour palette and richness of texture and material not seen since the sixteenth and seventeenth centuries. Velvet, corduroy, linen and seersucker were in. Ties were in! Kipper ties were of course the extreme, but men's ties back then were very expressive, colourful works of art. As hair grew longer, the entire menswear scene seemed to breathe a sigh of relief. The safari suit made an appearance (and become trendy again in 2010). Perhaps the ultimate expression for men was colourful platform shoes or was it my pop-art ice-cream shirt?

42

43

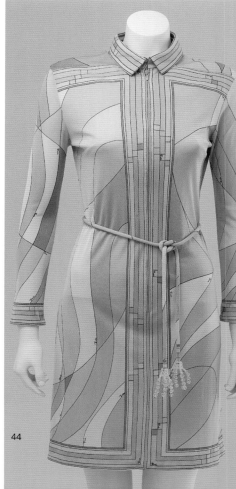

44

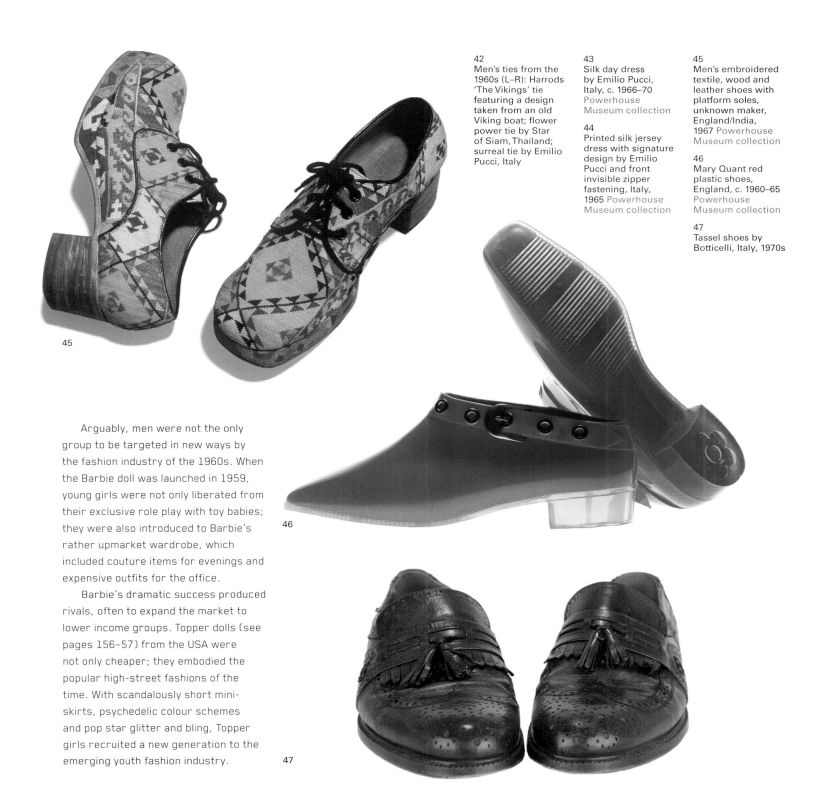

42
Men's ties from the 1960s (L–R): Harrods 'The Vikings' tie featuring a design taken from an old Viking boat; flower power tie by Star of Siam, Thailand; surreal tie by Emilio Pucci, Italy

43
Silk day dress by Emilio Pucci, Italy, c. 1966–70 Powerhouse Museum collection

44
Printed silk jersey dress with signature design by Emilio Pucci and front invisible zipper fastening, Italy, 1965 Powerhouse Museum collection

45
Men's embroidered textile, wood and leather shoes with platform soles, unknown maker, England/India, 1967 Powerhouse Museum collection

46
Mary Quant red plastic shoes, England, c. 1960–65 Powerhouse Museum collection

47
Tassel shoes by Botticelli, Italy, 1970s

Arguably, men were not the only group to be targeted in new ways by the fashion industry of the 1960s. When the Barbie doll was launched in 1959, young girls were not only liberated from their exclusive role play with toy babies; they were also introduced to Barbie's rather upmarket wardrobe, which included couture items for evenings and expensive outfits for the office.

Barbie's dramatic success produced rivals, often to expand the market to lower income groups. Topper dolls (see pages 156–57) from the USA were not only cheaper; they embodied the popular high-street fashions of the time. With scandalously short mini-skirts, psychedelic colour schemes and pop star glitter and bling, Topper girls recruited a new generation to the emerging youth fashion industry.

The 1970s

When The Beatles bowed out in 1969, they were more popular among photographers and fashion editors than any model or fashion designer. In this sense, the postmodern montage of looks they put together was as influential as their music and it is now becoming clear that they had far more than musical aspirations. This prepared the way for other rock and pop figures to position themselves firmly in the fashion world. This is why in the 1970s men in particular appeared to adopt a pop star look – possibly one of the strangest fashion events of all time?

Up until the 1970s, every man seemed to be more or less 'normal'. Sure, there were all sorts of people, but almost everyone was part of civilian, everyday life. In the 1950s, some of the kids took on an Elvis look and in the 1960s a lot of people grew their hair (but without looking very spectacular). I can remember my older brother's hair creeping over his collar, but it was the collar of the type of shirt my father wore, pretty much. Then at some point in the 1970s, everyone around me, including my brother (and, more disturbingly, my father) seemed to be dressed as if they were pop and rock stars.

This was the hirsute revolution, when almost every man went from the universal short-back-and-sides haircut down at the local barber's to something longer (and stranger) 'styled' by his 'hairdresser', in fancy downtown 'salons'. It was a new world. Men were getting a makeover, starting with their heads. I remember my childhood barber blowing jets of air around my face and neck as he

48

49

50

48
Men's cotton tapestry trousers, Milano Casuals, USA, 1970–72
Powerhouse Museum collection

49
1970s country-style jacket by DAKS of London, trousers by Jack Wills, shoes by Barker, England
Photo Brooke Franklin-Paddock

50
Sears 'Kings Road', 'Trim cut' shirt, USA, c. 1971

51
Platform shoes in leather and cork by Emilio (Gino) Pucci, Florence, Italy, c. 1973 Powerhouse Museum collection

52
Boot by Mary Shackman in hand painted cotton and leather, Sydney, 1971 Powerhouse Museum collection

53
Clog in leather, wood, metal and rubber, designer unknown, c. 1970–78 Powerhouse Museum collection

54
They said you could only look foolish in 70s gear: I disagree

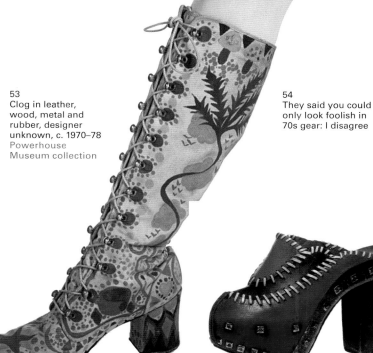

51

52

53

54

whistled wartime favourites to the snip of his scissors. But in the new salons it was wall-to-wall loud music; the cutters minced about like Rod Stewart and even spoke in a new rock star way. It was the point when 'like' became the first word of every sentence and everyone called you 'man'.

In the 1970s, London fashions were so extreme (selling more or less what David Bowie, Iggy Pop or Mick Jagger wore on stage), that I had to change out of them before I dared walk home from the railway station in Canterbury, some 80 km to the south of London. On one occasion, I remember nonchalantly buying a brown full-length, tailored trench coat, blue loon pants and 7.5 cm high plastic clogs with black and orange stripes. In this, I was relatively conservatively dressed: my mates were wearing knee-length, 7.5 cm high platform-soled yellow boots and wet-look plastic trench coats.

Even the bespoke look of Savile Row could not escape this madness. The traditional look was derailed and remodelled by the likes of Tommy Nutter, who played with the look of the fabric as well as its cut and style. After many years in exile, the dandy and the peacock were back on the streets of London, en masse.

We were all far-out, rock'n'roll animals back then. And it wasn't just the men. The young woman out in the Courrèges wet-look coat might have had cause for concern if she bumped into her father or grandmother on their way out to a date.

These were times of great experimentation and travel, especially to more exotic locations. The owner of a 1973 Biba pants-suit might have given her parents cause for concern with her trip to Istanbul. According to the Power House Museum notes for this Biba item that was donated to the museum, it was:

55

56

57

59

58

60

61

62

55
Punk leather jacket,
c. 1980–85
Powerhouse
Museum collection

56
DIY punk outfit
remade and worn
by Lewis Nicolson,
Australia, 2004
Powerhouse
Museum collection

57
'God Save the
Queen' screen
printed punk t-shirt,
Australia, c. 1977–80
Powerhouse
Museum collection

58, 60
Ben Sherman Retro-
Punk t-shirt, England,
2009

59
Punk/Two Tone
bracelet, England,
1980s

61
Silk evening dress,
Zandra Rhodes,
England, c. 1973–75
Powerhouse
Museum collection

62
Hotpants and blouse
by Gasworks,
Australia, c. 1972
Powerhouse
Museum collection

63

... worn by the donor Priscilla Shorne. She made the traditional 1960s trip to London as many young Australians did, lured by 'Swinging London'. She taught and travelled for three years before returning to Australia. She lived around the corner from the Biba Emporium and loved the atmosphere and clothes, buying the pants-suit in 1973 just before she returned to Australia. She also travelled to Istanbul on a fairly disorganised bus trip where she bought a coat in the Grand Bazaar in 1971. It was not a commercial trip but one put together by a group of people who wanted to travel to London and Istanbul and back.

The hot pants and see-through top by Gasworks were probably not a good idea to wear anywhere other than the epicentres of contemporary fashion, but even there the idea for many women was very much to shock and push the limits. Even footwear could be audacious.

As hinted at above, normal provincial society was a good deal less tolerant of these extremes, and for this reason the bulk of garments produced were toned down versions of the looks of London, New York, Paris and Melbourne. Here, Laura Ashley cashed in with designs that were wafty and floaty enough to suggest freedom, different enough to suggest 'new generation', yet conservative enough to be accepted. The same might be said of the Gucci dress still being sold in 1975, with its rather conservative themes and concern for 'modesty'. Even the Zandra Rhodes evening dress pictured here could be described as 'toned down'.

While we associate the 1970s with flowing, free and sexually liberating clothing, it would be wrong to think that the decade closed with the notion that it was dominated by progressive rock culture and hippy fashions. From at least 1976, 'punk rock' fashion, a netherworld associated with the young Vivienne Westwood's partnership with Malcolm McLaren, quickly became the latest look, but not one that built on its predecessors so much as demolished them (and then spat on them).

Punk very quickly brought in a harder, urban style that is now associated with anarchic, political and less commercial cultures. The look was anti-style and anti-fashion. Instead of matching jewellery, punks wore safety pins by way of protest. I can recall that the narrow profile was often based on cheaper, less fashionable cuts of jeans and trousers and particularly clothing from second-hand and charity shops. A lot of clothes were home [re]made or de-structured, in the case of women's clothes and men toned down to darker colours, with jackets covered with badges and ripped t-shirts often with hand-drawn slogans. Initially, there were anti-fashion fashion boutiques and these quickly became repetitive sellers of bondage trousers, kilts and mangled knits. The true punk spirits were never going to become clients of Paris fashion houses and for a while there was something of an impasse. The youth market that had fed fashion went into something of a decline. In the eighties, however, it would bounce back – with a vengeance.

63
Biba pants-suit,
England, 1973
Powerhouse
Museum collection

TIMELESS PAISLEY CHRISTINA SUMNER = CURATOR, DESIGN AND SOCIETY, POWERHOUSE MUSEUM

The design motif known as 'paisley' in the western world is more or less universally recognisable. A teardrop shape whose elongated tip curls gently over, sometimes looping elegantly back upon itself, the paisley motif is a true vintage classic to which textile designers in particular repeatedly and lovingly return. The design continues today as the standard for men's scarves, ties and cravats, while evidence of its retro power can be seen in the Mod fashions of Carnaby Street in the 1960s, and in the recent revival of '60s and '70s style. In another variation, Azerbaijan's team uniform for the 2010 Winter Olympics featured paisley patterned pants.

The paisley motif takes its modern name from the Scottish town of Paisley, famous in the 1800s for large woven shawls which featured this design. The origins of the paisley pattern are, however, much older and can be traced back to India, to the delicate tip-tilted flower or *buta* of Mughal art, and again back along the Silk Roads through Central Asia to ancient Persia (now Iran), from whose Zoroastrian cypress tree, symbol of life and time without end, it arguably came. Those paisley patterned shawls from Scotland and other weaving centres in Europe were woven in imitation of, and competition with, costly silk and wool shawls from Kashmir and India, imported by the East India Company from the late 1600s.

In naming one of her 1987 screenprint designs 'Aboriginal paisley', the influential Australian Indigenous artist Bronwyn Bancroft makes reference to the motif's everyday popularity. Bancroft's work is sometimes political as well as aesthetically compelling; it is also an intensely personal take on traditional themes and an exploration of her Aboriginality. Aboriginal art is an ancient, yet vibrant contemporary force with its own timeless motifs, its own paisley. This essentially Aboriginal design by Bancroft, who has a Scottish mother, stems however from the fondly remembered paisley-patterned quilts of her childhood. In seeking to create her own Aboriginal paisley pattern, Bancroft seems to blend Indigenous design with paisley's timeless properties, evoking the presence and fundamental importance of all inherited traditions to the vitality of emerging urban Aboriginal arts.

Women's outfit by Bronwyn Bancroft, cotton jersey bra top, t-shirt, skirt and pants screen printed with 'Aboriginal paisley', Sydney, 1987 Powerhouse Museum collection

192

67

65
Screen-printed
dress by
Studibaker Hawk,
Australia, c.1984–90
Powerhouse
Museum collection

64
'Waratah' ensemble
by Linda Jackson
in silk taffeta,
Australia, 1984
Powerhouse
Museum collection

66
Ensemble by
Comme de
Garcons, Japan
1987 Powerhouse
Museum collection

67
Men's vest with
detachable
'armour' sleeves,
from Vivienne
Westwood's
'Time Machine'
collection, England,
1988 Powerhouse
Museum collection

65

66

The 1980s

The mid- to late 1970s were a social and economic crisis period. An oil crisis fuelled a major fiscal crisis that would finally halt the tax-hungry welfare states of the western world. In 1979 Britain voted for a radical conservative prime minister, Margaret Thatcher, and in the USA Ronald Reagan formed a double act that would see more emulation than opposition. In the name of market freedom, these neoliberal leaders deregulated stock markets, rolled back state infrastructures, terminated inefficient nationalised industries and privatised as many operations as possible. The upshot was a great deal of pain, but emerging from the pain of change came a massive economic boom. Cities bent on redevelopment and regeneration filled up with an entirely new youth figure: the young urban professional or 'yuppie'. Their fast-track careers and fortunes made from stocks and property markets as well as media and information technologies

gave them a reputation for greed and consumerism, labels that were entirely appropriate.

Fashion was very clearly used as an expression of this new affluence and eighties fashions were characterised by a greater emphasis on designer label shopping and what came to be termed as 'power dressing'. Power dressing required that success and seniority, affluence and property, were marked by a more overt form of fashion one-up-man-ship. For both men and women, this began in the workplace, with very tailored, angular and massively padded silhouettes (the so-called 'Superbody' in the case of women) by a series of ascendant new names: notably, Gucci, Versace and Armani for men and Thierry Mugler, Jean Paul Gaultier and Issey Miyake for women. 'Masculinised' women became more significant in the corporate law firms and multinationals, and they dressed so as to emphasise that they meant business. Outside the

workplace, the powerful superwoman metaphor was kept up through androgynous role models like Grace Jones and Madonna and the new women of TV such as Sue Ellen (Linda Grey) in *Dallas*.

It would be a mistake, however, to see the entire decade as being determined by the commercial world of the yuppy. In many ways it was a very political era, with many civil rights battles being fought, not least the ascendance of more confident gay and lesbian communities, the end of apartheid in South Africa and, ultimately, the termination of the communist influence in Poland, East Germany and the Soviet Union. The first Sydney Gay Mardi Gras took place in 1981 and became a mainstream event on the social calendar.

Leisure scenes were dominated by a revival of 1950s middle American cool style. This was characterised by tailored chino pants, baggy shirts with playful and exotic motifs (the Hawaiian shirt made a comeback). Hair was brushed back, brilliantined and longish; glasses were in

JENNY KEE ARCHIVE   GLYNIS JONES = CURATOR, FASHION, POWERHOUSE MUSEUM

Beatlemania hit Australia in 1964, and among the thousands of screaming fans gathered for the group's arrival was Jenny Kee, primly clad in a tartan Mod suit. Kee managed to evade security at the Sheraton Hotel in Kings Cross and found herself singled out for an 'unforgettable' night with John Lennon. The encounter left Kee feeling restless and she was soon on her way to 'Swinging London'. Here she found fashion undergoing profound changes as the hippie movement's anti-fashion, anti-consumerist ethic took hold and young people turned to dressing in retro nostalgic fashions and ethnic clothing found in second-hand shops and markets.

Kee landed a job at the hub of this trend, in Vern Lambert's vintage clothing stall at the Chelsea Antique Market. Dressed in a mix of Pakistani dress, Moroccan jewellery and 1920s shawls, Kee was selling exquisite couture garments from Dior and Schiaparelli, Victorian and Edwardian underwear, and embroidered garments from Asia and the Middle East, to an equally eclectic clientele of pop stars, fashion designers and hippies. It was here that she started collecting hand-knitted garments, including a jumper embroidered with Richard Attenborough's signature and the titles of films he appeared in between 1942 and 1948.

Attracted by the encouraging cultural climate of the new Gough Whitlam-led Labor government, Kee

returned to Australia in 1972 and opened her Flamingo Park 'frock salon' in Sydney's Strand Arcade. The sign on the door invited customers to 'Step into Paradise', where they found the shop interior decked out in retro style with Clarice Cliff vases, Goldsheider ceramic heads and a 1950s counter, behind which stood Kee in her 1940s Richard Attenborough jumper. The salon initially sold a mix of retro fashions, Hawaiian shirts, 1950s-style garments made from 40s and 50s

fabrics, and original designs by Linda Jackson.

The Attenborough jumper sparked Kee's desire to create knits featuring Australian motifs. The use of text was the primary attraction for Kee and was to become a signature element in both her knitwear and silk designs. These were soon in great demand and even Diana, Princess of Wales, was seen sporting a 'Blinky Bill' koala jumper.

When Kee's archive was acquired by the Powerhouse Museum, it was considered important to also acquire a selection of her own personal retro garments to document the impact they had on her creative process.

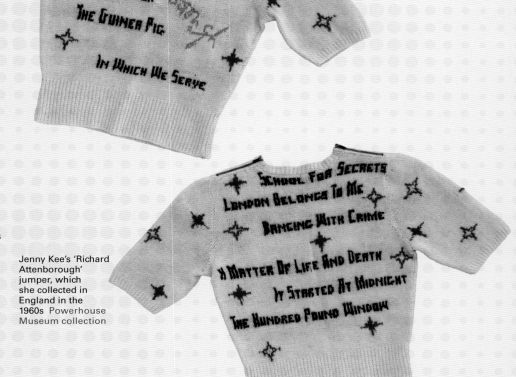

Jenny Kee's 'Richard Attenborough' jumper, which she collected in England in the 1960s Powerhouse Museum collection

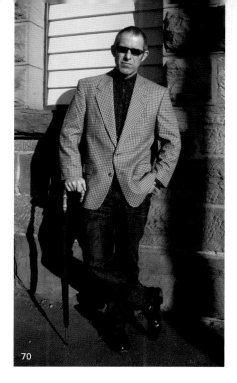

fashion and large – often in strange new plastic tones – and shoes were chunky, with Doc Martens and boat shoes ever popular. Many failed to notice the odd appearances by Memphis-inspired designers from Italy, but they were there.

1975 to 1984 was one of the strangest periods to live through because everyone went from a free and easy fashion aesthetic to the disciplined strictures of organisational and career imperatives. Looking back on my time then, it is difficult to see how we morphed from one to the other, but I do remember that the 1980s were exciting times, politically as well as economically, and in terms of popular culture – including fashion. We men smartened up significantly, we had good hair for the first time in a long time and we got back into wearing suits (and secretly rather liked to). I recall wearing an exorbitantly expensive green Boss suit with Church's black brogues and a black t-shirt. Black t-shirts were worn a lot at night back then and were a really cheap but almost unbeatable fashion statement. In the summer, I recall that the French designers had captured a market in smart but light and airy jackets, and one that I kept was a blue and white checked number by Yves Saint Laurent.

CHAPTER 7

GRAPHICS

DESPITE SHORTAGES, THEY WANTED NOT ONLY TO MAKE BOOKS THAT WOULD SELL TO A BOOK STARVED MARKET BUT TO PRODUCE BOOKS THAT WERE ATTRACTIVELY ILLUSTRATED. IT WAS DIFFICULT FOR ANYONE WHO HAD PRODUCED LAVISH BOOKS BEFORE THE WAR TO LEARN THE NEW RULES OF AUSTERITY.

BRIAN WEBB GRAPHIC DESIGN AND TOPOGRAPHY 2001:109

GRAPHIC ART EXPANDED EXPONENTIALLY into all areas of modern life after 1945, having established itself in stylistic terms from such sources as the Bauhaus, the advertising industry and public information services. It also benefitted from the expansion of graphic art courses and graduates emanating from the new art colleges. Far from being superseded by radio and TV, graphics persisted into this period as a largely paper medium and appeared strongly in poster design, vinyl record covers, books, postcards, advertising and packaging, and wallpaper. All of it is now subject to increased interest from historians, museums and collectors, and it has made substantial inroads towards being designated an art genre in its own right that sits alongside, rather than below the fine arts.

Posters arrived in the late nineteenth century as a result both of printing advances and of the massive expansion of metropolitan areas. Huge cities now concentrated markets, and their complex metropolitan transportation networks and hubs created the opportunity for focused marketing to people in transit. In subways, ticket halls, bus and underground rail carriages, along tunnels, at stops, stations and destinations, and alongside escalators, the poster became a principal marketing tool prior to radio and TV; but even after radio and TV, the poster continued to serve an important purpose. In the cacophony of images and messages surrounding modern life, the ability of a poster to reach out to its audience effectively was paramount. Hence, there emerged a specialised genre of graphic art and artists, a celebrity group of successful graphic artists and new styles of presentation.

Posters were initially mostly an advertising medium for performances, products and travel (especially) and in their earliest manifestations they were eagerly collected. In the twentieth century the poster was also drafted into wartime propaganda campaigns and public information, and later it was used in health and safety campaigns, the rock and pop industry, environmental campaigns and political or protest messages.

By the 1950s the number of products being marketed was far higher than it had been at any time previously, and the work of the Mad Men of Madison Avenue and the London advertising industry was never more important. The massive increase of road users meant that practically every available roadside space became an advertising opportunity, with the

TOSHIBA FLOWER BASKET RADIO
CAMPBELL BICKERSTAFF = CURATOR, SCIENCE AND INDUSTRY, POWERHOUSE MUSEUM

Where this transistor radio exhibits little technical sophistication, it stands out for its startlingly different appearance to other Japanese radios from the preceding period. Toshiba's Design Centre crew took the key design cue of the oriental (Japanese) interior and produced this plastic spherical flower basket transistor radio with more than a mild echo of traditional Japanese lacquer ware. A late 1950s penchant for westerners to 'orientalise' their interiors provided a rich consumer base for this design, and it was a modestly successful product. The company, so pleased with this product, exhibited the radio at Toshiba's showcase in Ginza, Tokyo for some time.

There is no denying that a certain attraction to novelty might also have induced the purchase of this hand-painted radio, but it must be said it is a most practical design. The centralised dial sits on top so that if the radio is placed in the centre of a table it can be operated and tuned from any direction. The speaker, mounted at the base of the sphere, is directed downwards, projecting sound toward the pedestal base, itself acoustically affable, affording audio in all directions.

Towards the late 1950s, Japanese designers had tended to follow their North American counterparts (the 'Cadillac' design school), conforming to popular taste by the judicious application of mock chrome trim to the casing of radios, televisions and refrigerators – the flower basket sees Japanese designers breaking from this and forging new ground with very Japanese styling.

The 'flower basket' transistor radio designed and manufactured by Toshiba in 1957
Powerhouse Museum collection

1

2

3

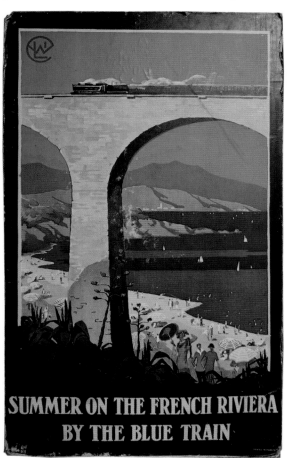

result that poster sizes and numbers increased. Postwar consumers became more sophisticated; consumers not only of products but also of product messages, of product quality and safety, and of their aesthetic presentation.

Even as early as 1954, the great poster designer Tom Eckersley wrote that 'in our lives today the poster plays an important role and enters every phase of it – the goods we buy, the entertainment we enjoy, the public services we use' (Tom Eckersley, *Poster Design*, The Studio Publications, London and New York, 1954, p. 6). Eckersley also wrote that 'emotional appeal is very important in the poster: Humour, Sentiment, Drama, all play their part and there is also a place for the abstract and

unusual'. Unlike the artist, whose work is pure self-expression, the poster designer is 'the man in the middle, the man who establishes contact between the advertiser and the consumer. It is for him to give pictorial expression to the message concerned in such a way that it may be instantly remembered and stored in the minds of all who see it' (ibid., p. 7).

In a rare passage, Eckersley takes his reader through the evolution of the poster he designed for Eno's Fruit Salt. He was told to create a cheerful impression suggesting the well-being that the product promises, and he used the simplest elements in its consumption: the glass, the spoon and the effervescent liquid. Originally the cheerful face was located on the bowl of the spoon but the face under water suggested drowning rather than wellbeing, so the familiar

1
Douglas Annand, travel poster for Qantas, Australia, 1972 Powerhouse Museum collection

2
Safety at work poster, National Safety Council of Australia, 1950s

3
Douglas Annand, 'Australia' poster with black swan for the Australian National Travel Association, 1954 Powerhouse Museum collection

4
Travel poster for the Blue Train, Compagnie Internationale des Wagons-Lits (CIWL), France, 1950s

AUSTRALIAN TRAVEL POSTERS

ANNE-MARIE VAN DE VEN = CURATOR, DESIGN AND SOCIETY, POWERHOUSE MUSEUM

Travel Posters 1930s–1950s (National Library of Australia, 1999), *Celebrating Australia: Identity by Design* (Powerhouse Museum for Australian Embassy, Washington DC, 2001), and Josef Lebovic's second major poster show, *Australian and International Travel Posters*, 2004.

The presence of travel posters in major auction houses further demonstrates the appeal of this type of object. 'At the moment, it is the pre-war and immediate postwar posters of Qantas Empire Airways, P&O and the various Federal and State Government tourist bureaus that are in demand', wrote James Cockington when reviewing Bonham & Goodman's auction of April 2005. In this piece,

he identified Harry Rogers's 'Qantas Japan' poster (illustrated) as one of the most striking posters on display. When a collection of mid-twentieth century Australian travel posters went under the hammer at Christie's rooms in London in 2007, about seventy people attended.

Qantas, in collaboration with Coverpoint Marketing, has recently paid further tribute to Harry Rogers's unique contribution to Qantas poster art by releasing a set of ten 'Qantas Retro posters'. Digitally remastered and released as giclée prints on archival paper, the posters are now highly collectable and have been acquired into private and corporate collections.

Australian travel posters are regarded as some of the best in the world. Ephemeral and disposable, they are now comparatively rare and do well at auction; the posters of Harry Rogers being especially sought after.

The revival of interest in this genre emerged when Sydney dealer Josef Lebovic held the watershed exhibition *Australian Travel Posters* in his Paddington gallery in 1990. This was followed by numerous other noteworthy poster displays, including *Trading Places: Australian Travel Posters 1909–1990* (Monash University Gallery, 1991), *The Street as Art Galleries – Walls Sometimes Speak: Poster Art in Australia* (National Gallery of Australia, 1993), *Follow the Sun: Australian*

Harry Rogers 'Japan' and 'Australia' posters screen printed by Posters Pty Ltd for Qantas Airways, Australia, late 1950s Powerhouse Museum collection

5

6

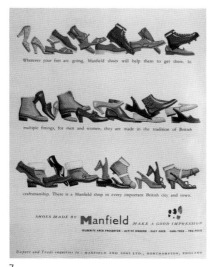

7

8

9

10

11

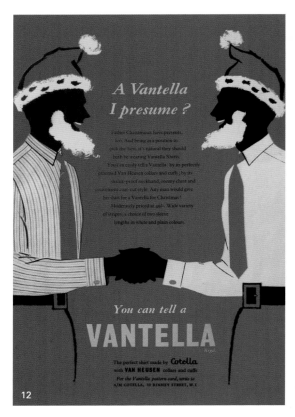

12, 13, 15
Advertisements from
*Illustrated London
News*, 1950s

14
Advertisement
from the Guide to
the South Bank
Exhibition, Festival
of Britain, 1951

16
Douglas Annand,
cover for catalogue
for the Australian
pavillion, World's
Fair, New York,
1939 Powerhouse
Museum collection

17
Reg Mombassa
(Chris O'Doherty)
poster for Mambo
Graphics, Sydney,
Australia, 1988
Powerhouse
Museum collection

18
Bruno Benini,
photograph of
Miki Gardner
modelling lurex
culotte by Jo Bond
1969 Powerhouse
Museum collection

19
David Mist, fashion
photograph for
Vanity Fair, London
1960 Powerhouse
Museum collection

20
Henry Talbot,
photograph of Penny
Pardey modelling
Pierre Cardin mini-
shift dress, Paris
1967 Powerhouse
Museum collection

21
David Mist,
photograph of
Jarmilla Lloyd
and Del Hancock
modelling for Flair
magazine, Sydney,
1965 Powerhouse
Museum collection

16

18

20

17

19

21

image of the apostle spoon was recruited to represent the demographic most likely to buy the product: a middle-aged man, now rendered cheerful after the night before.

Up until the 1980s posters were considered ephemeral and disposable; and indeed, from the 1970s they were widely and easily produced as flyers for a range of cultural, political and commercial products on extremely thin and fragile papers. However, as the creative and cultural industries became a more substantial part of late twentieth century society and economy, the history and aesthetic tradition of the poster became of great interest to museums, collectors and the art market itself. New poster businesses emerged and prices for the originals have become very high indeed. A band of poster designers has been elevated into a star category and their original vintage posters sell for very serious money. The key names include Zero (Hans Schleger), Abram Games, Tom Eckersley, Savignac, Cassandre, Percy Trompf, Villemot, Douglas Annand, Paul Rand, Lewitt-Him and Alexieff. An original Games poster from the 1950s, for example, can sell at auction for in excess of $US5000, thus the hunt to find them in charity shops, garage sales and car boot sales is really on.

True to the very best of retro design, many of these poster designs are currently being sold to eager collectors, both by commissioning companies, such as London Transport and by the estates of the artists, such as the estate of Abram Games. The longer this goes on, the more difficult it will be to discern an original print run from even good licensed reproductions.

However, the story of posters is even more convoluted, because in the late 1960s and early 1970s posters were produced for a new reason: not to inform, to advertise or to warn, but to brighten up the still bare walls of many homes. The so-called commercial 'art poster' trade may have begun a bit earlier as young students began the habit of removing 'working' posters to decorate their own rooms. The playwright Alan Bennett is a useful source of intelligence here. In his autobiographical essays *Writing Home* (first published by Faber and Faber, London, 1994), he reveals precisely what objects furnished and decorated his rooms at Oxford University when he was a student in the 1950s. He reveals that many things were still in very short supply and this included prints and other decorative materials. As a consequence, he filled his rooms with curiosities from local junk shops (this is before they took on the moniker of 'antiques' shops) and these gradually covered the bare mantelpieces and chests of drawers; but only a mirror could be used to punctuate the bare walls. That is until he stumbled on the decorative use of his jazz record covers, and these became widely used in students' rooms: literally, to jazz them up a bit.

It was from just such a habit that the first posters of rock and pop bands were also recruited onto the college bedroom walls of students in the late 1960s and then, more generally into 'teenagers' bedrooms. These walls, as I can testify myself, had been bare in the 1950s, apart from the odd crucifix or tasteful print. I never once thought to put a poster up in my bedroom and I did not leave home until 1973. Nor did I see posters on my friends' bedroom walls, and that leads me to conclude that the commercialisation of posters as aesthetic domestic objects must have come shortly afterwards. The first wave seemed to consist of commercial posters, particularly for old product adverts such as Pears soap. Also making a strong appearance in the early days were reproductions of Toulouse-Lautrec's posters for French theatre productions. It was only when lucrative and extensive rock and pop tour circuits became established that the world seemed to become flooded with music posters and these were used in a casual way to further adorn bed-sits

and college rooms. I suspect that few were kept for long but were updated as musical taste changed. I managed to miss the opportunity to amass posters from all the bands I saw, from Captain Beefheart to David Bowie, and from The Clash to the Pogues via The Jam, Ian Dury, Blondie and Status Quo. And there were parts of town, transit areas mainly, completely dominated by fly posters, all hectoring for attention to a band, a rally or happening of some other kind.

While posters certainly took over from record covers as the aesthetic wrapper of misspent youth, the vinyl record cover itself was an aesthetic joy until its last days as a mass-produced product (it has made a come-back of sorts but it is really only a minor genre today). Since the record itself was mostly dull and uninteresting (apart from the great period of picture discs), the graphics on the cover became a sophisticated surface for photography and design.

The record cover's square format and size were the perfect proportions to hold in the hands, perfect for loading with pictorial and textual information, and perfect for creating a graphical interpretation of the band and the music on the record. Further, because they were very thin and stacked in deep piles in record stores, the record buyer or peruser could stand in one position for a long period of time, being exposed to entire genres of music.

The earliest and perhaps some of the best graphics on vinyl record covers were created for jazz records in the 1950s. These days, many people collect jazz for the album cover art as much

as the amazing music, particularly for the masterpiece covers by David Stone Martin. His signed cover for Lester Young's *Collates No. 2* from 1953 is a great work of modern art. Although my copy is a little tatty, I just don't care: in the jazz world, tatty can be good. Often done using just a crow-quill pen and a wash in one or two colours, his designs have an incredible impact on the eye and suit jazz very well. There are over 400 album cover designs to collect, and the great jazz producer Norman Granz commissioned many of them. I imagine David Stone Martin sitting in the recording studio capturing Dizzy Gillespie, Skeeter Best and John Lewis for the legendary cover for *The Modern Jazz Sextet*, an album that would be in my top 5.

Other notable albums include *The Amazing Nina Simone* (Pye, USA, 1959) that features the three winning block colours of yellow, orange and pink, and the exquisite photo of the jazz queen by Herb Snitzer, the most significant jazz photographer of them all. The quality of the Japanese pressing of the Bobby Hackett Quartet album *An Evening with the Bobby Hackett Quartet Vol 1* from around 1959 makes it a real standout.

The 1960s and 1970s was a golden period of vinyl record production and the album sleeves represent a very significant art form. In the early 1960s the sleeves were simpler and tended to showcase the performer and performance rather than the idea of the album title. The Beatles early album *With the Beatles*, Stevie Wonder's *Greatest Hits*, Nancy Sinatra's timely (1966) appearance as 'Nancy in London', *The Stax-Volt Tour in London*

22
Album covers:
What A Party, Fats Domino, London, c. 1955; *Collates No 2,* Lester Young (cover art by David Stone Martin), Mercury/Clef, USA, 1953; *The Modern Jazz Sextet* (cover art by David Stone Martin), Norgram, USA, 1956; *Time Further Out,* The Dave Brubeck Quartet, CBS Records, England, 1961; *An Evening with the Bobby Hackett Quartet Vol 1,* Japanese pressing, Stateside Upsurge, Japan, c. 1959; *The Amazing Nina Simone* (photo by Herb Snitzer), Pye Records, USA, 1959; *Monk's Blues,* Thelonious Sphere Monk (cover art by Paul Davis), CBS, USA, 1969 Photo Di Quick

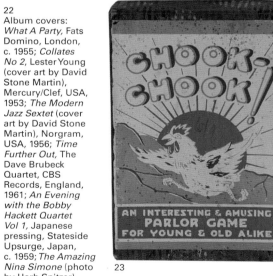

23

23
Box for *Chook Chook* card game, Australia, c. 1947

of 1967, and The Lovin' Spoonful all showcase the musicians, but by the late 1960s and 1970s the tendency was to suggest the idea or theme through abstraction and narrative. One thinks here of the Rolling Stones album *Sticky Fingers* (1971), Jimi Hendrix's *Electric Ladyland* (1968), and Pink Floyd's *Wish You Were Here* (1975).

By the late 1970s and into the 1980s 'the message' was often the key (and sometimes bleak) element and these ranged from The Sex Pistols *Never Mind the Bollocks* of 1977 to The Fall's *Perverted by Language* in 1983 and The Smiths *Hateful of Hollow* in 1984.

Better known for his travel posters, Douglas Annand was also drafted into other key marketing campaigns. The Australian exhibition at the 1939 World's Fair was a critical marketing exercise, since Australia was keen to create markets in the USA. Douglas Annand stepped up to the mark. His design was basically a kangaroo taking a leap into the future across the Australian flag. OK there was a bit of wattle blossom there too but all the action was around 'the leap' and 'the flag'. Clearly, the leaping kangaroo was Australia herself but the flag was not the familiar Australian flag: Annand cleverly changed that. The Union Jack

bit of the Australian flag seemed to suggest a strong, perhaps dependent connection with Britain, so Annand subtly changed it. The thick red lines became ultra thin, unmistakably like the red lines on the Stars and Stripes. Then, in case you hadn't been paying attention, he changed the solid stars of our Southern Cross to the silvery lines of stars on the US flag. In other words, this design made it clear that, yes, Australia was once a British colony, but now it envisaged an important part of its future with the USA. Here is an apt illustration of the suggestive powers of graphics, and the same is achieved for the actual brochure for the 1939 New York World's Fair. The brochure confirmed in graphic terms the promise of its futuristic title by showing a barely recognisable cityscape of a future modernity, and the laser-white lighting and acid reds confirmed it again in colour.

Even more subtly, Alistair Morrison's design for the exhibition catalogue cover *Architecture Today and Tomorrow* achieves maximum effect through a strong design using a minimal number of elements. Here, the rather dull title of the publication is given oxygen and appeal through a simple exercise in abstraction.

24
LP vinyl record covers from 1950s to 1980, various artists, USA and UK Photo Di Quick

25
Book covers from 1950s to 1980s, USA and UK Photo Di Quick

26
Detail from a film guide for Ned Kelly starring Mick Jagger, Director, Tony Richardson, United Artists, filmed in UK, 1970

27
Marc Bolan & T. Rex vinyl LP record (picture disc) *Across The Airwaves*, BBC Radio 1 sessions, Dakota / Cube / BBC ICSX 1004, England, 1982

28

29

As affluence spread across the western world after the Second World War, publishers of fiction and non-fiction vied with each other in an increasingly competitive commercial environment. Plain, monochromatic covers gave way to book covers with greater design input. Increasingly, booksellers gave this designed surface greater exposure through their display techniques, not least through the vertical, rotary stands that can display the front covers of an entire range or series. Thus were copies of Roland Barthes's *Mythologies* from 1957 given a second life in Palladin's brightly lit covers for 1970s audiences.

Ian Fleming's Bond series of spy-thrillers were particularly successful at deploying suggestive elements or fragments of a story onto book covers;

The Spy Who Loved Me being a case in point. Lesser cult figures such as Colin MacInnes's photographer hero Wizard from *Absolute Beginners*, also stood the test of time. This book, which was set in London's Notting Hill as the first race riots rocked the city, suggested the potential of cultural exchange, the transformative effects of the mixed race jazz clubs and the redemption offered by the an experimental teenage culture. If ever there was a story set to become a cult this was it, and in many ways it set down the coordinates for retro culture itself with its interest in beat poets, jazz, rebellion, ethnic tolerance and curiosity. *Absolute Beginners* was reissued by Allison and Busby and became a best seller again in the 1980s (alongside the other volumes of the London Trilogy: *City of Spades*

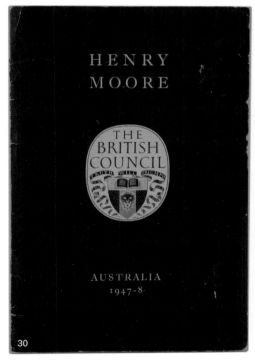

30

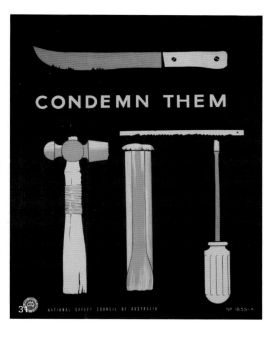

Claude Lévi-Strauss, Roland Barthes and Karl Marx carried covers with elegant structures that mirrored their structural theoretical writings. In the 1970s simple abstract designs with striking colour were a feature, as can be seen on the cover of Pitt-Rivers's ethnography of Spain, *People of the Sierra*.

However, by the mid-1970s the graphics changed from the self-assured structural codas to the social turmoil that was unleashed following a fiscal crisis of the welfare state, an oil crisis and an emerging environmental crisis. Titles like *Slump City* on de-industrialisation in the UK and *Farewell to the Working Class* showed images of disorder and decline and began to evaluate the churning nature of neoliberal politics in Europe and America. Added to that, feminism and other angry rights campaigns created political, cultural and ontological uncertainties. The cover of Judith Butler's *Gender Trouble* (1990) and *Aint No Black in the Union Jack* (1987) reflected this turmoil.

The work of Martin Amis was set within a London, a trans-Atlantic and a globalising world that was unravelling and disordered. The covers of his best novels, *Money* and *London Fields*, use blurred images to illustrate decay and the lack of definition, normality and ethics. It is no wonder that the very best of his covers, that of his book *Experience* (2000), shows him on a childhood Christmas day when, in his family, normality was suspended: he and his brother, for instance, were allowed to smoke and drink whisky.

During the 1980s a retro genre

and *Mr Love and Justice*) and a film was made of it that starred David Bowie. Retro is motivated by powerful urges to look back, remember, relive and review. Books that did that, particularly with stylish topics and people, were bound to attract attention; and one that captured a few Beatle reflections some ten years after they split up was Cynthia Lennon's *A Twist of Lennon* (Star Books, London, 1978). The cover featured an unposed shot of John and Cynthia Lennon at what is very obviously a tense moment. It reminds one of some of those moments captured between Prince Charles and Princess Diana, where their private life

had to be lived in front of the camera and an audience keen for the slightest scrap of private information.

As the tertiary education sector expanded massively, so also did the number of academic and scholarly titles. An educated readership subsequently elaborated the non-fiction market and this also became a competitive field where graphics were deployed to maximise market penetration.

Anthropology and popular sociology became sites for critical discussion about societies in states of flux, change and unfolding futures. Books by

209

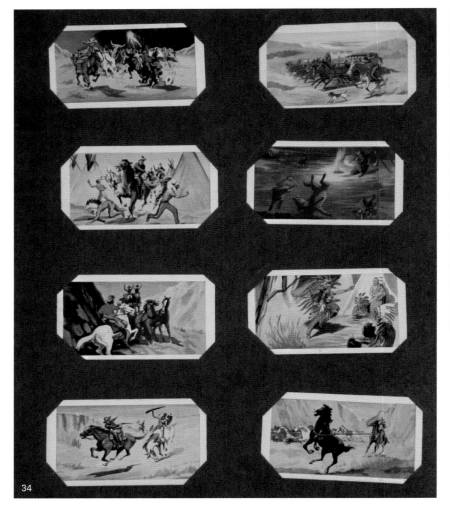

34

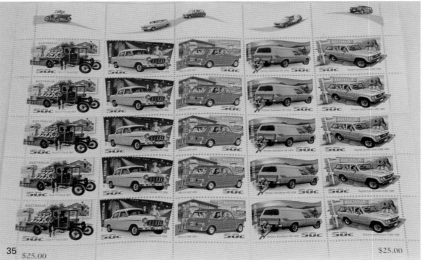

35

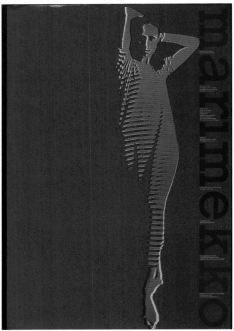

36

37

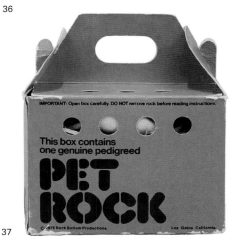

38

39

40

41

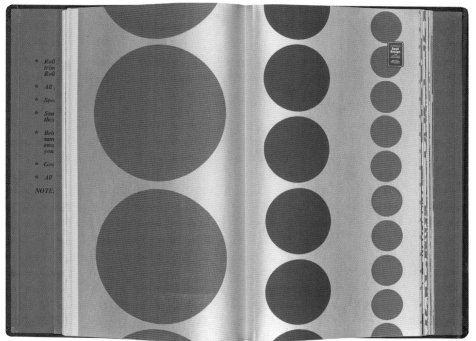

42

began to form around some seminal titles, not least of which was the Faber & Faber classic *The Hip* by Roy Carr, Brian Case and Fred Deller. Faber & Faber are recognised in the bookseller's trade as a leading light in book cover graphics, so it is hardly surprising that when retro became all-pervasive in the 2000s, there would be a retrospective book of their own book cover designs (Joseph Connolly, *Eighty Years of Book Cover Design,* Faber & Faber, London, 2009) as well as one by Penguin in 2010 (*Penguin 75: Designers, Authors,*

Commentary, Edited by Paul Buckley).

The retro years were largely wallpaper years, or at least, wallpaper loomed large in most homes across the western world. In the 1950s wallpaper occasionally let its hair down: I remember a glossy bright undersea world that covered my grandparents' 1950s bathroom, giving great joy to at least myself. During the 1960s there were some excellent wallpapers that came from the early psychedelic years but it was really the 1970s when wallpaper let rip and finally got the

34
'Wild West' series of picture cards by Hoadley's Chocolates Ltd, Melbourne, Australia, 1950s

35
Retro car stamps by Australia Post, c. 2009

36
Bruce Weatherhead, poster for Marimekko, Melbourne 1970-71, Powerhouse Museum collection

37
Packaging for Pet Rock, Rock Bottom Productions, Los Gattos, California, USA, 1975

38
Selection of clothing labels, 1980s – present

39
Packaging for Peace on Barrel toy, Hong Kong, 1967

40
Arthur Leydin, Australian animal wooden jigsaw puzzle, c. 1970, Powerhouse Museum collection

41
Ronald Hamilton Fraser, fabric design for David Whitehead, England, 1950s

42
David Miles, wallpaper sample book, Sydney, 1972 Powerhouse Museum collection

'AUBREY' WALLPAPER BY FLORENCE BROADHURST

ANNE-MARIE VAN DE VEN = CURATOR, DESIGN AND SOCIETY, POWERHOUSE MUSEUM

In 1966 the Victoria and Albert Museum (V&A) in London held a retrospective of a little-known, late nineteenth century graphic artist named Aubrey Beardsley. The scent of scandal following the seizure by London's Metropolitan Police of so-called 'obscene' Beardsley prints, from a shop not far from the museum, saw visitor numbers to the exhibition flourish.[1] After its showing at the V&A, the controversial exhibition travelled to the United States. The subsequent social and graphic influence of this licentiously gay, Art Nouveau exhibition, and the monograph published the following year, was widespread.

Klaus Voorman's famous Beatles *Revolver* album cover in 1966 echoes Beardsley's style, as does Martin Sharp's *Bob Dylan Mister Tambourine Man* poster from around 1966–67. And Milton Glaser and the Push Pin Studio in New York created the iconic, Art Nouveau–inspired *Bob Dylan Greatest*

> Florence Broadhurst Wallpapers Pty Ltd, white on metallic gold 'Aubrey' wallpaper sample from sample book, Sydney, 1973 Powerhouse Museum collection

Hits album poster at the same time.

The ripple effect of the Beardsley revival was also felt in Australia. Reproduction Beardsley blow-ups appear as backgrounds in a David Mist fashion photograph for Sekers Silks in 1967. Australian wallpaper producer Florence Broadhurst created a vibrant psychedelic tribute to Beardsley with her two-colour wallpaper design titled 'Aubrey', featuring a striking linear design for reproduction on shining foil or black surfaces. This design had a recent revival when Australian fashion designer Nicole Zimmermann selected it from the Broadhurst archive for a swimwear range in 2001. Helen Lennie from Signature Prints, which holds the rights to commercially reproduce Broadhurst designs worldwide, was surprised by the bikini's huge success in the United States. 'You wouldn't believe it! We had to print thousands of metres of "Aubrey" for the US market after Zimmermann's bikini featured on the cover of the Victoria's Secret magazine. For the tiny meterage required for the four small triangles of a string costume, that's a lot of bikinis!'[2]

< David Mist, photograph of Del Hancock and Maggi Eckardt modelling for Sekers Silk fashion, art direction by Rob Hatherley, Sydney, 1967 Powerhouse Museum collection

> Florence Broadhurst Wallpapers Pty Ltd, red and black 'Aubrey' wallpaper sample from sample book, Sydney, 1969–77 Powerhouse Museum collection

confidence to achieve its true potential. Op-art and pop-art papers are clear favourites, and anything influenced by Barbara Brown, or Barbara Hulanicki for Biba is particularly desirable. However, the undisputed queen of wallpaper was the colourful Florence Broadhurst. Broadhurst was born and raised in outback Queensland but acted for all the world like a refined lady from a Georgian park. Clearly a talented artist and businesswoman, as well as the kind of socialite who can become central to the lives of an entire clientele, Broadhurst created one of the most colourful design businesses of the retro period. It began in 1959 and became almost unable to satisfy demand some four years later. However, it was in the late 1960s and 1970s that her best work was created. A newspaper article covering the opening of her new Florence Broadhurst Wallpaper Studio in Paddington in 1969 carried the caption 'Palm trees and Psychedelics' and it was her designs far more than the counterculture that brought this vivid backcloth into the mainstream homes of suburban Australia. Such was the power of her designs that they have never been out of fashion since and have made a very significant comeback in the 2000s where they were adopted more widely onto furnishing fabrics by Customweave; fashion designs by Akira Isogawa, Zimmermann and Karen Walker; fashion accessories by Funkis; furniture designs by Matthew Butler of Blue Square; and interior design by Greg Natale.

43, 45
Postcards from 1939
New York World's Fair,
USA

44
Artist unknown,
cigarette cards, 'An
Album of Film Stars',
Second Series, John
Player and Sons,
England, 1937

46

47

48

49

46, 47
Safety at work
posters, National
Safety Council of
Australia, 1960s

48
Menu from Her
Majesty's Yacht
Britannia, July 2nd
1964

49
Menu from
JF Kennedy's
Inauguration Lunch
at the White House,
January 20th 1961

50
Cigarette cards,
Australian Sporting
Stars Series, B.V.D.
Cigaretttes, Australia,
1930s–40s

51
Paul Frank, vinyl
purse, USA, 1990s

52,
Mug, Official *Viz*
Merchandising,
House of Viz/John
Brown Publishing,
England, 1991

53
World Cup Willie,
England soccer team
merchandise, 1966

54,
Glass coaster
with hand painted
Aboriginal design,
Australia, 1940s

55
Unknown artist,
Velvet painting of
an Aboriginal man,
Australia, 1960s

56
Poodle design
playing cards, USA,
1950s

50

51

52

53

54

55

56

TECHNOLOGY

TO MEET THE GROWING NEED FOR
RECORD PLAYERS...THE DECCA COMPANY
PRODUCED IN 1949 THE DECCALION.
THIS WAS DESIGNED BY HARVEY SCHWARTZ
WHO HAD EARLIER DESIGNED THE DECCA
NAVIGATOR SYSTEM, AN EARLY FORM
OF RADAR USED IN THE NORMANDY
LANDINGS OF 1944.

RICHARD CAMBERLAIN AND GEOFFREY RAYNER, **DOMESTIC EQUIPMENT
AND PRODUCT DESIGN** 2001

THE RETRO PERIOD PROBABLY introduced more technologies, and variations on each one, than any other fifty-year period of human history. It is therefore difficult to choose which objects to include here. One could search the numerous top ten lists for design, cars and so on. These are interesting in that they tend to reflect popular taste (as does retro collecting generally) rather than design excellence per se, or the 'best' technology. So, for cars, lists commonly place the Model T Ford as number one for the twentieth century, closely followed by the Mini (the retro number one, therefore) followed by the Volkswagen Beetle, the Citroen DS and the Porsche 911. One has some sympathy with such lists. However, the 'best ofs' do not necessarily reflect the range of designs and products that were sold or succeeded in making their presence felt as iconic of their period, and it is this that has really been a guiding principle here, if not an absolute criterion.

The retro period is, if anything, quirky and fond of whimsy and flights of fancy. The romantic age bequeathed a strong love of *imagination* as the mother of invention and progress (and not merely function and use value). If it were not for imagination as a really important element of retro culture, we would surely never have had BMX bikes or Swatches, surfboards or tea diffusers that look like farmyard ducks. Nor would we have such iconic objects as Daleks from the mid-1960s.

Some things really do have to be included because of their undisputed brilliance of design, although how to define that is difficult. Some designers, like Dieter Rams, seemed to get it right every time and he certainly offered a description of what good design is. But if it were that simple, then everyone would be a brilliant designer and they are just not. Many designers merely followed those who could do it, like Rams. Sony's brilliant cylinder-shaped radio may not have copied Rams but it certainly followed the trend for this kind of shape and simplicity of design and switching.

Dieter Rams could turn his hand to anything – a radiogram, a shelving system, a table lighter or a coffee mill – and it came out beautifully every time. Some people got it right once and had to make do with that. Some say that great designs never cease to be loved. The Model T Ford seems to support that, and even more extraordinary is the design life of some things such as the Porsche 911, the Mini, the Bialetti espresso maker or Dieter Rams's shelving system (606 universal

1

2

5

6

3

7

8

shelving system for Vitsoe) or even his LE1 audio speaker for Braun (1960) that is acknowledged as the design inspiration for the Macintosh range of desk computers in the 2010s. That really is design longevity.

It is very difficult to choose a typical 1950s automobile since they include some at the beginning that were still influenced by the 1930s, and at the end of course we have the Mini. In between, there was a period in the USA of the huge-finned shiny monsters associated so much with this period. The Pontiac and Ford pictured, together capture the automotive spirit of these times. Built on a grand scale with an emphasis on extreme luxury and flashiness, they were not particularly fast or racy since they needed to be so heavy and lumbering. What they were very good at was getting attention and creating envy. How many people can look at the Pontiac shown here and not feel a twinge of envy?

To my mind, none of them can compare with the European cars that began to be produced during the 1950s and especially into the 1960s. The Mini Cooper is a classic example of an affordable car that was both stylish, fast, a great drive and efficient at cornering (which you do more in Europe than America, perhaps). The ultimate car of the 1960s, for me, was the Aston Martin DB5 that evolved out of an initial design for the DB4 by Touring of Milan

and that was only pipped by Ian Callum's incredible design for the DB7 in 1993. In 1967 urban style was possible on every budget and youth budgets stretched to another of the great designs of the twentieth century, the Vespa and the Lambretta scooters from Italy. Originally born of postwar austerity, the idea being to get Italy moving again (even if it was a bit underpowered and creaky), these

design legends evolved into the last word in urban chic and the centrepiece of the most successful and creative of the retro youth cultures, the Mods.

Not everyone was in the market for an Aston but many still wanted speed and racing performance. This came to a more affluent 1970s market in the form of the muscle car; a form the Australians specialised in and encouraged through their Bathurst racing tradition.

11

Televisions

In many ways, television defines
and forms the retro period. If the
radio allowed information and some
entertainment to reach the everyday
lives of most people, then TV extended
that and added theatre and spectacle.
If radio was more like literature and
records, TV was more like tourism:
it could place people in the thick of
things, and give them the impression of
a multitude of realities and events they
might never have experienced directly.

Vision became essential to a
world that became more and more
accessible through travel and tourism,
and television extended this idea into
politics, current affairs, international
and national events, sport, and theatre.
A mix of many of these things became,
for almost everyone, a daily fix that
extended significantly in terms of time
and coverage as each decade passed.
The television permitted us to follow
our own history in a way humans in the
past could not imagine, especially as
networks such as the BBC extended
their coverage into every corner of
the world. It is not surprising that we
experienced it emotionally, even if Elvis

12

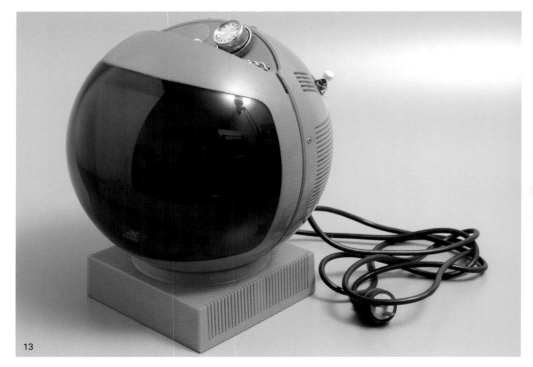

13

16

Presley was taking things a little far by shooting one.

Not surprisingly, the television became a social centre of western lives, not merely because it connected people nationally and internationally, but because it reorganised domestic space and family life. Throughout the 1950s to the 1980s, most households only possessed one TV and so watching it became a *social* ritual, of shared experience and time together and a negotiated program of viewing. The focus of this new way of life was the television set, and this meant seating and furnishing platforms needed to be lowered. Increasingly, TV sets became pieces of furniture, as with the Baird 727.

Through the first three decades of television, its shape and format was relatively standardised compared to what came later. Portable TVs arrived by the late 1960s, although most portables were less often moved about than moved into new spaces such as the kitchen and the bedroom. Clearly it was their small size that fitted them for this purpose rather than their portability.

In the 1970s the advent of colour extended television's transmission and consumer base and, as competition grew and as the TV markets diversified into different youth, age and lifestyle groups, so television designers created radically different housing – such as JVC's space-age model, the 'VideoSphere 3240' from 1970. Like a lot of designs at this time, including a Pucci hat for a flight attendant's uniform, this took its inspiration from the astronauts' space helmets from the Apollo moon missions.

Radios

Radio was by no means obsolete but in its case portability became almost essential. During the retro years valve technology gave way to transistors, which made radios considerably lighter and smaller – and thus readily portable. Beginning with pirate pop stations, it was through the free-to-air technology of radio that popular music became a youth phenomenon in the 1960s and 1970s. Radio was responsible for one

15

11
AWA model 'P4' 17-inch portable black and white television, designed by William F. Moody, manufactured by Amalgamated Wireless (Australasia) Ltd (AWA), Sydney, Australia, 1969 Powerhouse Museum collection

12
Baird '727' television, UK, c. 1965–70, Powerhouse Museum collection

13
JVC 'VideoSphere' model 3240 television, designed and made by Victor Company of Japan Ltd (JVC), Yokohama, Japan, c. 1970 Powerhouse Museum collection

14
Murphy 'A122' radio receiver, manufactured by Murphy Radio, England, 1947

15
AWA 'B320' 2-band alarm clock radio, Hong Kong, 1970s

16
Vega transistor radio, Soviet Union, c. 1970

SHARP GF-777Z PORTABLE STEREO CASSETTE AND RADIO PLAYER

CAMPBELL BICKERSTAFF = CURATOR, SCIENCE AND INDUSTRY, POWERHOUSE MUSEUM

The 'ghetto blaster', also known as a 'boombox', evolved as a consumer product in the late 1970s; its golden age arbitrarily framed around 1981–85. This particular player is regarded by the boombox cognoscente as the 'holy grail of boomboxes'; an accolade that may be attributed to its size – 752 mm wide x 379 mm high x 166 mm deep; weight – 12.2 kg (not including the required ten D-size batteries); amplification power factor – 90W with four amplifiers driving six speakers; and dual cassette drives. Its image also features on the reverse of Run DMC's debut album.

Two distinct types of portable music devices were used in the 1980s: the 'Walkman' and the boombox. The two were used in very different ways – the 'Walkman' as an extension of the user's private space, and the boombox for performance in public spaces. This factor in the boombox's appeal was driven by the communal nature of the places it was used, outside the confines of the home, where the type of music played, and volume level, may have been prohibited.

The ghetto blaster was used to play mix tapes or records (through a dedicated phono input) quite loudly, so that a small gathering could be entertained. The music was sometimes accompanied by rapping (through a mixed microphone input with built-in echo effect). This form of entertainment may in turn have been augmented with highly stylised street dancing or 'breaking' – a form of movement that borrowed and reciprocated extensively from popular culture performers.

Boomboxes of this calibre are presently undergoing a renaissance, with private collectors recognising them as a cultural relic of particular power from the 1980s. The museum was lucky enough to snap one up for its collection and put it on display in *The 80s are Back*, a recent exhibition exploring Australian life and popular culture in the 1980s.

Commonly referred to as a 'boombox' or 'ghetto blaster', the latter referring to the geographical epicentre of its popular use and a colourful reference to its musical amplification factor. It was also known to many in a more satirical or endearing frame as the 'Bronx briefcase'
Powerhouse Museum collection

17

18

17
Fleetwood globe
radio, USA, 1960

18
Citizen alarm radio,
Japan, c. 1976

19
Sony TR – 1829
transistor radio,
Japan, 1967

of the preconditions for the emergence, spread and commercial power of youth cultures. The increased affluence of this demographic meant that they drove a considerable design evolution in radios. Through FM broadcasting and receiving technologies, sound quality improved dramatically, leading to stereo FM by the 1980s.

Scaling down became an obsession for the designers of teenage 'transistors', with Sony and Panasonic driving the size down while maintaining build and sound quality. In addition, radios were designed with niche markets in mind – they became gendered as well as age targeted. By the 1980s the so-called ghetto blaster was developed, with some racial

groups in mind. In the 1970s alarm radios more or less undermined the role of alarm clocks in the bedroom, and again, there was a very specific bedside design to fit the purpose – back-lit, jump-hour alarm radios appeared first, followed by new LED and LCD displays that could provide low light displays during the sleeping hours. The end of the tyranny of the constant tick-tocking and jarring mechanical alarms was received with a collective sigh of relief. This is why I know of no retro collector who has replaced his or her alarm radio with a retro mechanical alarm clock. These days, they are more likely to find an 'early model' such as the bright orange Citizen from the 1970s.

19

20

Lighting

In the retro years lighting left its place as the shaded bulb on a hanging holder, to become something completely different. Once freed from hanging around on ceilings or casting low light satisfaction from standard lamps, lighting became an experimental field for designers. A few examples will suffice to show how wide-ranging it became.

Mention must be made of the TV lamp (see item 22, page 15 and also page 132) which was something of a white elephant. It was claimed that for successful TV viewing people needed more light around the set itself. Actually, we didn't, but we liked the TV lamp anyway, precisely because it was so new and so jazzy; especially the ones made of anodised aluminium cast in strange space-age shapes.

The French and the Italians in particular experimented with lighting in a way that made other nationalities appear conservative. Lighting could be mounted from any hollow sculptural form and thus many new designs along the lines of the 'Gherpe' lamp, designed by the Italian company Superstudio, came onto the market in the 1960s. One of the more interesting was the 'Pillola' lamp by Casati and Ponzio for Ponteur, Italy in 1968 (see page 158). Here was that old postmodern design trick, to take a functional object and give it an entirely different, ironic function.

21

22

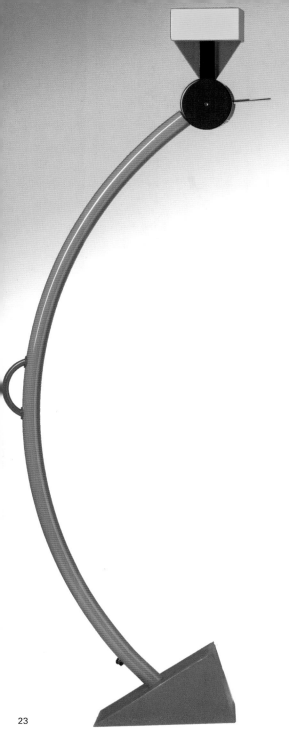

24

Classic Danish lighting design was the dominant look of this period, owing to Denmark's very successful export industries and efficient manufacturing. Poul Henningsen's designs such as his 'Artichoke', 'Kontrast' and 'Stammekrone' are standouts in this tradition, and many of his designs are still being manufactured today.

It would be very predictable of me to mention and describe the arrival of the 'Anglepoise' lamp. It regularly appears on lists of the top designs of the twentieth century, and rightly so, but the surprise is that George Carwardine's brilliant design was launched in *1934* and that it once advertised itself as 'the ideal light for the blackouts' (during the German blitz of British cities). So, though it has the look of retro technology, and though it was ahead of its time, it is not strictly speaking in the retro period. However,

it did spur even more innovation along similar lines in the period at hand, not least in the floor-standing versions beloved by draughtspersons and architects. In the hands of Marc Newson or Ettore Sottsass, floor lighting and sculpture became as one. The 'Tree Tops' design by Ettore Sottsass in 1981 has become a Memphis design classic; it is so simple: the base is a wedge-shaped chunk of cast metal, giving it the strong triangular shape so favoured by Memphis designers. This is then connected by a bright orange tube to a cluster of red triangles with a yellow and a black rectangular block and a blue circle that comprise the light unit itself. It has the distinct poise of a 'being' that seems to be looking your way, somewhat menacingly. This is merely because the shapes of the light housing provide, in the most abstract sense, the key features of a human face and head.

23

20
Richard Stevens and Peter Rodd, light fitting from the Chelsea Range for Atlas Lighting (subsidiary of Thorn Lighting of London), with glass shade by James Powell and Son (Whitefriars Glass), England, 1958

21
'PH Kontrast' ceiling light by Poul Henningsen for Louis Poulsen, Denmark, 1958–62
Vampt Vintage Designs

22
'Gherpe' table lamp, designed by Superstudio, made by Poltronova, Italy, 1967 Powerhouse Museum collection

23
'Tree Tops' floor lamp, designed by Ettore Sottsass, Italy, 1981, made by Memphis, Italy, 1981–86
Powerhouse Museum collection

24
'Stammekrone' ceiling light by Poul Henningsen for Louis Poulsen, Denmark, c. 1960
Vampt Vintage Designs

Audio

During the postwar period there was something of a sound revolution. Stereophonic sound systems appeared in large numbers through the 1960s and 1970s, and during their novelty phase became the focus for something of a men's cult. It was men who would spend inordinate sums of money on this very hi-tech equipment, it was they who championed the buying of large collections of music to play on it and it was largely they who tended to bore polite society with their ramblings on this favourite subject when all around would rather get back to gossip, fashion and life in general. I know

because I was just such a man and I felt the bitter chill of boredom around me as I was cranking up the sound to levels that killed conversation. Maybe I overemphasise the gendered nature of audio, but I also worked in a stereo shop for several years while in my last years of grammar school, so I know who bought this stuff and who stood around looking bored.

Music wasn't merely music to the stereo/hi-fi generations. It was an important expression of their values, politics and aspirations. It also connected them to the bands they saw live, the experiences of which were probably the most exciting of their lives. No wonder then that they

wanted to recreate that sound energy in their own living rooms or bedrooms, or, increasingly, their studies as they were abandoned to it by their female partners. This is why everything about the hi-fi design world, its technical names, its equipment, its architecture and presentation (with wires showing everywhere) has very little femininity or feminine appeal built into it. Rather, it is the personification of middle class masculinity in the mid-century. It is not only deliberately technical but it is an undressed form of technical, without, say, the cowling that makes the line of the Vespa scooter appealing to women.

The exception to these general remarks about hi-fi design is the less technically specified market in radiograms, which was more of a family, and thus feminised, domain. The star turn here is the 'Phonosuper', yet another design by Dieter Rams for Braun, dubbed 'Snow White's Coffin' owing to its pretty white housing and clear lid.

25

26

25
Yamaha 'TC 800D' stereo cassette deck, designed by Mario Bellini, manufactured by Yamaha, Nippon Gakki Co. Ltd, Hamamatsu, Japan, 1976, Powerhouse Museum collection

26
Sanyo hi-fi system, Japan, 1975

THE BRAUN SK4 'PHONOSUPER'

PAUL DONNELLY = CURATOR, DESIGN AND SOCIETY, POWERHOUSE MUSEUM

Braun 'Phonosuper' radiogram and record player combination, Braun A G, West Germany, 1956–60
Powerhouse Museum collection

The Braun SK4 'Phonosuper' radio record player combination, designed in 1956, represents a giant leap in design philosophy; born of the belief that new and increasingly miniaturised technology requires a correspondingly fresh form and functionality.

Braun's celebrated design-based corporate success story has been referred to as the 'Braun-Ulm symbiosis'.[1] In the early 1950s, Artur and Erwin Braun took over their father's company and, in a decision to broaden the company's product range, aligned themselves with the Ulm Academy of Art and Design (HfG/ Hoschschule für Gestaltung). The designers of the SK4, Ulm lecturer Hans Gugelot (1920–65) and devotee Dieter Rams (born 1932) pursued the functionalist ideals held at the academy, which had originated from the pre-war Bauhaus and was nurtured outside of Germany during the Second World War.

The functionalists valued honesty of materials and longevity of design, with the ultimate goal of creating products that were useful yet unobtrusive. Accordingly, the SK4 was designed to be only as large as necessary for its components and function, and was made of simple materials with no ornamentation and minimum controls. The SK4's perspex cover became the industry standard but was so startlingly new in 1957 that it acquired the moniker 'Snow White's Coffin'.

Rams was chief designer at Braun from 1962 to 1995, during which time the company became a world leader in product design. Today, the SK4 and other seminal Rams designs are extremely collectible, representing pivotal moments in the history of design. In this post–post modernist world, Dieter Rams enjoys renewed recognition among a new generation of designers, notably Jonathan Ive at Apple.[2]

Other sumptuous radiograms were designed by the Castiglioni brothers for Brionvega, Italy (see page 12); and clearly these were high-end products which had much larger numbers of lesser designs below them in the audio sections of department stores. Here were the largely teak-encased products from Grundig, Decca, HMV, Philips and GEC, most of them seeking to retain their historic market share built up from the golden years when radio sets were thought of as items of furniture. This was not going to last and in the end a hybrid, simplified and packaged version of hi-fi separates came to dominate the market. Some of these were marketed as music centres, largely one suspects to sell to the family market, while others offered themselves as stereo systems, a cheaper alternative for men.

While significant commercially, cassette tape recorders never quite matched the audio capabilities of the proper reel-to-reel tape recorders, although the Yamaha TC 800D came close. Mostly, cassette recorders and even the larger eight-track formats were a disappointment. They also allowed a massive, though illegal, copying of music that undermined the vibrant quality of the popular music business. This is something computing and the internet have compounded.

The biggest breakthrough was the Sony 'Walkman', which was designed in 1978, first marketed in 1979 and took off significantly in the 1980s. It was originally designed by Nobutoshi Kihara for Sony's co-chairman Akio Morita, to allow him to listen to opera on long-haul flights.

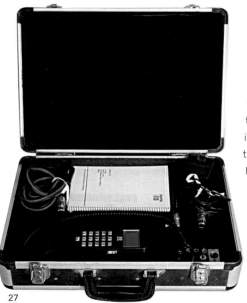

27

28

Telephones

While an old technology, the telephone has made several important transitions in its progress to mobile/internet telephony. Postwar demands for more colour and panache saw the arrival of the 'Ericofon' in 1954, although originally it was marketed especially for hospitals in order to give patients lying down greater ease of dialling and use. It struggled to break into the heavily protected US market but eventually found a way in for its eighteen different coloured phones. At one time it was so popular that demand outstripped supply by 500 per cent, something that rarely ever happens. But this ought not to surprise us in retrospect, since we now know that it was a rare and beautiful exception to a largely unchanging and conservative market, even though it had a major design fault: it cut a caller off if it was placed back on its base.

The 'Ericofon' is comparatively rare for collectors, and prices are very high and climbing still. Naturally, Ericsson has released an updated version of this phone.

29

27
Mobile radio-telephone with cables and instruction manual, designed and manufactured by NovAtel Communications Ltd, Canada, 1985, briefcase installation design by Allan Electronics (Aust) Pty Ltd, Australia, 1986 Powerhouse Museum collection

28
Sony 'Walkman', Japan, c. 1984 Powerhouse Museum collection

29
Ericsson 'Ericofon' telephone, designed by Gosta Thames, manufactured by L.M. Ericsson, Sweden, 1958–65

THE SAFNAT TELEPHONE, 1958

CAMPBELL BICKERSTAFF = CURATOR, SCIENCE AND INDUSTRY, POWERHOUSE MUSEUM

'SAFNAT 2+7' telephone, designed by Marcello Nizzoli, made by SAFNAT, Italy, **1958** Powerhouse Museum collection

The 'SAFNAT' telephone, with its cellulose acetate housing, low-slung stature and anthropomorphic arrangement of dial and buttons, clearly reflects the designer Marcello Nizzoli's attitude and methods. Nizzoli rejected the accepted theories of machine design of the time – 'form follows function' – for a tendency towards sculptural forms and organic shapes.

Nizzoli was a graduate of the Accademia di Belle Arti of Parma (1913) and his subsequent involvement in various avant-garde movements, as well as his success as a graphic artist, painter, fashion-accessory designer, architect, industrial designer and exhibition arch-itect, demonstrate the adeptness and adaptability of his design ideas and methods.

Nizzoli went on to design for Olivetti from the mid 1930s to the late 1950s. His award-winning work was recognised by the Italian design establishment as the epitome of Italian functionalist design. This school of thought sought to widen the role of industrial design within companies to encompass all aspects of product development, from concept onwards, to strive towards the achievement of a design devoid of ornament and to produce items for mass consumption. It was within this framework that Nizzoli very successfully combined industrial design and the plastic arts to create new designs for existing office and domestic products.

Nizzoli's work for Olivetti received recognition early on from New York's Museum of Modern Art (Nizzoli's 'Lettera 22' and 'Lexikon 80' typewriters have resided in the permanent collection of the MoMA since 1952); the inaugural Golden Compass award of 1954 in Italy; and in 1959 a jury of 100 designers formed by the Illinois Technology Institute chose Nizzoli's 'Lettera 22' as the first of the 100 best design products of the previous 100 years. Although deserving, the 'SAFNAT' telephone has not registered on the institutional collectors' radar and remains valued by a small group who appreciate Nizzoli's output.

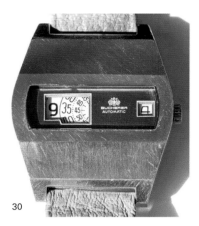

30

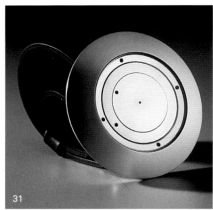

31

32

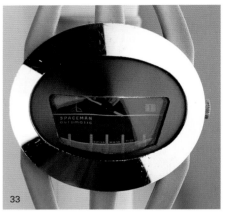

33

34

35

36

37

38

39

40

41

42

43

Watches

It is a topic of some speculation in the twenty-first century as to whether the watch will continue or become obsolete. Young mobile phone uses have never had the need for a watch and are out of the habit of using them. On the other hand, it is still the case that expensive and exotically engineered automatics are still highly prized by the most affluent among us – as any glossy magazine will testify. The reason for this is that compared to women, western men have few decorative elements to suggest their status and identity. While suits tend to standardise more than distinguish; shoes, cufflinks and watches permit the display of affluence and taste – and, apparently, these are closely, but discretely, inspected by others.

For a brief while back in the early 1970s, the grand mechanical automatics were in crisis when the executive class began to buy the expensive first-generation LED (light emitting diode display) digital watches. The 1974 Microma watch pictured dates back to this period and would have cost the price of a new car when it first came out. This Microma watch was the first product to integrate a complete electronic system chip, called a system-on-chip or SOC. Back in 1972 this watchmaking company had been bought by Intel, since digital watches were regarded as high-tech marvels

44

45

and sold for over \$200. The 1974 Microma featured a single Intel 5810 CMOS chip and in an area of less than 0.086 cm^2, over 1000 transistors translated the precise oscillations of the quartz crystal into a digital read-out. Fittingly of course, the rest of this watch was made with aerospace-precision engineering. Excessively rare, this watch would be worth a small fortune if only it worked, but it is still worth a lot to me as a piece of history. One day down the track I might see if there is a company that can restore it.

For now though, the high status of contemporary mechanical automatics means that there is an inevitable interest in their design pedigree and indeed, many of the vintage models are still good timekeepers and marvels of engineering. This is certainly true of Jaeger-LeCoultre watches. One of the first watches to feature a TV-shaped face, it was also a breakthrough in terms of its thinness in 1965.

In design terms, the 'Museum Watch', designed by Nathan George Horwitt, is interesting because while it looks as though it might be a very recent design it was actually designed in 1947, many years ahead of its time.

In the 1960s, and partly in response to the pop art phase of design, new jump-hour watches appeared, to give the watch a face-lift. These digital watches were not much in the way of a revolution, being

30
Bucherer jump-hour automatic watch, Switzerland, c. 1968

31
'Large Pod' watch, Marc Newson, Australia, 1986

32
Rado 'Diastar' automatic watch, Switzerland, c. 1976

33
Andre Le Marquand 'Spaceman' automatic watch, Switzerland, c. 1967

34
Microma first generation LED digital watch, USA, 1974

35
Basis manual wind watch, Switzerland, c. 1970s

36
Seiko divers watch, Japan, 1978

37
Swatch Watch with Native North American Indian design, Switzerland, 1988

38
Pulsar-Spoon digital watch, USA/Japan, c. 1998

39
Pulsar-Spoon digital watch, USA/Japan, c. 2006

40
Jaeger-LeCoultre manual gold watch, Switzerland, c. 1965

41
Timex automatic watch, England, c. 1960

42
Tressa automatic watch, Switzerland, c. 1974

43
Skagen Aktiv watch, Denmark, c.1990

44
Movado 'Museum' watch for Zenith, Switzerland, 1948

45
Swatch Watch with peace/smiley/flowerpower design, Switzerland, 1992

TWO 1960s CLOCKS
DEBBIE RUDDER = CURATOR, SCIENCE AND INDUSTRY, POWERHOUSE MUSEUM

The Powerhouse Museum purchased these two clocks new in 1969. They are now being considered for display in the proposed *Energy* gallery, because one is powered by a solar cell and the other by small changes in atmospheric conditions. The idea of using such distributed sources of renewable energy is of vital interest today.

An old, hand-written display label about the Patek Philippe clock explains that its solar cell charges a battery, which drives a 'micro-motor specially constructed of corrosion-resistant precious metal alloys', which winds the 'extremely sensitive though robust 29-jewelled movement'. The unwritten subtext is that this is a thoroughly modern clock, made to the exacting standards traditionally associated with the Swiss clock industry.

The Jaeger-LeCoultre clock,

dubbed the 'Atmos', is even more ingenious and built to even more exacting standards. It contains a small capsule of a gas that expands and contracts as atmospheric temperature or pressure changes; this small movement is sufficient to wind the mainspring, as all the clock's parts are made with low friction and accurate balance in mind.

When the museum acquired the Powerhouse site and developed a series of exhibitions to open in 1988, the clocks were considered for display in our hands-on science exhibition, *Experimentations*. They did not make the final cut and have since languished on their basement shelf. But much has changed since 1988: even if they miss the cut again, the clocks can be seen by anyone at any time, online with most of the other objects in our collection.

The brass and teak veneer Patek Philippe 'light energy' clock and the brass and glass Jaeger-LeCoultre 'Atmos' clock are both very desirable timepieces. Atmos clocks were first made in 1929 and are still being made today; a series of design changes over that time makes older versions very collectible
Powerhouse Museum collection

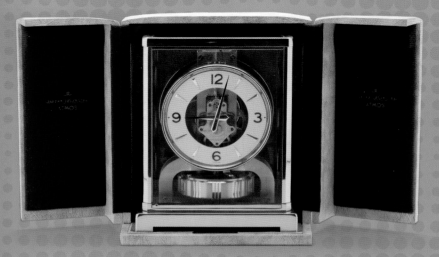

46
Smiths CL39 'Torre'
pendulum kitchen
wall clock, designer
unknown, UK,
1952–61

47
Kienzle automatic
electric kitchen clock,
c.1961

48
Kaiser transparent
mantle clock, West
Germany, 1958

49
Junghans Repetition
alarm clock, designer
unknown, Germany,
1958

50
Junghans Silentic
Trivox alarm clock,
designer unknown,
Germany, 1962

51
Junghans Silentic
Bivox alarm clock,
designer unknown,
Germany, 1958

52

still based on existing mechanical movements, but the new watch face, achieved by innovating three revolving discs, was a success and sold well until the true digital technology came on line in the 1970s. The Bucherer was among the finest of these.

Throughout the retro period, watches had been very conservative and largely unchanging until the digital age, when the cheaper-to-produce and more reliable LCD displays were made in massive quantities and began to displace all mechanical makes, apart from the very top end. But even there the claims to greatest accuracy that justified their premium price could no longer bear scrutiny against the cheap Japanese digitals. In the 1970s when digital technology vied with the rather conservative Swiss-dominated industry, the Swiss response was to improve and update their designs. Companies such as Rado were fresh and new and especially popular in the

Middle Eastern markets. Tressa was another sought-after brand. Then there were other product launches such as Andre Le Marquand's 'Spaceman' watch in 1972. This was a watch for David Bowie, and immediately had a following. However, sales generally continued to decline and it was not until Swatch was launched in 1983 that the Swiss industry got back on its feet.

Swatch has been incredibly successful at producing low-cost designer pieces and still holds a massive market share, partly through buying out many of the remaining Swiss elite brands.

Instead of trying to compete with the digital technology (which was presented in a dry, technical manner) Swatch decided that watches could be ironic, fun works of art. So, one idea was to repackage the classical-looking mechanical timepieces in plastic, give them a contemporary designer look and make them every bit as accurate as their boring-looking rivals. The second great

idea was to challenge established watch-wearing habits by suggesting that we all have several watches, to suit our mood, clothing or whim. The name Swatch is actually a contraction of 'second watch'.

Swatch was launched in 1983 and the marketing for it was spectacular. Very quickly they were putting out new designs in a wide range of single block colours, including the defining primary colours of the decade, but also moodier, quirkier and crazier, rock'n'roll patterns. All this aligned them nicely with the fashion and art worlds.

Swatch was also important in sociological and cultural terms. It was a major influence on that '80s' revolution where individual forms of self-expression became more important and standardised forms of consumption, product design and production became more flexible. Swatch was among the first to release small numbers of a single design, to aim designs at specific markets and to release large numbers of new designs to keep pace with fashion and events. Swatches have thus become one of the most vibrant collectables in history. They have made around 100 million of them but many are rare and sought after.

53

Computing and office technologies

The office and its technologies, as seen in the TV show *Madmen*, were to be completely transformed by digital technology. Some design top-twenties place the elegant Olivetti 'Lettera' typewriter among the giants and I can never pass one without a flutter of the heart. Ettore Sottsass's masterful 'Valentine' typewriter design for Olivetti is another stroke of genius. I find the complete wipe-out of typewriters by computers quite a sad story. One has to admire them; their story is tragic, but their bodies, like beached whales, no longer give the thrill they did when they were alive and well. So for me the typewriter is, paradoxically, less interesting and compelling now than the first generation of displaced computers. While equally washed-up, they still have that quality of being pioneers and prototypes. This is why I have included the Mac Plus and the iMac in my own collection – and I have three of the latter sitting opposite me as I write (a blue, a red and a neutral coloured one).

I can remember the arrival of the Mac Plus and its astonishing desktop publishing capabilities when I still struggled daily with the awkward first generation PCs. When I changed jobs in 1991, I also moved into a Macintosh environment and I immediately took renewed pleasure in my work. It's like driving a great car; it's a pleasure in its own right. Macintosh re-awakened many of the thrills associated with entirely new technologies that really make an improvement to life; and through their iPod and iPad this knack of theirs carries on. The Macintosh take on computing was to humanise the potentially alienating technology, and to make it part of our cyborg being – an extension of ourselves rather than a new techno-master

52
Watches are, L–R Pulsar Spoon space age LED watch, Japan/USA, c.1990; Seiko M154 4019 LCD watch, Japan c.1977; Seiko UC2000 Japan, 1984; Pulsar LCD Alarm Chronograph Y486 4030, Japan, 1982; Unknown brand, early LED watch, c.1974, Switzerland; Seiko Sports 100 1982, Japan; Micronta Quartz Chrono-Alarm, custom made in Hong Kong for Radio Shack, USA, c. 1980

53
Pulsar LCD Alarm Chronograph Y486 4030, Japan, 1982

54
Olivetti 'Lettera 22' typewriter, designed by Marcello Nizzoli and Giuseppe Beccio, Italy, 1950, made by Olivetti, Glasgow, Scotland, 1961 Powerhouse Museum collection

54

as the old factory machines once were. I typed this book with a MacBook Air. I have never loved a machine more than this one and was so glad I fought prejudices about computing power and storage capability when I wrestled with cheaper, more powerful and heavier alternatives. But this machine demonstrates to me the importance of combining a machine for the purpose with the pleasure of working with something that is both beautiful and sympathetic. This is the combination of elements that Dieter Rams always got right too.

55

55
Ettore Sottsass
'Valentine'
typewriter, Olivetti,
Glasgow, Scotland,
1976

Photography

The visual image and its reproducibility is yet another defining feature of the retro period. Never before have we been able to produce photographic images of our own and at the same time be subject to the bombardment of the images of others, as in this period. At the beginning of the period, photography was expensive and undertaken only occasionally by some and not at all by others. Just sixty years later, it is difficult to possess a phone or computing device that does not produce photographic images very easily and affordably. Regular photography produces a lasting trail of narration about a life or a family, organisation or locality, and over the retro period there has been a growing sense of documentation and narration of everyday life.

The growth of photography owes something to the growing individualism of the late twentieth century. The more a society individualises, the more individuals value their own personal lives, the events they were a part of and the story of their developing careers and life histories. All of this places greater value on recording themselves more frequently and perhaps on more and more occasions.

In the 1940s photos might only have been taken at weddings and on holidays but by the 1970s photos might have been taken during sporting competitions, outings in the car, school events, community events, hens nights, office parties, graduations and so on. New photographic technology is partly the result of greater demands for it, but equally it makes more photography a possible thing to desire.

Box cameras were widely available before the Second World War but their quality was fairly poor and the costs of film and developing were expensive. The arrival of the 'Brownie 127' changed everything because this was a camera that was easy to use but which also produced high quality photos. As millions of these sold, the demand for more photos created greater capacity and reduced unit costs, thus leading to new photographic habits. The 'Brownie 127' had a special look and feel. It had stylish art deco lines and felt modern and up-to-date. Flash units could be bought for them, thus extending photography into the night-time, leading to the recording of hitherto unrecorded aspects of everyday culture.

The instant camera first produced as the 'Land' camera, after its inventor Edwin Land, arrived in 1947 but it was not until the 1960s with the Polaroid camera that instant cameras could produce colour photographs. By the late 1970s the technology had improved and they became the fastest selling cameras of any type. However, while the immediate results had great appeal, the key demand was for quality photography and high quality lenses; and single lens reflex cameras gradually came down

first semi-professional quality camera to be offered to a mass market and prefigured the arrival of cheap digital photography in the 2000s.

The technology of the retro period thus revolutionised modern life immeasurably. In the affluent west, most people acquired personal transport; entertainment systems for their homes; fast, cheap and efficient telephone and internet communication, as well as a machine that could replace all office functions and permit its owners to be publishers and to participate in public discussions and debates around the world. They could create, reproduce and share perfect images with great ease. This fifty-year period changed human life and the planet we live on more than at any time in human history and the objects and technologies that made this possible will be remembered for this very reason.

in price. As a halfway stage in this long development, special mention must be reserved for Pentax's hit camera, the 'Auto 110'. Released in 1978, it sold as a system with three lenses, a flash unit and carrying case and thus became a complete photographic toolbox. It was easy to master, it had excellent lenses and was relatively cheap to use. It was also light to carry and enrolled several prominent professional photographers as supporters. Arguably, it was the

56
'Brownie 127' camera by Kodak, England, 1952

57
Pentax 'Auto 110' single lens reflex camera that used the 110 film cartridge. The only complete ultra-miniature SLR System for the 110 film format. Japan, 1978

RETRO REISSUED

NOT ONLY HAS THERE NEVER BEFORE BEEN A SOCIETY SO OBSESSED WITH ITS OWN IMMEDIATE PAST, BUT THERE HAS NEVER BEEN A SOCIETY THAT IS ABLE TO ACCESS THE IMMEDIATE PAST SO EASILY AND SO COPIOUSLY.

SIMON REYNOLDS, RETROMANIA 2011:XXI

CONTEMPORARY DESIGN STORES, fashion boutiques, kitchenware chains and giftware shops have become spellbound by the retro era. Many new designs take inspiration from retro colour palettes, retro shapes and retro patterns; and indeed many of the famous designs have been reissued – in even greater numbers than they were initially. This is astonishing.

Clearly, insufficient items from the original period survived, or at least, not enough have made their way back into the market to satisfy the incredibly escalating demand that has developed since the 1980s. At different times, prices on many of these designs have reached epic proportions. Examples include Whitefriars 'Banjo' vases by Geoffrey Baxter, aluminium designs by Russel Wright, furniture by Charles and Ray Eames and robots by Horikawa. Many companies had folded way before their star designs reached their new retro audience (Whitefriars Glass, Midwinter Pottery and many Czech glass manufacturers of the Sklo Union all disappeared in the 1980s) and were unable to cash in on the bonanza in the way Cassina, Vitra, Iitalla, Erickson, Kartell, Herman Miller and Robert Welch could.

Many, such as Herman Miller, had never stopped producing their most timeless pieces by Charles and Ray Eames but they probably never imagined the magnitude of the sudden *retro* demand for their products from the 1940s and 1950s. In their current on-line catalogue, Herman Miller asks you to consider:

> Who's coming to dinner? How about inviting the masters of modern design – George Nelson, Charles and Ray Eames, Alexander Girard, Isamu Noguchi? Or extend the invitation to younger designers – Mark Goetz, Sam Hecht and Kim Colin, Ayako Takase and Cutter Hutton. Whatever your choice, know that these designs for dining are as alluring as fine food and good conversation.

And even if you were to run with something new, like a Mark Goetz sofa perhaps, there is something reassuringly *retroid* about its design features. Not a copy or even a resemblance, but the inspiration from the mid-twentieth century is undeniable (see page 245).

Alongside continuing manufacturers like Herman Miller, a new form of design retailer has emerged that has been responsible, in no small measure, for propelling retro design into the mainstream of interior fashion. I can remember a

ARNE JACOBSEN'S 'CYLINDA LINE' FOR STELTON

EVA CZERNIS-RYL = CURATOR, DESIGN AND SOCIETY, POWERHOUSE MUSEUM

'Cylinda line' teapot and coffeepot in polished 18/8 stainless steel and thermoset plastic, designed by Arne Jacobsen in 1964 for Stelton, Copenhagen, Denmark, made in 1990 Powerhouse Museum collection

The 'Cylinda line' was Scandinavia's first tea and coffee service designed for the home, directly for production in stainless steel. It has also been the most revisited 1960s tableware – by its maker, users and collectors – in any material, over the last four decades.

Cylinda was created in 1964 when the Danish architect and designer Arne Jacobsen sketched some cylindrical shapes on a napkin for Peter Holmblad, export manager, and later owner, at Stelton. It took Stelton three years to develop the technology to produce Cylinda's seamless cylindrical forms in stainless steel. The original Cylinda series, released in 1967, consisted of seventeen items, including jugs, bowls and an ice bucket.

Cylinda's neo-functionalist, yet sensuous design was awarded one of two 1967 ID prizes by the Danish Society of Industrial Designers. An award from the American Institute of Interior Designers followed in 1968, and it wasn't long until Cylinda was acquired into museum collections, beginning with the Museum of Modern Art in New York.

Holmblad continued to add items to the original Cylinda group following Jacobsen's death in 1971.

A photograph of the items lined up like a cityscape is seen as iconic, and one of the most recognised images in design books. In 2004 the Cylinda coffeepot featured in two films: the science fiction film *I, Robot* and *Alfie*, alongside other Cylinda items.

In 2010, to mark the fiftieth anniversary of Stelton, British designer Paul Smith was commissioned to create his interpretation of Cylinda. The limited-edition AddColour Cylinda LIne (teapot, coffeepot and jug, and press coffeemaker) sports handles in twelve different colours in place of the original black plastic.

time when people who wanted classy interiors chose an antiques-rich path. Some still do but the majority have been seduced by top-end modern; and indeed, one has seen a marked decline in the number of antiques shops in most cities of the world. Stores such as Space have seen them off!

On a recent trip to a Space store, I was amazed by the depth and breadth of retro designers and manufacturers they stocked. Being surrounded by stuff by Accademia, Acerbis, B&B Italia, Edra, Fiam Italia, Foscarini, Giorgetti, Ingo Maurer, Italamp, Kartell, Poltronova, Vitra and Zanotta is a heady

shop, where you can walk home with the objects you like best. Space even greets you with a table full of design literature so that you can savour its sumptuous lines and colour prior to shopping. Unlike most other contemporary furniture products, the stuff they stock is *legendary* and part of the consumption experience is to understand how and why it was designed – and by whom. Top designers are also artists and their products have an

unmistakable aura that can be appreciated just like any work of art. Yes, it is expensive, but it is a lot less expensive than many other forms of art, and this is art that you can use on a daily basis.

I could not quite believe that I could just pick up a brand new George Nelson 'Ball Clock' or the 'Eye Clock' I have always wanted. These are made to the exacting quality standards of the original designs,

experience, particularly when you have spent so much time hunting down the occasional example of any one of their originals on the second-hand market. Normally you only ever see collections of these designs in museums, but a store like Space is like a giant museum

1
Gaetano Pesce's 'Up5/Up6' chair for B&B Italia, 1969 Space Furniture

2
Reissued Bitossi pottery: Aldo Lundi 'Rimini Blue' cat for Bitossi, Italy, c. 1955

3
Eames House Bird for Vitra Space Furniture

4
Reissued Iittala 'Aalto' vase Space Furniture

THE MINI
MARGARET SIMPSON = CURATOR, TRANSPORT AND TOYS, POWERHOUSE MUSEUM

The Mini is one of the few cars to have combined innovative body design, creative engine arrangement, performance and sales, with a unique place in both motoring and popular culture.

The two-door Mini, designed in England by Alex Issigonis and built by BMC from 1959, was the first small car to accommodate four adults in a deceptively roomy interior. This was achieved by turning the four-cylinder engine around to an east-west configuration and using front-wheel-drive, which incorporated the gearbox and differential.

Throughout the 1960s the Mini Cooper and Mini Cooper S (the sporty versions) were unbeatable at Monte Carlo rallies. Famously easy to drive, with road-hugging performance, the Mini crossed social boundaries as a fun car for the wealthy, an inexpensive city runabout, and even a police car in Australia. The car's iconic status was reinforced after three Mini Coopers starred in the 1969 film *The Italian Job,* racing along alleyways and down steps in Rome.

The last Mini rolled off the production line in Britain in 2000 and the following year BMW produced the 'New Mini'. Included were 1960s retro touches such as large round headlight frames, a centre-mounted speedo and old fashioned toggle switches for windows and fog lights. Gone were the space-saving external body seams, light body weight and basic construction, to be replaced by modern brakes, twenty-first century comfort and safety, alongside its original razor-sharp handling. Three New Minis appeared in the 2003 remake of *The Italian Job.*

Minis were made in Sydney at BMC's Zetland plant between 1961 and 1978. The Model K, introduced in 1969, comprised 80 per cent local content, complete with kangaroo decals.

Model K Mini
made in Sydney,
1970 Powerhouse
Museum collection

using more or less the same materials and so one does not feel that these are any less than the period pieces, even if a serious collector might prefer one. One's resolve to have only originals is seriously tested in stores such as these.

I wanted an Eames elephant for a friend's child, I wanted an entire plastic table setting by Philippe Starck, I wanted the 'Clover Chair' by Ron Arad, I wanted a 'Birillo Chair' by Joe Colombo and I so wanted a 'Cité Chair' by Jean Prouvé! Sadly, my house is already full to overflowing with furniture so I had to concentrate on their smaller stock of accessories. Here, there were many brands and designers to please. There were some lovely Iitalla glass vases; I was tempted to get two of Anna Castelli Ferrieri's 'Componibili' (for Kartell)

cylindrical storage units as bedside cupboards, I wondered whether it was time to get Arne Jacobsen's 'Cylinda Line' coffee- and teapots (by Stelton) and I definitely wanted a set of Olaf Von Bohr wall wet-look clothes hooks (for Kartell).

Although we are very lucky to have these magnificent period pieces made by their original manufacturers (or those licensed by them), a new phenomenon arose after the 1980s that bypassed copyright laws and protocols: China. Chinese manufacturers or western businesses operating from China quickly realised the

potential of copying, in full or in part, some of the classic retro rarities, and by the 2000s western markets were flooded with many cheap alternatives.

The ethical considerations here are interesting. Against the Chinese copies there is of course the copyright issue, whereby designers and their estates have been robbed of their intellectual property. Clearly China, alongside the Russian Soviet states, did not respect the ownership rights of the individual designer. Indeed, as Graham Cooley writes in the foreword to Mark Hill's catalogue for the *Hi Sklo Lo Sklo* exhibition of Czech glass (Mark Hill Publishing, London, 2008), 'one of

6

5

7

5
Cushions covered in 'Tistlar' fabric by Dagmar Lodén for Jobs, Sweden, 1949

6
Eames Elephant for Vitra Space Furniture

7
Cilla Ramnek 'Lusy Blom' cushion for IKEA, Sweden, 2011

Communism's central tenets is the elimination of the cult of the individual which left many great designs unattributed to the artists responsible for them'.

While this rejection of western copyright law will remain a contentious issue, at the very heart of the great modern political divide, quality won't be; and many object to the poor quality of the Chinese reissued products. While American and Danish furniture that was reissued by their original or relicensed manufacturers maintained or even improved on the original manufacturing quality (after all, new and better materials could be used where it did not compromise the design), very often the Chinese products are poor by comparison. My Eames chairs are a great example. While they look fine in a catalogue or showroom window, the standard of manufacturing is poor, as are the fixtures used to hold them together. I am constantly retightening

8
Olaf Von Bohr clothes hooks for Kartell Space Furniture

9
Birillo Chair by Joe Colombo for Zanotta Space Furniture

10
Cité Chair by Jean Prouvé for Vitra Space Furniture

11
Model of Pierre Paulin's 'Ribbon' chair (originally 1966), China, c. 2008 (the lighter is shown for scale)

12
Arden candlestick by Robert Welch, chromed stainless steel, c. 2008

13
Mark Goetz sofa for Herman Miller, USA, 2000s

14
Verner Panton's 'Living Tower' for Vitra Space Furniture

fixtures that do not work and I fear that one day they will collapse or break!

On the positive ethical side, the Chinese entry into the market has made it possible for far more people of slender financial means to enjoy these designs. And, it has to be said, most of them were never originally intended to be expensive luxuries, exclusive to a wealthy minority; and one wonders what Charles Eames or the owners of G-Plan furniture in the UK would make of the massive hike in auction prices for their products over the past twenty years. Indeed, many of those trained in industrial design were fervent believers in the democratising nature of modern manufacturing and designed their products willingly for such (affordable) ends.

Almost alone, the Swedish company IKEA has managed to uphold both the democratising value of mass manufacturing as well as the attribution of design to the artists involved. Whereas the Chinese manufacturers have tended to be parasitical for their designs by providing a vibrant market for designers, IKEA has kept the retro dream alive. When so many other western manufacturers went under as a result of the freeing up of international markets from the 1980s onwards, IKEA developed new manufacturing and retailing techniques that kept design and manufacturing quality high while delivering prices that competed internationally.

IKEA designers have recycled many retro ideas and influences without copying previous designs directly. More than that, they have produced hybrid designs that mix and match older themes with more contemporary ideas. The result is that we have not seen design atrophy around a new set of classics.

Alongside IKEA there are many other companies whose products continue to

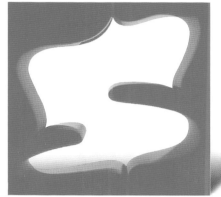

14

13

be directly inspired by the retro period. Robert Welch, whose 1960s designs in stainless steel are pictured in chapter 4, has continued to design into the present period. I particularly like his dramatic, sweeping 'Arden' candlesticks.

I also like to wear contemporary fashions that reference the retro period, particularly the Mod and psychedelic period. Ben Sherman has enjoyed a massive surge in demand a second time

around. I can remember buying their button-down collared shirts from the early 1970s and then their long, round-collared shirts in the late 1970s. Since 2005, I have bought a large number of their new designs, including their Lambretta summer shirt and a very nice Beatles shirt with fab detailing. I am also a fan of the German company Chenaski, whose contemporary retro designs are bold and dramatic.

For the contemporary kitchen, popular new stores such as Cath Kidston have almost exclusively referenced the retro period in both colour palette and design. I see a lot

12

of teenage kids and uni students in Kidston stores, and it is surely through these new manifestations of older ideas that younger generations will continue to be recruited into the retro aesthetic.

Which brings me rather neatly to an ending for this book. We are always tempted to see modernity as a procession of new things, each one gradually superseding previous forms and products. We rarely see it as a style in itself, in the same way we might characterise antique periods such as Georgian, Jacobean or Elizabethan; however, it is becoming clear to me that in centuries to come, it may well be. One has only to consider the set designs for Stanley Kubrick's film *2001: A Space Odyssey* (released in 1968), which featured the furniture, lighting and technologies (such as TV screens set into seatbacks on spaceship airlines), that were inspired by designers of that period, to realise that homes, office spaces and airline cabins of the present have not moved very far in all the intervening time. That some kind of design aesthetic has held us in its gravity and that very few *entirely new* interventions have distracted us away from it.

Of course, this period has seen a great deal of technological change but it is interesting to consider how even the most advanced forms, such as contemporary flat-profiled Apple computers, were directly inspired by designs by Dieter Rams (for Braun) hi-fi speakers back in 1966!

While we can discern the different looks of the 50s, 60s, 70s and 80s, they have a great deal in common too; and when collected together into interior designs, they do not jar – in fact they often compliment each other very well. One of the reasons why this period has an integrity and commonality, and one of the reasons why we are nostalgic for it and won't let it go, has to do with the values contained within it but also because we have our identities and souls wrapped up in it.

Initially, retro designs can appear flimsy, flippant, ephemeral, hedonistic and disposable but in fact they do contain and embody many of our most cherished modern values. The fact that things are made cheaply and abundantly so that most

15
'Clover Chair' by Ron Arad for Driade

16
Chenaski op-art shirt, Germany, 2010

17
Nuutajarvi/Notsjo glass candle holders by Oiva Toikka, Finland, 1964

16

17

18

people can aspire to having them is more or less restricted to the modern period, because many designed objects from previous periods were restricted to wealthier clients and consumers. It forms a material culture that is widely shared, widely appreciated, and widely available. It pushed its way across former ethnic, national and political boundaries which had hitherto contained more regionalised material cultures. In these various ways therefore it provided the basis for a shared culture generally, an everyday culture that was shared from Finland

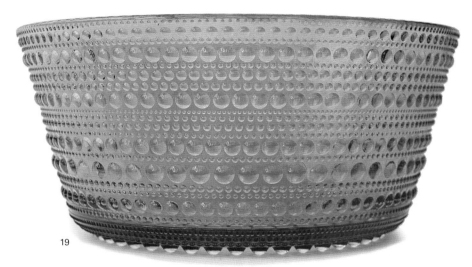

19

20

21

22

20
1980s reimagined: Claudia Chan Shaw models a multi-coloured geometric print jersey dress by Non è Vero, Australia, summer collection 2010

21
'Lampan' table lamp by Magnus Elbäck and Carl Öjerstam for IKEA, Sweden, 1990s

22
Tosh Licensing fine bone china mug in their Street Speak Range to commemorate the Wedding of HRH Prince William and Catherine Middleton, April 29th 2011. This was sold from Heal's, the top London design store, England, 2011

18
Cath Kidston mug (stylised Formula 1 race track from the 1950s)

19
Nuutajarvi/Notsjo blue bowl by Oiva Toikka, Finland, 1964

to Italy and from San Francisco to Christchurch. At the heart of this modern sensibility was the idea that everyone could live an aesthetically enriched life – we have a name for it, *lifestyle* – and this made modern life qualitatively different from previous periods, where art and aesthetics were restricted to high culture and the social elites.

Very importantly, most retro is not so much consumed just like any other goods but collected, cherished, valued and even adored. Anthropologists might argue that retro has many ritual qualities which are social in origin – and this is relatively easy to explain. Modern societies, unlike unchanging traditional societies, are predicated on change and progress. Objects, technologies, bureaucratic systems, science, medicine, education and design are all subject to the improving ethic. Nothing

is perfectly acceptable as it is and almost everything is undergoing transformation and change. Although we modern human beings are getting very used to this state of affairs, we do find it unsettling. After all, much of our social identity is bound up with our various pasts, our childhood, our school days, our adolescence, parenting years and so on. Each of these eras formed a technical, social and material place that was our home and our environment. It was the world of our everyday and a familiar, shared cultural milieu. Naturally, when these worlds change, when familiar music is replaced with new music, when loved old car models go to the scrap-heap, when steam trains and steam rollers no longer create the noise and smell of our industrial heartlands and when the trams disappeared from (some) of our cities, we miss them. Naturally, we have to embrace the new, but we do not forget the older stuff because to do that would mean to forget ourselves, who we are.

So collecting retro objects can be understood as a form of memory. Safe and sound in our collections, we know our past is not going to disappear off the face of the earth, but will stay close to us like old family photos. We can get it out whenever we want and relive past moments, associations and eras. As a phenomenon, collecting is a relatively recent, modern thing. It is a way of coping with being modern and having to lose a lot of the things that are part of our lives.

There is just one final thing that is also important to remember. Modern societies were always in danger of swamping us and making our lives dull with standardised, highly regulated lifestyles, dominated by bureaucratic procedures; both in our private lives and at work. Early in the twentieth century, some likened life in modern times to living in an iron cage where one is increasingly controlled by machines, regulations and standardised forms of consumption. The spectre of a modern hell was dramatised in films such as *Metropolis* and *Brazil* and in real life its worst excesses were witnessed in Nazi Germany and in the Stalinist Soviet Union.

It occurs to me that a lot of the objects that we value as retro buck this tendency, or subvert it even. A lot of the designers we celebrate through our consumption of retro items were revolutionaries who brought pleasure as much as function to the process of its consumption, first time round – as well as now. This is illustrated through furniture, for example, when French designers of the 1960s and 1970s began to imagine a new way of living by changing the style and architecture of living spaces. Grant Featherston's music chair ran with this idea as did Verner Panton's 'Living Tower' (see page 245).

Retro tends to elevate the importance of pleasing design, things that will surprise and delight us. It was the antidote to the mantra 'form follows function' and introduced *aesthetic appeal* while not losing any sense of functionality. Indeed, many retro objects delight us with their sheer ingenuity.

23

Tiny transistor radios in the 1960s or iPhones today make us smile and talk about them. Who did not like the Sony 'Walkman'? We do not merely perform functions with them, we live with them, and we live well. All of which means we have not, and will not turn into drones, slaves to the machine age, but will remain, happily and playfully human.

However, it also remains true that the retro period was one of great social and cultural innovation; of great political and technical projects related to extending wellbeing in a really audacious manner. Artists, designers, technocrats, companies and politicians formed a relatively strong alliance on these issues, back then. There was actually a Ministry of Design in France! It was a heady period of reform, churning social movements and ferment. Sadly, with politicians now in short-term and re-election mode and with the manufacturing base of the west all but dismantled, we might

24

say that modernity ran out of steam, politicians lost their nerve and the general public was sent into a period of nostalgia for the heroic modern past. By comparison with today the retro years were an inspiration, a golden age, and, not surprisingly, we reconnect to its ideas, values and example through its triumphant, life-affirming material culture.

23
Panton Chair, one piece plastic manufactured by Vitra, released 1967, still on sale Space Furniture

24
Anna Castelli Ferrieri's 'Componibili' cylindrical storage units for Kartell Space Furniture

25
Ben Sherman 'Beatles' shirt and belt in faded Union Jack design Photo Di Quick

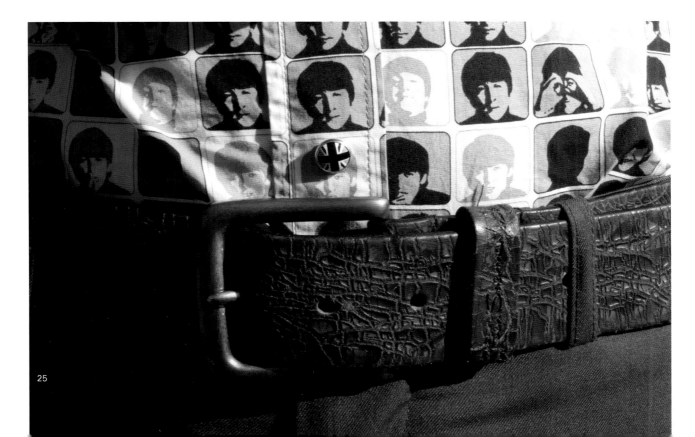

25

POWERHOUSE MUSEUM

NOTES

P34
The 1960s chairs of Olivier Mourgue and Pierre Paulin
1 Anne Watson, *Mod to Memphis*, Powerhouse Publishing, Sydney, 2002.
2 Peter Smithson (1986), quoted in Fiell, Charlotte and Peter, *1000 Chairs*, Taschen, 2005.

P62
Argenta ware ceramics – Further reading
A Duncan, 'Wilhelm Käge's Argenta', *American Ceramics*, vol. 14, no. 3, 2004, pp. 46–50.

P106
Crown Corning 1970s–80s domestic glassware
1 Australian Consolidated Industries (ACI) owned and operated Crown Crystal Glass and in 1972 it merged with the Australian subsidiary of the Corning Glass Works of USA to form Crown Corning Limited. Production at Waterloo, Sydney, ceased in 1990.
2 'Charles Furey', in Michael Bogle (ed), *Designing Australia, Readings in the History of Design*, Sydney, 2002, pp. 83–86.

P200
Australian travel posters – References
James Cockington (2005) 'Flights of fancy', Collect page, Money supplement, *Sydney Morning Herald*, 18 May.
Richard Jinman (2004) 'Images from a golden age', *Sydney Morning Herald*, 9–10 October.
Terry Ingram (2007) 'Well worth the journey', Saleroom, *Australian Financial Review*, 20 September.
Roger Butler (curator), *The Street as Art Galleries – Walls Sometimes Speak: Poster Art in Australia* held at the National Gallery of Australia, 1993.
Exhibition catalogue, *Australian Travel Posters*, Josef Lebovic Gallery, Paddington, 1990.

P212
'Aubrey' wallpaper by Florence Broadhurst
1 For an excellent overview of the Beardsley exhibition and its influence on popular culture, refer to the introduction of Elizabeth Guffey's book, *Retro: The Culture of Revival* (Reaktion Books, London, 2006), where she writes, 'Beardsley's posthumous exhibition offered harmless excitement and an intoxicating whiff of official disapproval'. Interestingly, Guffey also writes '"Retro" has crept into daily usage over the past thirty years. But there have yet been few attempts to define it. Half-ironic, half-longing "retro" considers the recent past with an unsentimental nostalgia. It doesn't bother with tradition and doesn't try to reinforce social values. Instead, it often suggests a form of subversion while sidestepping historical accuracy.' I wonder if this definition could apply to Florence's 'Aubrey' design?
2 Helen Lennie, conversation with author, 2011.

P227
The Braun SK4 'Phonosuper'
1 Marion Godau and Bernd Polster, *Design Directory*, Germany, Universe, Bonn/London, 2000.
2 Compare, for example, Braun's ET44 calculator of 1977 with Apple's 2010 i-Phone graphic version.

OBJECT CREDITS

INTRODUCTION
P12 Brionvega radiogram, gift of Belinda Franks through the Australian Government's Cultural Gifts program, 2003. 2003/23/1

FURNITURE
P19-5 'Antelope' chair, purchased 1985. 85/1840
P19-6 Eames chair, purchased 1985. 85/387
P20-7 Eames chair and ottoman, gift of Herman Miller (Aust) Pty Ltd, 1987. 87/1138D
P20-8 Eames chair, purchased 1985. 85/386
P20-9 'Ant' chair, purchased 1988. 87/810
P20-10 Jacobsen armchair and footstool, purchased 1988. 88/379
P29-34 'Rondo' chair, purchased 1995. 95/179/1
P30-35 'Gazelle' chair, purchased 1989. 89/499
P31-37 'Michael Hirst' chair, purchased 1991. 91/1326
P31-38 Snelling chair and stool, purchased 1992. 92/1949
P32-39 Fler 'SC55' chair, purchased 1992. 92/1946
P32-40 'R152 Contour' chair, gift of Mr & Mrs J Warner, 1993. 93/265/1
P33-41 p34 '577' chair, purchased 1987. 87/1284
P34 'Djinn' chaise longue, purchased 1985. 85/1451
P34 '582' chair, purchased 1987. 87/1283
P35-42 'Up 1' armchair, purchased 1985. 85/115
P36 'Sacco' bean bag, purchased 1987. 87/809
P36 'Mies' chair and footstool, donated by Mike Dawborn through the Australian Government's Cultural Gifts Program, 2008. 2008/54/1
P37-43 'Divano Gonfiabile', purchased 1984. A10194
P38 'Mark I Sound' chair, purchased 2008. 2008/144/1
P38 'Mark II Sound' chair, gift of BHP, 1986. 86/1308
P39-44 'Joe' chair, purchased 1995. 95/272/1
P39-45 'Marilyn' sofa, purchased 1985. 85/83
P40-46 Philippe Starck chair, purchased 1988. 88/662
P40-48 'Wiggle' chair, purchased 2003. 2003/83/1
P41-49 'Wink' chaise lounge, purchased 1985. 85/1830
P41-51 'Lido' couch, purchased 1986. 86/1013
P43-53 Paul Kafka cocktail cabinet, purchased 1984. A10559
P44-55 'Carlton' room divider, purchased 1986. 86/1015
P46-58 Paul Kafka coffee table, purchased 1981.
P46-61 John Smith Coffee table, purchased with the assistance of the Crafts Board of the Australia Council and Monahan Dayman Adams Pty Ltd, 1986. 86/120
P46-62 Philippe Starck table vase, purchased 1996. 96/402/1
P46-63 Douglas Snelling coffee table, gift of Irene Rolfe, 1983. A9251
P46-64 Robert Klippel coffee table, purchased 1994. 94/256/1

CERAMICS
P59 Ramekins, gift of Mr Alex Sikkes. 91/872
P 62 'Argenta' ware bowl, purchased 1956. A4712
P 62 'Argenta' ware bowl, purchased 1956. A4713
P 62 'Argenta' ware dish, purchased 1956. A4714
P68-47 Jenny Orchard tea set, gift of Paul van Reyk, 1998. 98/140
P79-80 'Le Noyau de la Force' vase, donated by Graeme Hindmarsh through the Australian Government's Cultural Gifts Program, 2004. 2004/30/1
P92-142 Animal figure, gift of Alan Landis, 1984. A10629
P97-153 William Ricketts earthenware vase, purchased 1938. A3138
P97-154, 157 Man and child ceramic sculpture, purchased 1951. A4317
P97-155 'Mind thought, beauty wrought' ceramic sculpture, purchased 1948. A4123
P97-156 Earthenware mug, gift of William Ricketts, 1961. A5154
P97-154,157 William Ricketts man and child ceramic sculpture, purchased 1951. A4317
P97-155 William Ricketts 'Mind thought, beauty wrought' ceramic sculpture, purchased 1948. A4123
P97-156 William Ricketts earthenware mug, gift of William Ricketts, 1961. A5154
P101-179 'Sepik' teapot, purchased 1986. 86/ 1016

GLASS
P105-3 'Serpentiini' vase, gift of Robert Bleakley under the Tax Incentive for the Arts Scheme, 1997. 2000/106/1
P105-4 'Jester's hat' vase, purchased 1984. A10648
P106 Crown Corning glass designs and brochures, gift of Denise Larcombe, 2011. P.1275
P107 Glassware, gift of Crown Corning Ltd, 1987. 87/236
P114-26 'Apple' vase, purchased 1986. 86/1440
P115-29 'Sommerso' vase, gift of Robert Bleakley under the Tax Incentive for the Arts Scheme, 1997. 2000/106/15
P116-30 'Piume' vase, purchased 1984. A10643
P119-41 'Zebra' vase, purchased 1985. 85/15
P119-44 Warff plate, purchased 1972. A6091

MODERN METAL
P132 TV Lamp, purchased 2005. 2008/145/1
P135 Tumblers, purchased 1991. 91/72
P137-20 Electric car kettle, gift of Mr George Hamill, 2002. 2002/34/1
P142-43 Knife and scabbard, gift of Wiltshire International, 1997. 97/125/1
P144-45 'Murmansk' fruit stand, purchased 1986. 86/1018
P145-48 Kettle, bequest of Ian Neil Whalland, 1996. 2005/66/1

PLASTIC
P152 Bakelite collection, gift of Stephen Cummings, 1983. K1027
P153-2 Hair comb, purchased 1950. H5075
P154-3 Rouge container, purchased 1985. 85/2530
P154-6 Shell bowser ornament, purchased 1997. 97/288/1
P158 'Pillola' lamp set, purchased 1985. 85/1977
P159-19 'Panton' chair, purchased 1985. 85/1976
P161-31 Beatles figures, purchased 1993. 93/438/1
P163 'Cafe Bar Compact', gift of Cafe Bar International, 1990. 90/1049
P166-49 Eveready Torch, gift of Design Field Pty Ltd, 1991. 91/1313
P169-59 Wine cask cooler, gift of Decor Corporation, 1987. 87/117
P169-60 Wine carrier, gift of Decor Corporation, 1987. 87/70

FASHION
P173 Givenchy evening coat, gift of Margie and Andrew Isles, 2002. 2002/98/1
P175-6 Skirt, gift of Mary Eichner, 1997. 97/201/1
P176-10 Johnny O'Keefe suit, gift of Sydney Opera House Trust, 1998. 98/32/2
P176-11 Annette Kellerman swimsuit, gift of Sydney Opera House Trust, Dennis Wolanski Library, 1983. A9180
P177-14 Dior evening dress, gift of the Fashion Group International of Sydney, 1994. 94/47/1
P177-15 Dior cocktail dress, gift of Anne Schofield, 1983. A8680
P177-16 Balenciaga evening dress and jacket, gift of Phyllis Kendall, 1989. 89/250
P178-17 Dress, gift of Sister Marie O'Regan, 1993. 94/271/1
P179-19 Sports jacket, gift of Mrs Rhonda & Mr David Travis, 1992. 92/1945
P179-20 Winkle-pickers shoes, gift of Terence Mooney, 1997. 97/218/1
P179-21 Beth Levine shoes, purchased 1997. 97/185/2
P180-22 Chanel suit, gift of the Fashion Group International of Sydney, 1983. A8945
P182-28 Courrèges mini dress, gift of Lady Fairfax, 1986. 86/1487
P182-29 Courrèges mini dress, gift of Lady Fairfax, 1986. 86/1488
P182-30 Courrèges ensemble, gift of the Fashion Group International of Sydney, 1983. A8939
P183-31 Mary Quant dress, gift of R H Taffs Pty Ltd, 1973. A6234
P183-32 Expo 67 hostess uniform, gift of Kate Burke, 2008. 2008/133/1
P183-33 Louis Féraud mini dress, purchased 1979. A7197
P183-34 Beth Levine boots, purchased 1997. 97/222/1
P184-35 Paper dress, gift of Jenifer Elliot, 1990. 90/1039
P186-43 Pucci dress, gift of

INDEX

A Bloomsbury book

First published in Australia and NewZealand by
NewSouth Publishing
University of New South Wales Press Ltd
University of New South Wales
Sydney NSW 2052
AUSTRALIA
www.newsouthpublishing.com.au

Published in the rest of the world by
Bloomsbury Publishing Plc
50 Bedford Square
London
WC1B 3DP
ENGLAND
www.bloomsbury.com

In association with **ph**ᵐ

© Adrian Franklin 2011
First published 2011
This edition 2013

A CIP catalogue record for this book is available from the British Library.

Design Di Quick
Printer Everbest

This book is printed on paper using fibre supplied from plantation or sustainably managed forests.

Photographs without credits are courtesy of the author.

Powerhouse contributions © Powerhouse Museum.

As a NSW Government cultural institution, the Powerhouse Museum is not able to validate or endorse the estimates of value contained in this book.

Powerhouse Museum object photography by Sotha Bourn, Penelope Clay, Scott Donkin, Geoff Friend, Andrew Frolows, Peter Giaprakas, Ryan Hernandez, Marinco Kojdanovski, Jean-François Lanzarone, Kate Pollard, Sue Stafford, Jane Townsend and Nitsa Yioupros.

All reasonable efforts were taken to obtain permission to use copyright material reproduced in this book, but in some cases copyright could not be traced. The author welcomes information in this regard.

Page 1 Three Flying Ducks, unknown manufacturer, England, 1950s–1960s

Above Sootie and Sweep are waving goodbye. Rare, unmarked ceramic figures from England in the early 1950s. Sootie and Sweep were the creation of Harry Corbett and first appeared on the BBC in 1952. They have rarely been off-air ever since and a new series commenced on CITV in 2011.